WASHINGTON'S
TRAVEL GUIDE
2018

SHOPS, RESTAURANTS, **ARTS,** ENTERTAINMENT **& NIGHTLIFE**

★★★★★

The Most Positively
Reviewed And Recommended
Places In The City

EGP
Editorial

WASHINGTON DC
TRAVEL GUIDE
2018

SHOPS, RESTAURANTS, ARTS, ENTERTAINMENT & NIGHTLIFE

WASHINGTON DC TRAVEL GUIDE 2018
Shops, Restaurants, Arts, Entertainment & Nightlife

© Anthony M. Harrison, 2018
© E.G.P. Editorial, 2018

Printed in USA.

ISBN-13: 978-1545011614
ISBN-10: 1545011613

I N D E X

WASHINGTON TRAVEL GUIDE 2018

Shops, Restaurants, Arts, Entertainment & Nightlife

*This directory is dedicated to Washington Business Owners and Managers
who provide the experience that the locals and tourists enjoy.
Thanks you very much for all that you do and thank for being the "People Choice".*

*Thanks to everyone that posts their reviews online and
the amazing reviews sites that make our life easier.*

*The places listed in this book are the most positively reviewed
and recommended by locals and travelers from around the world.*

*Thank you for your time and enjoy the directory that is
designed with locals and tourist in mind!*

TOP 500 SHOPS

The Most Recommended by Locals & Trevelers
(From #1 to #500)

#1
Books For America
Category: Bookstore
Average Price: Inexpensive
Address: 1417 22nd St NW
Washington, DC 20037
Phone: (202) 835-2665

#2
Violet Boutique
Category: Women's Clothing, Accessories
Average Price: Modest
Area: Adams Morgan
Address: 2439 18th St NW
Washington, DC 20009
Phone: (202) 621-9225

#3
Fia's Fabulous Finds
Category: Thrift Store, Used, Vintage
Average Price: Modest
Area: Petworth
Address: 806 Upshur St NW
Washington, DC 20011
Phone: (202) 492-8278

#4
Politics & Prose
Category: Bookstore, Coffee, Tea
Average Price: Modest
Area: Chevy Chase
Address: 5015 Connecticut Ave NW
Washington, DC 20008
Phone: (202) 364-1919

#5
Glover Park Hardware
Category: Hardware Store
Average Price: Modest
Area: Glover Park
Address: 2251 Wisconsin Ave NW
Washington, DC 20007
Phone: (202) 333-6378

#6
Labyrinth Games & Puzzles
Category: Hobby Shop, Toy Store
Average Price: Modest
Area: Capitol Hill, Southeast
Address: 645 Pennsylvania Ave SE
Washington, DC 20003
Phone: (202) 544-1059

#7
Hugh & Crye
Category: Men's Clothing
Average Price: Modest
Area: Georgetown
Address: 3212 O St NW
Washington, DC 20007
Phone: (202) 250-3807

#8
Nordstrom Rack
Category: Department Store,
Men's Clothing, Women's Clothing
Average Price: Modest
Address: 1800 L St NW
Washington, DC 20036
Phone: (202) 627-3650

#9
National Gallery Of Art Sculpture Garden & Ice Rink
Category: Skating Rinks, Art Gallery,
Landmark/Historical
Average Price: Inexpensive
Address: 700 Constitution Ave NW
Washington, DC 20565
Phone: (202) 289-3360

#10
Goodwood
Category: Antiques, Thrift Store,
Furniture Store
Average Price: Expensive
Area: U Street Corridor
Address: 1428 U St NW
Washington, DC 20009
Phone: (202) 986-3640

#11
Market Street Diamonds
Category: Jewelry
Average Price: Modest
Area: Georgetown
Address: 2914 M St NW
Washington, DC 20007
Phone: (202) 552-5744

#12
T.J. Maxx
Category: Department Store
Average Price: Modest
Address: 601 13th St NW
Washington, DC 20005
Phone: (202) 637-1261

#13
Capitol Hill Books
Category: Bookstore
Average Price: Inexpensive
Area: Capitol Hill, Southeast
Address: 657 C St SE
Washington, DC 20003
Phone: (202) 544-1621

#14
Patagonia
Category: Sports Wear, Outdoor Gear
Average Price: Expensive
Area: Georgetown
Address: 1048 Wisconsin Ave NW
Washington, DC 20007
Phone: (202) 333-1776

#15
Modern Mobler Vintage Furnishings
Category: Home Decor,
Furniture Store, Antiques
Average Price: Expensive
Area: Takoma
Address: 7313 Georgia Ave NW
Washington, DC 20012
Phone: (571) 594-2201

#16
Ella-Rue
Category: Used, Vintage, Accessories,
Women's Clothing
Average Price: Modest
Area: Georgetown
Address: 3231 P St NW
Washington, DC 20007
Phone: (202) 333-1598

#17
Willow
Category: Accessories,
Women's Clothing, Used, Vintage
Average Price: Modest
Area: Petworth
Address: 843 Upshur St NW
Washington, DC 20011
Phone: (202) 643-2323

#18
Miss Pixie's
Category: Antiques, Furniture Store
Average Price: Modest
Area: Logan Circle
Address: 1626 14th St NW
Washington, DC 20009
Phone: (202) 232-8171

#19
Paper Source
Category: Cards, Stationery, Art Supplies
Average Price: Modest
Area: Georgetown
Address: 3019 M St NW
Washington, DC 20007
Phone: (202) 298-5545

#20
Ginger Root/Revamp Design
Category: Sewing, Alterations,
Men's Clothing, Women's Clothing
Average Price: Modest
Area: U Street Corridor
Address: 1530 U St NW
Washington, DC 20009
Phone: (202) 567-7668

#21
All Fired Up
Category: Arts, Crafts
Average Price: Modest
Area: Cleveland Park
Address: 3413 Connecticut Ave NW
Washington, DC 20008
Phone: (202) 363-9590

#22
The Flea Market At Eastern Market
Category: Antiques
Average Price: Modest
Area: Capitol Hill, Southeast
Address: 7th And C St
Washington, DC 20003
Phone: (703) 534-7612

#23
Tabletop
Category: Home Decor, Jewelry,
Kitchen & Bath
Average Price: Expensive
Area: Dupont Circle
Address: 1608 20th St NW
Washington, DC 20009
Phone: (202) 387-7117

#24
Barston's Child's Play
Category: Toy Store
Average Price: Modest
Area: Chevy Chase
Address: 5536 Connecticut Ave NW
Washington, DC 20015
Phone: (202) 244-3602

#25
Betsy Fisher
Category: Women's Clothing, Accessories
Average Price: Expensive
Area: Dupont Circle
Address: 1224 Connecticut Ave NW
Washington, DC 20036
Phone: (202) 785-1975

#26
Treasury
Category: Used, Vintage,
Women's Clothing
Average Price: Modest
Address: 1843 14th St NW
Washington, DC 20009
Phone: (202) 332-9499

#27
Lululemon Athletica
Category: Sports Wear,
Women's Clothing, Yoga
Average Price: Expensive
Area: Logan Circle
Address: 1461 P St NW
Washington, DC 20005
Phone: (202) 518-4075

#28
Hirshhorn Museum
& Sculpture Garden
Category: Museum, Art Gallery
Average Price: Inexpensive
Address: 7th St & Independence Ave SW
Washington, DC 20560
Phone: (202) 633-4674

#29
Frugalista
Category: Used, Vintage, Bridal
Average Price: Inexpensive
Address: 3069 Mount Pleasant St NW
Washington, DC 20009
Phone: (202) 328-2135

#30
National Postal Museum
Category: Landmark/Historical,
Museum, Art Gallery
Average Price: Inexpensive
Area: Noma
Address: 2 Massachusetts Ave NE
Washington, DC 20001
Phone: (202) 357-1300

#31
Lou Lou
Category: Accessories, Jewelry
Average Price: Modest
Area: Dupont Circle
Address: 1601 Connecticut Ave NW
Washington, DC 20009
Phone: (202) 588-0027

#32
Redeem
Category: Men's Clothing,
Women's Clothing
Average Price: Expensive
Address: 1810 14th St NW
Washington, DC 20009
Phone: (202) 332-7447

#33
Nordstrom Rack
Category: Discount Store
Average Price: Modest
Area: Friendship Heights
Address: 5333 Wisconsin Ave
Washington, DC 20015
Phone: (202) 697-4100

#34
Lululemon Athletica
Category: Yoga, Sports Wear,
Women's Clothing
Average Price: Expensive
Area: Georgetown
Address: 3265 M St NW
Washington, DC 20007
Phone: (202) 333-1738

#35
Pacers
Category: Sporting Goods
Average Price: Modest
Area: Logan Circle
Address: 1427 P Street NW
Washington, DC 20005
Phone: (202) 506-2029

#36
Hu's Wear
Category: Women's Clothing
Average Price: Exclusive
Area: Georgetown
Address: 2906 M St NW
Washington, DC 20007
Phone: (202) 342-2020

#37
Federal
Category: Men's Clothing
Average Price: Modest
Address: 2216 14th St NW
Washington, DC 20009
Phone: (202) 518-3375

#38
The Smithsonian Institution
Category: Landmark/Historical,
Museum, Art Gallery
Average Price: Inexpensive
Address: 1000 Jefferson Dr SW
Washington, DC 20560
Phone: (202) 357-1300

#39
Wake-Up Little Suzie
Category: Jewelry, Home Decor,
Children's Clothing
Average Price: Modest
Area: Cleveland Park
Address: 3409 Connecticut Ave NW
Washington, DC 20008
Phone: (202) 244-0700

#40
Commonwealth
Category: Men's Clothing, Women's
Clothing, Shoe Store
Average Price: Expensive
Area: Adams Morgan
Address: 1781 Florida Ave NW
Washington, DC 20009
Phone: (202) 265-1155

#41
Costco
Category: Discount Store, Wholesale Store
Average Price: Modest
Address: 2441 Market St NE
Washington, DC 20018
Phone: (202) 269-8540

#42
The Container Store
Category: Shopping Center
Average Price: Modest
Area: Tenleytown
Address: 4500 Wisconsin Ave NW
Washington, DC 20016
Phone: (202) 478-4000

#43
Junction
Category: Used, Vintage
Average Price: Modest
Area: U Street Corridor
Address: 1510 U St NW
Washington, DC 20009
Phone: (202) 483-0261

#44
Kramerbooks & Afterwords Cafe
Category: Bookstore, American
Average Price: Modest
Area: Dupont Circle
Address: 1517 Connecticut Ave NW
Washington, DC 20036
Phone: (202) 387-1400

#45
The Lantern
Category: Bookstore
Average Price: Inexpensive
Area: Georgetown
Address: 3241 P St NW
Washington, DC 20007
Phone: (202) 333-3222

#46
Room & Board
Category: Furniture Store, Home Decor
Average Price: Expensive
Address: 1840 14th St NW
Washington, DC 20009
Phone: (202) 729-8300

#47
India Art & Craft
Category: Women's Clothing, Accessories
Average Price: Modest
Area: Woodley Park
Address: 2602 Connecticut Ave NW
Washington, DC 20008
Phone: (202) 299-0067

#48
Georgetown Running Company
Category: Sports Wear, Shoe Store
Average Price: Modest
Area: Georgetown
Address: 3401 M St NW
Washington, DC 20007
Phone: (202) 337-8626

#49
Lush
Category: Cosmetics, Beauty Supply
Average Price: Modest
Area: Georgetown
Address: 3066 M St NW
Washington, DC 20007
Phone: (202) 333-6950

#50
Georgia Avenue Thrift Store
Category: Thrift Store
Average Price: Inexpensive
Address: 6101 Georgia Ave NW
Washington, DC 20011
Phone: (202) 291-4013

#51
Proper Topper
Category: Jewelry, Women's Clothing
Average Price: Expensive
Area: Dupont Circle
Address: 1350 Connecticut Ave NW
Washington, DC 20036
Phone: (202) 842-3055

#52
Secondi
Category: Used, Vintage
Average Price: Modest
Area: Dupont Circle
Address: 1702 Connecticut Ave NW
Washington, DC 20009
Phone: (202) 667-1122

#53
Hu's Shoes
Category: Shoe Store
Average Price: Exclusive
Area: Georgetown
Address: 3005 M St NW
Washington, DC 20007
Phone: (202) 342-0202

#54
Urban Outfitters
Category: Men's Clothing,
Women's Clothing
Average Price: Modest
Area: Chinatown
Address: 737 7th St NW
Washington, DC 20001
Phone: (202) 737-0259

#55
Sullivan's Toy Store & Art Supplies
Category: Toy Store, Art Supplies
Average Price: Modest
Area: Tenleytown
Address: 4200 Wisconsin Ave NW
Washington, DC 20016
Phone: (202) 362-1343

#56
Carpe Librum
Category: Bookstore, Used, Vintage
Average Price: Inexpensive
Address: 1030 17th St NW
Washington, DC 20006
Phone: (202) 347-9841

#57
Everard's Clothing
Category: Men's Clothing, Women's
Clothing, Bespoke Clothing
Average Price: Exclusive
Area: Georgetown
Address: 1802 Wisconsin Ave NW
Washington, DC 20007
Phone: (202) 298-7464

#58
Anthropologie Store
Category: Fashion
Average Price: Expensive
Address: 950 F St NW
Washington, DC 20004
Phone: (202) 347-2160

#59
TJ Maxx & Homegoods
Category: Department Store
Average Price: Modest
Area: Georgetown
Address: 3222 M St NW
Washington, DC 20007
Phone: (202) 333-1040

#60
Le Bustiere Boutique
Category: Lingerie
Average Price: Expensive
Area: Adams Morgan
Address: 1744 Columbia Rd NW
Washington, DC 20009
Phone: (202) 745-8080

#61
Busboys And Poets
Category: Bookstore, Coffee, Tea,
Vegetarian
Average Price: Modest
Address: 1025 5th St NW
Washington, DC 20001
Phone: (202) 789-2227

#62
Madewell
Category: Accessories, Women's Clothing
Average Price: Expensive
Area: Georgetown
Address: 1237 Wisconsin Ave
Washington, DC 20007
Phone: (202) 333-3599

#63
Crossroads Trading
Category: Women's Clothing,
Men's Clothing, Used, Vintage
Average Price: Modest
Area: U Street Corridor
Address: 2015 14th Street NW
Washington, DC 20009
Phone: (202) 986-9382

#64
Second Story Books & Antiques
Category: Bookstore
Average Price: Modest
Area: Dupont Circle
Address: 2000 P St NW
Washington, DC 20036
Phone: (202) 659-8884

#65
Tempo Bookstore
Category: Bookstore
Average Price: Modest
Area: Tenleytown
Address: 4905 Wisconsin Ave NW
Washington, DC 20016
Phone: (202) 363-6683

#66
Old School Hardware
Category: Hardware Store
Average Price: Modest
Area: Mount Pleasant
Address: 3219 Mount Pleasant St NW
Washington, DC 20010
Phone: (202) 462-1431

#67
Secret Pleasures Boutique
Category: Adult Entertainment, Adult
Average Price: Modest
Area: U Street Corridor
Address: 1510 U St NW
Washington, DC 20009
Phone: (202) 664-1476

#68
Crafty Bastards Arts & Crafts Fair
Category: Art Gallery, Arts, Crafts
Average Price: Expensive
Address: 1309 5th St NE
Washington, DC 20002
Phone: (202) 332-2100

#69
Idle Time Books
Category: Bookstore
Average Price: Inexpensive
Area: Adams Morgan
Address: 2467 18th St NW
Washington, DC 20009
Phone: (202) 232-4774

#70
Trohv
Category: Furniture Store,
Home Decor, Cards, Stationery
Average Price: Expensive
Area: Takoma
Address: 232 Carroll St NW
Washington, DC 20012
Phone: (202) 829-2941

#71
Jack Spade
Category: Accessories,
Men's Clothing, Women's Clothing
Average Price: Expensive
Area: Georgetown
Address: 1250 Wisconsin Ave NW
Washington, DC 20007
Phone: (202) 333-1905

#72
Anthropologie
Category: Fashion, Home & Garden
Average Price: Expensive
Area: Georgetown
Address: 3222 M St NW
Washington, DC 20007
Phone: (202) 337-1363

#73
Buffalo Exchange
Category: Used, Vintage,
Men's Clothing, Women's Clothing
Average Price: Inexpensive
Area: Logan Circle
Address: 1318 14th St NW
Washington, DC 20005
Phone: (202) 299-9148

#74
Walgreens
Category: Drugstore, Cosmetics, Beauty
Supply, Convenience Store
Average Price: Inexpensive
Area: West End
Address: 1217 22Nd St Nw
Washington, DC 20037
Phone: (202) 776-9084

#75
Vineyard Vines
Category: Women's Clothing,
Men's Clothing, Children's Clothing
Average Price: Expensive
Area: Georgetown
Address: 1225 Wisconsin Ave NW
Washington, DC 20007
Phone: (202) 625-8463

#76
Palace 5ive
Category: Shoe Store, Sports Wear,
Men's Clothing, Women's Clothing
Average Price: Modest
Address: 2216 14th St NW
Washington, DC 20009
Phone: (202) 299-9008

#77
Homebody
Category: Furniture Store,
Home Decor, Jewelry
Average Price: Expensive
Area: Capitol Hill, Southeast
Address: 715 8th St SE
Washington, DC 20003
Phone: (202) 544-8445

#78
Mercedes Bien Vintage
Category: Used, Vintage
Average Price: Modest
Area: Adams Morgan
Address: 2423 18th St NW
Washington, DC 20009
Phone: (202) 360-8481

#79
Sky Valet Shoes
Category: Shoe Store
Average Price: Expensive
Area: Georgetown
Address: 1800 Wisconsin Ave NW
Washington, DC 20007
Phone: (202) 337-4333

#80
Sassanova
Category: Shoe Store, Accessories,
Women's Clothing
Average Price: Expensive
Area: Georgetown
Address: 1641 Wisconsin Ave NW
Washington, DC 20050
Phone: (202) 471-4400

#81
City Sports
Category: Sporting Goods, Shoe Store
Average Price: Modest
Address: 1111 19th St NW
Washington, DC 20036
Phone: (202) 467-4100

#82
J.Crew
Category: Men's Clothing,
Women's Clothing, Accessories
Average Price: Expensive
Area: Georgetown
Address: 3222 M Street NW
Washington, DC 20007
Phone: (202) 965-4090

#83
Leica Store Washington DC
Category: Photography Store, Services
Average Price: Exclusive
Address: 977 F St NW
Washington, DC 20004
Phone: (202) 787-5900

#84
Smash Records
Category: Music, Dvds,
Men's Clothing, Vinyl Records
Average Price: Modest
Area: Adams Morgan
Address: 2314 18th St NW
Washington, DC 20009
Phone: (202) 387-6274

#85
Sephora
Category: Cosmetics, Beauty Supply
Average Price: Modest
Area: Georgetown
Address: 3065 M St NW
Washington, DC 20007
Phone: (202) 338-5644

#86
Goethe-Institut
Category: Cinema, Art Gallery,
Language School
Average Price: Inexpensive
Area: Chinatown
Address: 812 7th St NW
Washington, DC 20001
Phone: (202) 289-1200

#87
Caramel
Category: Women's Clothing,
Men's Clothing
Average Price: Modest
Area: U Street Corridor
Address: 1603 U Street NW
Washington, DC 20009
Phone: (202) 265-1930

#88
JEMS Optical
Category: Eyewear, Opticians, Optometrists
Average Price: Modest
Address: 1401 New York Ave NW
Washington, DC 20005
Phone: (202) 638-4700

#89
Current Boutique
Category: Accessories,
Women's Clothing, Used, Vintage
Average Price: Modest
Address: 1809 14th St NW
Washington, DC 20009
Phone: (202) 588-7311

#90
The Coach Store
Category: Leather Goods
Average Price: Expensive
Area: Georgetown
Address: 3259 M St NW
Washington, DC 20007
Phone: (202) 333-3005

#91
Riverby Books
Category: Arts, Crafts, Bookstore
Average Price: Inexpensive
Address: 417 E Capitol St SE
Washington, DC 20003
Phone: (202) 543-4342

#92
The Phillips Collection
Category: Museum, Art Gallery
Average Price: Inexpensive
Area: Dupont Circle
Address: 1600 21st St NW
Washington, DC 20009
Phone: (202) 387-2151

#93
Lettie Gooch Boutique
Category: Women's Clothing
Average Price: Expensive
Area: U Street Corridor
Address: 1517 U St NW
Washington, DC 20001
Phone: (202) 332-4242

#94
Tibet Shop
Category: Flowers, Gifts
Average Price: Modest
Area: Adams Morgan
Address: 2407 18th St NW
Washington, DC 20009
Phone: (202) 387-1880

#95
Second Time Around
Category: Used, Vintage, Thrift Store
Average Price: Modest
Area: Georgetown
Address: 3289 M St NW
Washington, DC 20007
Phone: (202) 333-2355

#96
Village Art & Craft
Category: Hobby Shop
Average Price: Expensive
Area: Georgetown
Address: 1353 Wisconsin Ave NW
Washington, DC 20007
Phone: (202) 333-1968

#97
H&M
Category: Men's Clothing,
Women's Clothing, Accessories
Average Price: Modest
Address: 1025 F St NW
Washington, DC 20005
Phone: (202) 347-3306

#98
Fleet Feet Sports
Category: Shoe Store, Sporting Goods
Average Price: Modest
Area: Adams Morgan
Address: 1841 Columbia Rd NW
Washington, DC 20009
Phone: (202) 387-3888

#99
Dr. K's Vintage
Category: Used, Vintage
Average Price: Modest
Area: U Street Corridor
Address: 1534 U St NW
Washington, DC 20009
Phone: (240) 888-6284

#100
Macy's
Category: Department Store,
Men's Clothing, Women's Clothing
Average Price: Modest
Address: 1201 G St NW
Washington, DC 20005
Phone: (202) 628-6661

#101
Tennis Zone
Category: Tennis, Sporting Goods
Average Price: Modest
Area: Glover Park
Address: 2319 Wisconsin Ave NW
Washington, DC 20007
Phone: (202) 362-7575

#102
Toro Mata
Category: Art Gallery, Arts, Crafts
Average Price: Expensive
Area: Adams Morgan
Address: 2410 18th St NW
Washington, DC 20009
Phone: (202) 232-3890

#103
Urban Chic
Category: Women's Clothing
Average Price: Expensive
Area: Georgetown
Address: 1626 Wisconsin Ave NW
Washington, DC 20007
Phone: (202) 338-5398

#104
Lord & Taylor
Category: Department Store,
Men's Clothing, Women's Clothing
Average Price: Modest
Area: Friendship Heights
Address: 5255 Western Ave.
Washington, DC 20015
Phone: (202) 362-9600

#105
City Sports
Category: Sporting Goods
Average Price: Expensive
Area: Chinatown
Address: 715 7th St NW
Washington, DC 20001
Phone: (202) 638-3115

#106
Groovy DC Cards & Gifts
Category: Cards, Stationery
Average Price: Modest
Area: Capitol Hill, Southeast
Address: 321 7th St SE
Washington, DC 20003
Phone: (202) 544-6633

#107
Copenhaver
Category: Cards, Stationery
Average Price: Expensive
Area: Dupont Circle
Address: 1301 Connecticut Ave NW
Washington, DC 20036
Phone: (202) 232-1200

#108
DC Vape Joint
Category: Vape Shop
Average Price: Modest
Area: Adams Morgan
Address: 2337 18th St NW
Washington, DC 20009
Phone: (202) 939-1360

#109
Foer's Pharmacy
Category: Drugstore
Average Price: Modest
Address: 2141 K St NW
Washington, DC 20037
Phone: (202) 296-7190

#110
American Rescue Workers Thrift
Category: Used, Vintage
Average Price: Inexpensive
Area: H Street Corridor, Atlas District
Address: 1107 H Street NE
Washington, DC 20002
Phone: (202) 397-6149

#111
The Old Post Office Pavilion
Category: Shopping Center
Average Price: Inexpensive
Area: Federal Triangle
Address: 1100 Pennsylvania Ave NW
Washington, DC 20004
Phone: (202) 289-4224

#112
Martha's Table
Category: Thrift Store
Average Price: Inexpensive
Address: 2114 14th Street NW
Washington, DC 20009
Phone: (202) 328-6608

#113
The Corner Store
Category: Art Gallery,
Performing Arts, Music Venues
Average Price: Inexpensive
Area: Capitol Hill, Southeast
Address: 900 S Carolina Ave SE
Washington, DC 20003
Phone: (202) 544-5807

#114
Lou Lou
Category: Jewelry, Accessories
Average Price: Modest
Area: Georgetown
Address: 1304 Wisconsin Ave NW
Washington, DC 20007
Phone: (202) 333-3574

#115
Target
Category: Department Store
Average Price: Modest
Area: Columbia Heights
Address: 3100 14th St NW
Washington, DC 20010
Phone: (202) 777-3773

#116
Barneys New York
Category: Department Store
Average Price: Expensive
Area: Georgetown
Address: 3040 M Street NW
Washington, DC 20007
Phone: (202) 350-5832

#117
Walmart Supercenter
Category: Discount Store, Grocery
Average Price: Inexpensive
Area: Noma
Address: 99 H St NW
Washington, DC 20001
Phone: (202) 289-5254

#118
Simon Vintage Furniture
& Homegoods
Category: Antiques, Home Decor,
Furniture Store
Average Price: Modest
Address: 1911 9th St NW
Washington, DC 20001
Phone: (202) 629-2517

#119
Second Affair Consignments
Category: Used, Vintage
Average Price: Inexpensive
Area: Dupont Circle
Address: 1904 18th St NW
Washington, DC 20009
Phone: (202) 265-1829

#120
Sherman Pickey
Category: Women's Clothing,
Men's Clothing
Average Price: Expensive
Area: Georgetown
Address: 1647 Wisconsin Ave
Washington, DC 20007
Phone: (202) 333-4212

#121
Ruff & Ready
Category: Antiques
Average Price: Modest
Address: 4722 14th St NW
Washington, DC 20011
Phone: (202) 726-2600

#122
Annie's Ace Hardware
Category: Hardware Store
Average Price: Modest
Address: 1240 Upshur St NW
Washington, DC 20011
Phone: (202) 726-2658

#123
Beadazzled
Category: Jewelry
Average Price: Modest
Area: Dupont Circle
Address: 1507 Connecticut Ave NW
Washington, DC 20036
Phone: (202) 265-2323

#124
Barnes & Noble Booksellers
Category: Bookstore, Toy Store,
Music, Dvds
Average Price: Modest
Address: 555 12th St NW
Washington, DC 20004
Phone: (202) 347-0176

#125
Upstairs On 7th
Category: Women's Clothing
Average Price: Expensive
Address: 555 12th St NW
Washington, DC 20004
Phone: (301) 351-8308

#126
The Breastfeeding Center
For Greater Washington
Category: Lactation Services,
Baby Gear, Furniture
Average Price: Modest
Address: 2141 K St NW
Washington, DC 20037
Phone: (202) 293-5182

#127
Wink
Category: Women's Clothing
Average Price: Expensive
Area: Georgetown
Address: 3109 M St NW
Washington, DC 20007
Phone: (202) 338-9465

#128
Salt & Sundry
Category: Kitchen & Bath,
Home Decor, Furniture Store
Average Price: Expensive
Address: 1309 5th St NE
Washington, DC 20002
Phone: (202) 556-1866

#129
Alton Lane
Category: Men's Clothing
Average Price: Expensive
Area: Dupont Circle
Address: 1506 19th St NW
Washington, DC 20036
Phone: (888) 800-8616

#130
Banana Republic
Category: Department Store
Average Price: Expensive
Area: Georgetown
Address: 3200 M St NW
Washington, DC 20007
Phone: (202) 333-2554

#131
Tangerine Boutique
Category: Women's Clothing
Average Price: Modest
Area: Woodley Park
Address: 2643 Connecticut Ave
Washington, DC 20008
Phone: (202) 652-1461

#132
Amani Ya Juu
Category: Jewelry, Accessories
Average Price: Modest
Area: Mount Pleasant
Address: 3166 Mt Pleasant St NW
Washington, DC 20010
Phone: (202) 536-5303

#133
Meeps
Category: Used, Vintage
Average Price: Modest
Area: Adams Morgan
Address: 2104 18th St NW
Washington, DC 20009
Phone: (202) 265-6546

#134
Forever 21
Category: Fashion
Average Price: Inexpensive
Address: 1025 F St NW
Washington, DC 20004
Phone: (202) 347-0150

#135
Zara
Category: Fashion
Average Price: Modest
Address: 1025 F St NW
Washington, DC 20050
Phone: (202) 393-2810

#136
Buffalo Exchange
Category: Men's Clothing,
Women's Clothing, Used, Vintage
Average Price: Inexpensive
Area: Georgetown
Address: 3279 M St NW
Washington, DC 20007
Phone: (202) 333-2829

#137
T.J. Maxx
Category: Department Store
Average Price: Modest
Area: Friendship Heights
Address: 5300 Wisconsin Ave NW
Washington, DC 20015
Phone: (202) 537-3023

#138
A Brighter Image
Category: Eyewear, Opticians, Optometrists
Average Price: Expensive
Address: 1720 Connecticut Ave NW
Washington, DC 20009
Phone: (202) 328-0300

#139
Lou Lou
Category: Shopping
Average Price: Modest
Address: 950 F Street NW
Washington, DC 20004
Phone: (202) 737-0545

#140
**Bentley's Vintage Furniture
& Collectibles**
Category: Antiques
Average Price: Inexpensive
Area: Petworth
Address: 810 Upshur St NW
Washington, DC 20011
Phone: (202) 251-0527

#141
DSW Designer Shoe Warehouse
Category: Shoe Store
Average Price: Modest
Area: Columbia Heights
Address: 3100 14th Street NW
Washington, DC 20010
Phone: (202) 688-2758

#142
Lou Lou
Category: Jewelry
Average Price: Modest
Address: 1802 14th St
Washington, DC 20009
Phone: (202) 232-6333

#143
The B Spot
Category: Art Gallery, Juice Bar
Average Price: Inexpensive
Area: Capitol Hill, Southeast
Address: 1123 B Pennsylvania Ave SE
Washington, DC 20003
Phone: (202) 546-7186

#144
LOFT
Category: Women's Clothing, Accessories
Average Price: Modest
Address: 707 Seventh Street Nw
Washington, DC 20001
Phone: (202) 628-1224

#145
Bluemercury
Category: Cosmetics, Beauty Supply,
Day Spa
Average Price: Expensive
Area: Dupont Circle
Address: 1619 Connecticut Avenue NW
Washington, DC 20009
Phone: (202) 462-1300

#146
Hunted House
Category: Furniture Store
Average Price: Modest
Area: H Street Corridor, Atlas District
Address: 510 H St NE
Washington, DC 20002
Phone: (202) 549-7493

#147
Burberry
Category: Men's Clothing, Women's
Clothing, Children's Clothing
Average Price: Exclusive
Address: 1155 Connecticut Ave
Washington, DC 20036
Phone: (202) 463-3000

#148
Kickk Spott
Category: Sporting Goods, Shoe Store,
Men's Clothing
Average Price: Expensive
Area: Georgetown
Address: 1436 Wisconsin Ave NW
Washington, DC 20007
Phone: (202) 333-5191

#149
J.Crew
Category: Men's Clothing,
Women's Clothing, Accessories
Average Price: Expensive
Area: Friendship Heights
Address: 5335 Wisconsin Avenue, N.W.
Washington, DC 20015
Phone: (202) 537-3380

#150
DURKL
Category: Men's Clothing
Average Price: Modest
Address: 443 Eye St NW
Washington, DC 20001
Phone: (202) 543-0586

#151
Madame Tussauds
Category: Museum, Art Gallery
Average Price: Modest
Address: 1001 F St NW
Washington, DC 20004
Phone: (866) 823-9565

#152
Home Rule
Category: Home Decor, Kitchen & Bath
Average Price: Modest
Address: 1807 14th St NW
Washington, DC 20009
Phone: (202) 797-5544

#153
Enzo Custom Clothiers
Category: Men's Clothing,
Bespoke Clothing
Average Price: Expensive
Address: 1001 Connecticut Ave NW
Washington, DC 20036
Phone: (202) 223-0000

#154
Brookland True Value Hardware
Category: Hardware Store
Average Price: Modest
Area: Brookland
Address: 3501 12th St NE
Washington, DC 20017
Phone: (202) 635-3200

#155
Suitsupply
Category: Men's Clothing
Average Price: Modest
Address: 2828 Pennsylvania Ave NW
Washington, DC 20007
Phone: (202) 800-7800

#156
The Shops At Georgetown Park
Category: Shopping Center
Average Price: Modest
Area: Georgetown
Address: 3222 M St NW
Washington, DC 20007
Phone: (202) 342-8190

#157
Old City Farm & Guild
Category: Nursery, Gardening
Average Price: Modest
Area: Shaw
Address: 925 Rhode Island Ave NW
Washington, DC 20001
Phone: (202) 412-2489

#158
Jon Wye
Category: Leather Goods, Accessories
Average Price: Modest
Area: Capitol Hill, Southeast
Address: 723 Independence Ave SE
Washington, DC 20003
Phone: (202) 368-4996

#159
**Reiter's Scientific
& Professional Books**
Category: Bookstore
Average Price: Modest
Area: Foggy Bottom
Address: 1900 G St NW
Washington, DC 20006
Phone: (202) 223-3327

#160
Walmart Supercenter
Category: Discount Store,
Grocery, Drugstore
Average Price: Modest
Address: 5929 Georgia NW
Washington, DC 20011
Phone: (202) 719-3770

#161
Big Planet Comics
Category: Comic Books
Average Price: Modest
Area: U Street Corridor
Address: 1520 U St NW
Washington, DC 20009
Phone: (202) 342-1961

#162
Urban Outfitters
Category: Accessories,
Men's Clothing, Women's Clothing
Average Price: Expensive
Area: Georgetown
Address: 3111 M St NW
Washington, DC 20007
Phone: (202) 342-1012

#163
Marshalls
Category: Department Store
Average Price: Modest
Address: 529 14th St NW
Washington, DC 20045
Phone: (202) 637-9890

#164
G-Star Raw Store Washington DC
Category: Women's Clothing,
Men's Clothing
Average Price: Expensive
Area: Dupont Circle
Address: 1666 Connecticut Avenue NW
Washington, DC 20009
Phone: (202) 232-8520

#165
Chocolate Moose
Category: Candy Store, Cards, Stationery
Average Price: Modest
Address: 1743 L St NW
Washington, DC 20036
Phone: (202) 463-0992

#166
Vastu
Category: Furniture Store, Interior Design
Average Price: Expensive
Address: 1829 14th St NW
Washington, DC 20009
Phone: (202) 234-8344

#167
Victoria's Secret
Category: Lingerie, Cosmetics,
Beauty Supply
Average Price: Expensive
Address: 1050 Connecticut Ave NW
Washington, DC 20036
Phone: (202) 293-7530

#168
Millennium Decorative Arts
Category: Antiques, Furniture Store,
Home Decor
Average Price: Modest
Area: U Street Corridor
Address: 1528 U St NW
Washington, DC 20009
Phone: (202) 483-1218

#169
Banana Republic
Category: Fashion
Average Price: Modest
Address: 601 13th St NW
Washington, DC 20005
Phone: (202) 638-2724

#170
Apple Store
Category: Computers
Average Price: Expensive
Area: Georgetown
Address: 1229 Wisconsin Ave NW
Washington, DC 20007
Phone: (202) 572-1460

#171
Just Paper & Tea
Category: Cards, Stationery,
Average Price: Expensive
Area: Georgetown
Address: 3232 P St NW
Washington, DC 20007
Phone: (202) 333-9141

#172
Gap
Category: Sports Wear, Men's Clothing,
Women's Clothing
Average Price: Modest
Address: 1120 Connecticut Av Nw
Washington, DC 20036
Phone: (202) 429-0691

#173
Starr's 2nd Story
Consignment Boutique
Category: Used, Vintage,
Jewelry, Women's Clothing
Average Price: Modest
Address: 3903 Georgia Ave NW
Washington, DC 20011
Phone: (202) 722-1626

#174
T.J. Maxx
Category: Discount Store
Average Price: Modest
Area: Brentwood
Address: 1060 Brentwood Rd
Washington, DC 20018
Phone: (202) 529-0630

#175
Potter's House Coffee House
Category: Coffee, Tea, Bookstore, Church
Average Price: Inexpensive
Address: 1658 Columbia Rd NW
Washington, DC 20009
Phone: (202) 232-5483

#176
Catch Can
Category: Women's Clothing, Home Decor
Average Price: Expensive
Area: Chevy Chase
Address: 5516 Connecticut Ave NW
Washington, DC 20015
Phone: (202) 686-5316

#177
Infoshop
Category: Bookstore
Average Price: Inexpensive
Address: Corner 18th St And Pennsylvania
Ave NW Washington, DC 20433
Phone: (202) 458-4500

#178
The Chic Shack
Category: Used, Vintage
Average Price: Inexpensive
Area: H Street Corridor, Atlas District
Address: 1307 H St NE
Washington, DC 20002
Phone: (202) 733-3194

#179
B&B Music Lessons
Category: Musical Instruments
Average Price: Expensive
Area: Eckington
Address: 14 Q St NE
Washington, DC 20002
Phone: (301) 655-4460

#180
Saks Fifth Avenue Men's Store
Category: Department Store
Average Price: Exclusive
Area: Friendship Heights
Address: 5300 Wisconsin Ave NW
Washington, DC 20015
Phone: (202) 363-2059

#181
English Rose Garden
Category: Florist
Average Price: Expensive
Area: Georgetown
Address: 3209 O Street, NW
Washington, DC 20007
Phone: (202) 333-3306

#182
Urban Essentials
Category: Furniture Store
Average Price: Modest
Area: Logan Circle
Address: 1401 14th St NW
Washington, DC 20005
Phone: (202) 299-0640

#183
Pinktini
Category: Women's Clothing, Accessories
Average Price: Modest
Area: Capitol Hill, Southeast
Address: 705 N Carolina Ave SE
Washington, DC 20003
Phone: (202) 546-1234

#184
L'occitane Inc
Category: Cosmetics, Beauty Supply
Average Price: Expensive
Area: Georgetown
Address: 3106 M St NW
Washington, DC 20007
Phone: (202) 337-6001

#185
Art Enables
Category: Art Gallery,
Average Price: Modest
Address: 2204 Rhode Island Ave NE
Washington, DC 20018
Phone: (202) 554-9455

#186
Hudson Trail Outfitters
Category: Bikes, Sports Wear
Average Price: Expensive
Area: Tenleytown
Address: 4530 Wisconsin Ave NW
Washington, DC 20016
Phone: (202) 363-9810

#187
Lee's Flower & Card Shop
Category: Florist
Average Price: Modest
Area: U Street Corridor
Address: 1026 U St NW
Washington, DC 20001
Phone: (202) 265-4965

#188
Meridian House
Category: Landmark/Historical,
Venues, Event Space, Art Gallery
Average Price: Expensive
Address: 1630 Crescent Pl NW
Washington, DC 20009
Phone: (202) 667-6800

#189
Five Below
Category: Discount Store
Average Price: Inexpensive
Area: Columbia Heights
Address: 3100 NW 14th St
Washington, DC 20010
Phone: (202) 319-3584

#190
BCBG
Category: Women's Clothing, Accessories
Average Price: Expensive
Area: Georgetown
Address: 3210 M St NW
Washington, DC 20007
Phone: (202) 333-2224

#191
J.Crew
Category: Women's Clothing,
Men's Clothing, Accessories
Average Price: Expensive
Address: 950 F Street NW
Washington, DC 20004
Phone: (202) 628-8690

#192
Periwinkle
Category: Home Decor, Candy Store
Average Price: Modest
Area: Chevy Chase
Address: 3815 Livingston St NW
Washington, DC 20015
Phone: (202) 364-3076

#193
Edible Arrangements
Category: Flowers, Gifts
Average Price: Modest
Address: 1740 M St NW
Washington, DC 20036
Phone: (202) 955-5660

#194
Caribbean Crescent
Category: Grocery, Wholesale Store, Halal
Average Price: Modest
Address: 1280 5th St NE
Washington, DC 20002
Phone: (202) 547-3101

#195
Bonobos Guideshop
Category: Men's Clothing, Formal Wear
Average Price: Expensive
Area: Georgetown
Address: 3320 Cady's Alley
Washington, DC 20007
Phone: (202) 333-7949

#196
Sangaree
Category: Women's Clothing
Average Price: Expensive
Area: Georgetown
Address: 3288 M St NW
Washington, DC 20007
Phone: (202) 333-4690

#197
Kiehl's Since 1851
Category: Cosmetics,
Beauty Supply, Skin Care
Average Price: Modest
Area: Georgetown
Address: 3110 M Street Nw
Washington, DC 20007
Phone: (202) 333-5101

#198
Appalachian Spring
Category: Jewelry, Arts, Crafts,
Home Decor
Average Price: Modest
Area: Georgetown
Address: 1415 Wisconsin Ave NW
Washington, DC 20007
Phone: (202) 337-5780

#199
Marshalls
Category: Department Store
Average Price: Inexpensive
Area: Columbia Heights
Address: 3100 14th St NW
Washington, DC 20010
Phone: (202) 265-3402

#200
Morgan Care Pharmacy
Category: Drugstore
Average Price: Modest
Area: Georgetown
Address: 3001 P St NW
Washington, DC 20007
Phone: (202) 337-4100

#201
Sterling & Burke Ltd
Category: Accessories, Leather Goods
Average Price: Exclusive
Area: Georgetown
Address: 2824 Pennsylvania Ave NW
Washington, DC 20007
Phone: (202) 333-2266

#202
H&M
Category: Women's Clothing,
Accessories, Men's Clothing
Average Price: Modest
Area: Georgetown
Address: 3222 M St NW
Washington, DC 20007
Phone: (202) 298-6792

#203
Barbour
Category: Men's Clothing, Women's Clothing
Average Price: Exclusive
Area: Georgetown
Address: 3221 M St NW
Washington, DC 20007
Phone: (202) 298-6032

#204
Transcendence-Perfection-Bliss Of The Beyond
Category: Toy Store, Cards, Stationery
Average Price: Expensive
Area: Cleveland Park
Address: 3428 Connecticut Ave NW
Washington, DC 20008
Phone: (202) 363-4797

#205
Inga's Once Is Not Enough
Category: Used, Vintage
Average Price: Expensive
Area: Palisades
Address: 4830 Macarthur Blvd NW
Washington, DC 20007
Phone: (202) 337-3072

#206
Georgetown Tees
Category: Sports Wear
Average Price: Inexpensive
Area: Georgetown
Address: 1075 Wisconsin Ave NW
Washington, DC 20007
Phone: (202) 337-2996

#207
Mazza Gallerie Mall
Category: Shopping Center
Average Price: Expensive
Area: Friendship Heights
Address: 5300 Wisconsin Ave NW
Washington, DC 20015
Phone: (202) 966-6114

#208
Allen Edmonds Shoe Corporation
Category: Shoe Store
Average Price: Expensive
Address: 1027 Connecticut Ave NW
Washington, DC 20036
Phone: (202) 429-9494

#209
Alex And Ani Georgetown
Category: Jewelry
Average Price: Modest
Area: Georgetown
Address: 3068 M Street, NW
Washington, DC 20007
Phone: (202) 333-4195

#210
Swiss Watch Works
Category: Watches
Average Price: Modest
Area: Georgetown
Address: 1512 Wisconsin Ave NW
Washington, DC 20007
Phone: (202) 333-4550

#211
Muléh
Category: Furniture Store, Women's Clothing
Average Price: Exclusive
Address: 1831 14th St NW
Washington, DC 20009
Phone: (202) 667-3440

#212
Georgetown Emporium
Category: Used, Vintage, Antiques
Average Price: Expensive
Area: Georgetown
Address: 2613 P St Nw
Washington, DC 20007
Phone: (202) 944-8449

#213
These Eyes Of Mines
Category: Eyewear, Opticians
Average Price: Expensive
Address: 3828 26th St NE
Washington, DC 20018
Phone: (202) 269-0624

#214
Miss Sixty / Energie
Category: Men's Clothing
Average Price: Expensive
Area: Georgetown
Address: 1239 Wisconsin Ave NW
Washington, DC 20007
Phone: (202) 965-6430

#215
Judy's Beauty & Barber Supply
Category: Cosmetics, Beauty Supply
Average Price: Inexpensive
Area: Brentwood
Address: 520 Rhode Island Ave NE
Washington, DC 20002
Phone: (202) 832-1300

#216
Kim's Watchmaker & Jewelers
Category: Jewelry, Watch Repair
Average Price: Inexpensive
Area: Dupont Circle
Address: 1813 18th St.
Washington, DC 20009
Phone: (202) 667-4002

#217
Hill's Kitchen
Category: Kitchen & Bath, Cooking School
Average Price: Modest
Area: Capitol Hill, Southeast
Address: 713 D St SE
Washington, DC 20003
Phone: (202) 543-1997

#218
Passport Clothing
Category: Women's Clothing,
Men's Clothing
Average Price: Expensive
Area: U Street Corridor
Address: 2003 11th St NW
Washington, DC 20001
Phone: (202) 332-4111

#219
Rite Aid
Category: Drugstore, Convenience Store
Average Price: Inexpensive
Address: 1815 Connecticut Avenue Nw
Washington, DC 20009
Phone: (202) 332-1718

#220
Camper
Category: Shoe Store
Average Price: Expensive
Area: Georgetown
Address: 3219 M Street NW
Washington, DC 20007
Phone: (202) 333-0507

#221
M & M Appliance Sales & Service
Category: Appliances & Repair, Appliances
Average Price: Expensive
Address: 6201 Blair Rd NW
Washington, DC 20011
Phone: (202) 882-7100

#222
Georgetown University Bookstore
Category: Bookstore
Average Price: Expensive
Area: Georgetown
Address: 3800 Reservoir Rd NW
Washington, DC 20057
Phone: (202) 687-7482

#223
Troy Montana Jewelry
Category: Jewelry
Average Price: Modest
Area: Dupont Circle
Address: 1614 17th St NW
Washington, DC 20009
Phone: (202) 370-6401

#224
Toolbox
Category: Pilates, Art Gallery,
Venues, Event Space
Average Price: Expensive
Area: Dupont Circle
Address: 1627 R Connecticut Ave NW
Washington, DC 20009
Phone: (202) 664-3808

#225
DSW Designer Shoe Warehouse
Category: Shoe Store
Average Price: Modest
Area: Friendship Heights
Address: 5333 Wisconsin Ave, NW
Washington, DC 20015
Phone: (202) 688-2759

#226
Lost Boys
Category: Men's Clothing
Average Price: Expensive
Area: Georgetown
Address: 1033 31st St NW
Washington, DC 20007
Phone: (202) 333-0093

#227
Ann Taylor
Category: Accessories, Women's Clothing
Average Price: Modest
Address: 1140 Connecticut Ave
Washington, DC 20036
Phone: (202) 659-0120

#228
The Brass Knob
Architectural Antiques
Category: Antiques, Lighting
Fixtures, Equipment
Average Price: Expensive
Area: Adams Morgan
Address: 2311 18th St NW
Washington, DC 20009
Phone: (202) 332-3370

#229
Lucky Brand Blue Jeans
Category: Men's Clothing,
Women's Clothing
Average Price: Expensive
Area: Georgetown
Address: 3273 M St NW
Washington, DC 20007
Phone: (202) 333-6377

#230
Via Gypset
Category: Used, Vintage
Average Price: Modest
Area: Woodley Park
Address: 2311 Calvert St
Washington, DC 20008
Phone: (202) 803-2874

#231
L'Enfant Plaza La Promenade
Category: Shopping Center
Average Price: Modest
Address: 429 L'Enfant Plaza SW
Washington, DC 20024
Phone: (202) 485-3300

#232
Rizik Bros
Category: Bridal, Accessories,
Women's Clothing
Average Price: Expensive
Address: 1100 Connecticut Ave NW
Washington, DC 20036
Phone: (202) 223-4050

#233
City Sports
Category: Sporting Goods
Average Price: Modest
Area: Georgetown
Address: 3338 M St NW
Washington, DC 20007
Phone: (202) 944-9600

#234
The North Face
Category: Sports Wear, Outdoor Gear
Average Price: Expensive
Area: Georgetown
Address: 3333 M St NW
Washington, DC 20007
Phone: (202) 298-5510

#235
CB2
Category: Furniture Store
Average Price: Expensive
Area: Georgetown
Address: 3307 M St NW
Washington, DC 20007
Phone: (202) 333-6204

#236
Point Of It All
Category: Hobby Shop
Average Price: Expensive
Area: Chevy Chase
Address: 5232 44th Street NW
Washington, DC 20015
Phone: (202) 966-9898

#237
Safeway
Category: Grocery, Drugstore
Average Price: Modest
Area: Georgetown
Address: 1855 Wisconsin Ave NW
Washington, DC 20007
Phone: (202) 333-3223

#238
Hill & Dale
Category: Vinyl Records
Average Price: Modest
Area: Georgetown
Address: 1054 31St St NW
Washington, DC 20007
Phone: (202) 333-5012

#239
Best Buy
Category: Electronics, Computers
Average Price: Expensive
Area: Tenleytown
Address: 4500 Wisconsin Ave NW
Washington, DC 20016
Phone: (202) 895-1580

#240
Neiman Marcus Mazza Gallerie
Category: Department Store
Average Price: Exclusive
Area: Friendship Heights
Address: 5300 Wisconsin Ave NW
Washington, DC 20015
Phone: (202) 966-9700

#241
Hugo Boss
Category: Men's Clothing, Watches
Average Price: Expensive
Area: Georgetown
Address: 1517 Wisconsin Ave NW
Washington, DC 20007
Phone: (202) 625-2677

#242
**Clothes Encounters
Of A Second Kind**
Category: Used, Vintage
Average Price: Modest
Area: Capitol Hill, Southeast
Address: 202 7th St SE
Washington, DC 20003
Phone: (202) 546-4004

#243
G.R.U.M.P.
Category: Festival, Arts, Crafts
Average Price: Inexpensive
Area: Capitol Hill, Southeast
Address: 224 D St SE
Washington, DC 20003
Phone: (202) 543-9163

#244
Primp Beauty Bar
Category: Cosmetics, Beauty Supply
Average Price: Exclusive
Area: U Street Corridor
Address: 1515 U St NW
Washington, DC 20009
Phone: (202) 387-1000

#245
Ross
Category: Department Store
Average Price: Inexpensive
Area: Carver, Langston
Address: 1600 Benning Rd N E
Washington, DC 20002
Phone: (202) 388-1222

#246
DUO
Category: Women's Clothing, Jewelry
Average Price: Modest
Area: Georgetown
Address: 1624 Wisconsin Ave NW
Washington, DC 20007
Phone: (202) 652-0837

#247
The Washington Design Center
Category: Kitchen & Bath, Furniture Store,
Appliances, Home Decor
Average Price: Exclusive
Address: 300 D St SW
Washington, DC 20024
Phone: (202) 646-6114

#248
CVS Pharmacy
Category: Drugstore
Average Price: Modest
Address: 2000 M St NW
Washington, DC 20036
Phone: (202) 862-8417

#249
CVS/Pharmacy
Category: Drugstore
Average Price: Inexpensive
Area: U Street Corridor
Address: 1000 U St NW
Washington, DC 20050
Phone: (202) 518-2978

#250
Bespoke Design
Category: Sewing, Alterations,
Men's Clothing, Women's Clothing
Average Price: Modest
Address: 1100 New York Ave NW
Washington, DC 20006
Phone: (202) 547-0000

#251
Safeway
Category: Grocery, Drugstore
Average Price: Modest
Area: Capitol Hill, Southeast
Address: 415 14th St SE
Washington, DC 20003
Phone: (202) 547-4333

#252
LOFT
Category: Women's Clothing, Accessories
Average Price: Modest
Area: Dupont Circle
Address: 1611 Connecticut Avenue Nw
Washington, DC 20009
Phone: (202) 299-9845

#253
Crate & Barrel
Category: Furniture Store, Kitchen & Bath
Average Price: Expensive
Area: Spring Valley
Address: 4820 Massachusetts Ave NW
Washington, DC 20016
Phone: (202) 364-6100

#254
Modell's Sporting Goods
Category: Sporting Goods
Average Price: Modest
Area: Columbia Heights
Address: 3100 14th St NW
Washington, DC 20010
Phone: (202) 299-1003

#255
Fantom Comics
Category: Comic Books
Average Price: Inexpensive
Area: Dupont Circle
Address: 2010 P St NW
Washington, DC 20036
Phone: (202) 241-6498

#256
American/Holiday
Category: Accessories,
Home Decor, Furniture Store
Average Price: Modest
Area: Georgetown
Address: 1319 Wisconsin Ave NW
Washington, DC 20007
Phone: (202) 684-2790

#257
Sheyla's Boutique Of Georgetown
Category: Women's Clothing,
Men's Clothing
Average Price: Modest
Area: Georgetown
Address: 3251 Prospect St
Washington, DC 20007
Phone: (703) 887-6568

#258
Expressions
Category: Women's Clothing
Average Price: Expensive
Area: Foggy Bottom
Address: 2000 Pennsylvania Ave NW
Washington, DC 20006
Phone: (202) 775-9299

#259
Bed Bath & Beyond
Category: Kitchen & Bath
Average Price: Modest
Area: Columbia Heights
Address: 3100 14th St NW
Washington, DC 20010
Phone: (202) 232-4310

#260
Artisan Lamp
Category: Home Decor, Antiques
Average Price: Modest
Area: Cleveland Park
Address: 3331 Connecticut Ave NW
Washington, DC 20008
Phone: (202) 244-8900

#261
Victoria's Secret
Category: Lingerie
Average Price: Expensive
Address: 50 Massachusetts Ave NE,
Ste 41, Washington, DC 20002
Phone: (202) 682-0686

#262
Stussy
Category: Women's Clothing,
Men's Clothing, Shoe Store
Average Price: Modest
Area: Adams Morgan
Address: 1781 Florida Ave NW
Washington, DC 20009
Phone: (202) 265-1155

#263
Comfort One Shoes
Category: Shoe Store
Average Price: Expensive
Area: Dupont Circle
Address: 1630 Connecticut Ave NW
Washington, DC 20235
Phone: (202) 232-2480

#264
United Colors Of Benetton
Category: Men's Clothing,
Women's Clothing
Average Price: Expensive
Area: Dupont Circle
Address: 1666 Connecticut Ave NW
Washington, DC 20050
Phone: (202) 232-1770

#265
Royal Beauty Supply
Category: Cosmetics, Beauty Supply
Average Price: Modest
Area: Capitol Hill, Southeast
Address: 422 8th Street SE
Washington, DC 20003
Phone: (202) 544-6852

#266
Zara
Category: Men's Clothing,
Women's Clothing
Average Price: Modest
Area: Georgetown
Address: 1238 Wisconsin Ave NW
Washington, DC 20007
Phone: (202) 944-9797

#267
SCRAP DC
Category: Art Supplies, Thrift Store
Average Price: Inexpensive
Area: Brookland
Address: 3101 12th St NE
Washington, DC 20017
Phone: (202) 827-4547

#268
Painting Classes - Dana Ellyn
Category: Art Gallery,
Average Price: Expensive
Address: 916 G St NW
Washington, DC 20001
Phone: (202) 737-6161

#269
Massimo Dutti
Category: Men's Clothing,
Women's Clothing
Average Price: Modest
Area: Georgetown
Address: 1220 Wisconsin Ave NW
Washington, DC 20007
Phone: (202) 944-8780

#270
The Newsroom
Category: Coffee, Tea, Newspapers
Average Price: Inexpensive
Address: 1803 Connecticut Ave NW
Washington, DC 20009
Phone: (202) 332-1489

#271
The Art Of Shaving
Category: , Cosmetics, Beauty Supply
Average Price: Expensive
Address: 1050 Connecticut Ave
Washington, DC 20036
Phone: (202) 223-1433

#272
Boconcept Georgetown
Category: Furniture Store, Home Decor
Average Price: Expensive
Area: Georgetown
Address: 3342 M St NW
Washington, DC 20007
Phone: (202) 333-5656

#273
Compton Jewelers
Category: Jewelry, Watches, Watch Repair
Average Price: Expensive
Area: Foggy Bottom
Address: 1709 G St NW
Washington, DC 20006
Phone: (202) 393-2570

#274
Best Kitchen Supply
Category: Kitchen & Bath
Average Price: Modest
Address: 413 Morse St NE
Washington, DC 20002
Phone: (202) 544-2525

#275
The C.A.T.WALK Boutique
Category: Women's Clothing
Average Price: Modest
Area: H Street Corridor, Atlas District
Address: 1000 H St NE
Washington, DC 20002
Phone: (202) 398-1818

#276
**America's Best Contacts
& Eyeglasses**
Category: Eyewear, Opticians, Optometrists
Average Price: Modest
Address: 1100 Connecticut Ave NW
Washington, DC 20036
Phone: (202) 223-1050

#277
And Beige
Category: Furniture Store
Average Price: Exclusive
Area: Adams Morgan
Address: 1781 Florida Ave NW
Washington, DC 20009
Phone: (202) 234-1557

#278
Pronto Press Printing
Category: Office Equipment,
Average Price: Expensive
Address: 1133 20th St NW
Washington, DC 20036
Phone: (202) 745-0047

#279
Rosies And Rockers Boutique
Category: Women's Clothing,
Men's Clothing, Accessories
Average Price: Modest
Area: U Street Corridor
Address: 2001 13th St NW
Washington, DC 20009
Phone: (202) 328-7625

#280
Gary Taylor Fine Art & Framing
Category: Framing
Average Price: Exclusive
Area: Adams Morgan
Address: 1843 Columbia Rd NW
Washington, DC 20009
Phone: (202) 483-5853

#281
Capital Consignments
Category: Furniture Store, Home Decor
Average Price: Modest
Area: Georgetown
Address: 1614 Wisconsin Ave NW
Washington, DC 20007
Phone: (202) 339-9478

#282
Nine West
Category: Shoe Store
Average Price: Modest
Address: 1008 Connecticut Ave NW
Washington, DC 20036
Phone: (202) 452-9163

#283
Tenleytown Ace Hardware
Category: Hardware Store
Average Price: Modest
Area: Tenleytown
Address: 4500 Wisconsin Ave NW
Washington, DC 20016
Phone: (202) 364-1902

#284
Petals Ribbons & Beyond
Category: Florist
Average Price: Modest
Address: 3906 12th St NE
Washington, DC 20017
Phone: (202) 636-2048

#285
The Forecast
Category: Women's Clothing
Average Price: Expensive
Area: Capitol Hill, Southeast
Address: 218 7th St SE
Washington, DC 20003
Phone: (202) 547-7337

#286
Woven History & Silk Road
Category: Home Decor
Average Price: Exclusive
Area: Capitol Hill, Southeast
Address: 311-315 7th St SE
Washington, DC 20003
Phone: (202) 543-1705

#287
De Louice Custom Tailors
Category: Sewing, Alterations,
Men's Clothing
Average Price: Modest
Address: 4936 Wisconsin Ave NW
Washington, DC 20016
Phone: (202) 803-2915

#288
Ginkgo Gardens
Category: Nursery, Gardening
Average Price: Modest
Address: 911 11th St SE
Washington, DC 20003
Phone: (202) 543-5172

#289
CVS Pharmacy
Category: Drugstore
Average Price: Modest
Area: Foggy Bottom
Address: 2550 Virginia Ave NW
Washington, DC 20037
Phone: (202) 333-5031

#290
UGG Australia
Category: Shoe Store, Accessories
Average Price: Expensive
Area: Georgetown
Address: 1249 Wisconsin Ave NW
Washington, DC 20007
Phone: (202) 640-1208

#291
M29 Lifestyle
Category: Arts, Crafts
Average Price: Expensive
Area: Georgetown
Address: 2800 Pennsylvania Ave NW
Washington, DC 20007
Phone: (202) 295-2829

#292
CVS Pharmacy
Category: Drugstore
Average Price: Modest
Area: Glover Park
Address: 2226 Wisconsin Ave NW
Washington, DC 20007
Phone: (202) 944-8670

#293
The Gallery Shop
Category: Drugstore, Coffee, Tea,
Convenience Store
Average Price: Inexpensive
Address: 600 Maryland Ave SW
Washington, DC 20024
Phone: (202) 554-2900

#294
Douglas Cosmetics
Category: Cosmetics, Beauty Supply
Average Price: Modest
Address: 1145 Connecticut Ave NW
Washington, DC 20036
Phone: (202) 628-5567

#295
Timothy Paul Home
Category: Home Decor, Rugs,
Furniture Store
Average Price: Expensive
Area: Logan Circle
Address: 1529B 14th St NW
Washington, DC 20005
Phone: (202) 234-2020

#296
Allen Edmonds
Category: Shoe Store
Average Price: Expensive
Address: 1071 H St NW
Washington, DC 20001
Phone: (202) 842-5163

#297
Department Of Interior
Category: Shopping,
Average Price: Inexpensive
Area: Foggy Bottom
Address: 1840 C St, NW
Washington, DC 20240
Phone: (202) 789-2345

#298
Foundry Gallery
Category: Art Gallery
Average Price: Modest
Area: Dupont Circle
Address: 1314 18th Street, N.W
Washington, DC 20036
Phone: (202) 463-0203

#299
The Dandelion Patch
Category: Bridal, Cards, Stationery
Average Price: Expensive
Area: Georgetown
Address: 1663 Wisconsin Ave NW
Washington, DC 20007
Phone: (202) 333-8803

#300
Capitol Hill Arts Workshop
Category: Art Gallery, Performing Arts
Average Price: Modest
Area: Capitol Hill, Southeast
Address: 545 7th St SE
Washington, DC 20003
Phone: (202) 547-6839

#301
Mike's Thrift Store
Category: Thrift Store
Average Price: Inexpensive
Address: 1425 H St NE
Washington, DC 20002
Phone: (202) 384-2535

#302
Walgreens
Category: Drugstore, Discount Store
Average Price: Inexpensive
Area: Chinatown
Address: 801 7th St NW
Washington, DC 20001
Phone: (202) 789-5345

#303
CVS Pharmacy
Category: Drugstore
Average Price: Inexpensive
Address: 2000 L St NW
Washington, DC 20036
Phone: (202) 452-6193

#304
Staples Copy & Print Centers
Category: Office Equipment
Average Price: Modest
Address: 1250 H Street NW
Washington, DC 20005
Phone: (202) 638-3907

#305
Zenith Gallery
Category: Art Gallery
Average Price: Expensive
Area: Shepherd Park
Address: 1429 Iris St NW
Washington, DC 20012
Phone: (202) 783-2963

#306
It'sugar
Category: Desserts, Gift Shop,
Candy Store
Average Price: Modest
Address: 714 7th St Nw
Washington, DC 20001
Phone: (202) 737-0403

#307
District Of Columbia Arts Center
Category: Performing Arts,
Cinema, Art Gallery
Average Price: Inexpensive
Area: Adams Morgan
Address: 2438 18th St NW
Washington, DC 20009
Phone: (202) 462-7833

#308
Emporium
Category: Women's Clothing, Accessories
Average Price: Expensive
Area: Dupont Circle
Address: 1666 Connecticut Ave
Washington, DC 20009
Phone: (202) 232-1770

#309
American Apparel
Category: Men's Clothing,
Women's Clothing, Accessories
Average Price: Expensive
Area: Georgetown
Address: 3025 M St. N.W.
Washington, DC 20007
Phone: (202) 572-0166

#310
AT&T
Category: Mobile Phones
Average Price: Exclusive
Address: 1050 Connecticut Ave NW
Washington, DC 20036
Phone: (202) 822-1350

#311
Staples
Category: Office Equipment
Average Price: Expensive
Area: Columbia Heights
Address: 3100 14th St NW
Washington, DC 20010
Phone: (202) 939-0290

#312
Finials
Category: Antiques, Home Decor, Furniture
Store
Average Price: Modest
Area: Chevy Chase
Address: 3813 Livingston Street NW
Washington, DC 20015
Phone: (202) 362-8400

#313
Tugooh Toys
Category: Toy Store, Baby Gear, Furniture
Average Price: Expensive
Area: Georgetown
Address: 1355 Wisconsin Ave NW
Washington, DC 20007
Phone: (202) 338-9476

#314
Fairy Godmother-Childrens Books & Toys
Category: Toy Store, Bookstore
Average Price: Modest
Area: Capitol Hill, Southeast
Address: 319 7th Street SE
Washington, DC 20003
Phone: (202) 547-5474

#315
Julia Farr
Category: Women's Clothing
Average Price: Modest
Area: Friendship Heights
Address: 5232 44th St NW
Washington, DC 20015
Phone: (202) 364-3277

#316
Best Buy
Category: Electronics,
Appliances, Computers
Average Price: Modest
Area: Columbia Heights
Address: 3100 14th St NW
Washington, DC 20010
Phone: (202) 387-6150

#317
Sprint Store
Category: Mobile Phones
Average Price: Expensive
Area: Dupont Circle
Address: 1208 18Th St Nw
Washington, DC 20036
Phone: (202) 496-9400

#318
Secrète Fine Jewelry
Category: Jewelry, Watch Repair
Average Price: Exclusive
Area: Dupont Circle
Address: 1607 Connecticut Ave NW
Washington, DC 20009
Phone: (202) 588-7275

#319
Charm Georgetown
Category: Jewelry, Accessories
Average Price: Expensive
Area: Georgetown
Address: 2910 M St NW
Washington, DC 20007
Phone: (202) 298-0420

#320
Encore Consignment
Category: Women's Clothing,
Used, Vintage, Accessories
Average Price: Modest
Address: 3715 Macomb St NW
Washington, DC 20016
Phone: (202) 966-8122

#321
Veracruz
Category: Art Gallery
Average Price: Inexpensive
Address: 2108 Vermont Ave
Washington, DC 20001
Phone: (202) 906-9209

#322
Ralph Lauren
Category: Fashion
Average Price: Expensive
Area: Georgetown
Address: 1245 Wisconsin Ave NW
Washington, DC 20007
Phone: (202) 965-0905

#323
Ramer's Shoes
Category: Shoe Store
Average Price: Exclusive
Area: Chevy Chase
Address: 3810 Northampton St NW
Washington, DC 20015
Phone: (202) 244-2288

#324
Giant
Category: Grocery, Drugstore
Average Price: Modest
Area: Columbia Heights
Address: 1345 Park Rd NW
Washington, DC 20010
Phone: (202) 777-1077

#325
Dress Barn
Category: Accessories
Average Price: Modest
Address: 1009 Connecticut Ave NW
Washington, DC 20036
Phone: (202) 293-3875

#326
AT&T
Category: Mobile Phones
Average Price: Expensive
Area: Dupont Circle
Address: 1518 Connecticut Avenue NW
Washington, DC 20036
Phone: (202) 462-1643

#327
Lustre Formal Wear
Category: Men's Clothing
Average Price: Modest
Area: Capitol Hill, Southeast
Address: 311 Pennsylvania Ave SE
Washington, DC 20003
Phone: (202) 546-5451

#328
Grubb's Specialty Pharmacy
Category: Drugstore
Average Price: Expensive
Area: Dupont Circle
Address: 1517 17th St NW
Washington, DC 20036
Phone: (202) 503-2644

#329
Artjamz
Category: , Art Gallery
Average Price: Modest
Address: 1728 Connecticut Ave NW
Washington, DC 20009
Phone: (202) 709-8096

#330
H&M
Category: Accessories, Women's Clothing
Average Price: Modest
Address: 5335 Wisconsin Ave NW
Washington, DC 20015
Phone: (855) 466-7467

#331
CVS Pharmacy
Category: Drugstore
Average Price: Inexpensive
Address: 400 Massachusetts Ave NW
Washington, DC 20001
Phone: (202) 289-2236

#332
Dcfootwear
Category: Shoe Store, Accessories
Average Price: Modest
Area: U Street Corridor
Address: 1348 U St NW
Washington, DC 20009
Phone: (202) 232-2332

#333
CVS/Pharmacy
Category: Drugstore
Average Price: Modest
Address: 1201 Maryland Ave SW
Washington, DC 20024
Phone: (202) 488-0243

#334
Casa Lebrato
Category: Grocery, Wholesale Store
Average Price: Inexpensive
Area: Adams Morgan
Address: 1733 Columbia Rd NW
Washington, DC 20009
Phone: (202) 234-0099

#335
CVS/Pharmacy
Category: Drugstore
Average Price: Modest
Address: 1100 New Jersey Ave SE
Washington, DC 20003
Phone: (202) 488-2364

#336
Baker Georgetown
Category: Furniture Store
Average Price: Expensive
Area: Georgetown
Address: 3330 M St NW
Washington, DC 20007
Phone: (202) 342-7080

#337
Gant
Category: Men's Clothing
Average Price: Expensive
Area: Georgetown
Address: 3239 M St NW
Washington, DC 20007
Phone: (202) 625-1949

#338
Decatur House
Category: Landmark/Historical,
Venues, Event Space, Flowers, Gifts
Average Price: Exclusive
Address: 1610 H St NW
Washington, DC 20006
Phone: (202) 842-0920

#339
Sequels Consignment Shop
Category: Used, Vintage
Average Price: Modest
Area: Tenleytown
Address: 4115 Wisconsin Ave NW
Washington, DC 20016
Phone: (202) 966-7467

#340
Hamiltonian Gallery
Category: Art Gallery
Average Price: Expensive
Area: U Street Corridor
Address: 1353 U Street, NW
Washington, DC 20009
Phone: (202) 332-1116

#341
CVS Pharmacy
Category: Drugstore
Average Price: Modest
Area: Woodley Park
Address: 2601 Connecticut Ave NW
Washington, DC 20008
Phone: (202) 332-1446

#342
The Dutch Lady
Category: Antiques, Home Decor
Average Price: Modest
Area: Georgetown
Address: 2914 M St NW
Washington, DC 20007
Phone: (202) 669-0317

#343
Dr. Martens
Category: Shoe Store
Average Price: Expensive
Area: Georgetown
Address: 3108 M St NW
Washington, DC 20007
Phone: (202) 506-4654

#344
Goorin Bros.
Category: Hats, Accessories
Average Price: Modest
Area: Georgetown
Address: 1214 Wisconsin NW
Washington, DC 20007
Phone: (202) 338-4287

#345
Railway Newsstand
Category: Newspapers & Magazines
Average Price: Inexpensive
Address: 900 2nd St NE
Washington, DC 20002
Phone: (202) 682-0059

#346
Artist's Proof Gallery
Category: Venues, Event Space, Art Gallery
Average Price: Expensive
Area: Georgetown
Address: 3323 Cady's Alley NW
Washington, DC 20007
Phone: (202) 803-2782

#347
Myeyedr.
Category: Optometrists, Eyewear, Opticians
Average Price: Expensive
Area: Dupont Circle
Address: 1330 Connecticut Ave NW
Washington, DC 20036
Phone: (202) 785-5700

#348
Alpha Drugs
Category: Drugstore
Average Price: Inexpensive
Area: Dupont Circle
Address: 1638 R St NW
Washington, DC 20009
Phone: (202) 265-7979

#349
Conner Contemporary Art
Category: Art Gallery
Average Price: Exclusive
Address: 1358 Florida Ave NE
Washington, DC 20002
Phone: (202) 588-8750

#350
The Bike House
Category: Bikes
Average Price: Inexpensive
Address: 1240 Upshur St NW
Washington, DC 20542
Phone: (202) 248-6423

#351
Dan & Bryan's Christmas Trees
Category: Nursery, Gardening
Average Price: Inexpensive
Address: 3810 Massachucets Ave NW
Washington, DC 20016
Phone: (202) 243-0642

#352
Anacostia Arts Center
Category: Art Gallery
Average Price: Modest
Area: Anacostia
Address: 1231 Good Hope Rd Se
Washington, DC 20020
Phone: (202) 631-6291

#353
Kate Spade
Category: Women's Clothing, Accessories
Average Price: Expensive
Area: Georgetown
Address: 3061 M St NW
Washington, DC 20007
Phone: (202) 333-8302

#354
Thomas Pink
Category: Men's Clothing,
Women's Clothing
Average Price: Exclusive
Address: 1127 Connecticut Ave NW
Washington, DC 20036
Phone: (202) 223-5390

#355
Caruso Florist
Category: Florist
Average Price: Expensive
Address: 1717 M St NW
Washington, DC 20036
Phone: (202) 223-3816

#356
Nine West
Category: Shoe Store, Accessories
Average Price: Modest
Area: Georgetown
Address: 1227 Wisconsin Ave NW
Washington, DC 20007
Phone: (202) 337-7256

#357
CVS/Pharmacy
Category: Drugstore
Average Price: Modest
Area: Dupont Circle
Address: 6 Dupont Cir NW
Washington, DC 20036
Phone: (202) 833-5704

#358
Dupont Optical
Category: Eyewear, Opticians, Optometrists
Average Price: Expensive
Area: Dupont Circle
Address: 1615 17th St NW
Washington, DC 20009
Phone: (202) 483-9440

#359
Artful Gallery
Category: Art Gallery
Average Price: Modest
Area: H Street Corridor, Atlas District
Address: 1349 Maryland Ave NE
Washington, DC 20002
Phone: (301) 270-2427

#360
Honest Abe's Souvenirs
Category: Hobby Shop
Average Price: Modest
Address: 1000 F St NW
Washington, DC 20004
Phone: (202) 783-0505

#361
Diana's Couture & Bridal
Category: Bridal, Sewing, Alterations
Average Price: Expensive
Area: Georgetown
Address: 1624 Wisconsin Ave NW
Washington, DC 20007
Phone: (202) 333-5689

#362
Lou Lou
Category: Jewelry
Average Price: Modest
Address: 1742 L St
Washington, DC 20036
Phone: (202) 223-2023

#363
Rag & Bone
Category: Accessories,
Men's Clothing, Women's Clothing
Average Price: Expensive
Area: Georgetown
Address: 3067 M St Nw
Washington, DC 20007
Phone: (202) 295-9072

#364
Washington National Cathedral Gift Store
Category: Gift Shop
Average Price: Modest
Address: 3101 Wisconsin Ave NW
Washington, DC 20016
Phone: (202) 537-6267

#365
CVS/Pharmacy
Category: Drugstore,
Photography Store, Services
Average Price: Modest
Area: Spring Valley
Address: 4851 Massachusetts Ave NW
Washington, DC 20016
Phone: (202) 244-2001

#366
Lacoste
Category: Accessories,
Men's Clothing, Women's Clothing
Average Price: Expensive
Area: Georgetown
Address: 3146 M St NW
Washington, DC 20007
Phone: (202) 965-1893

#367
Unique Boutique
Category: Women's Clothing
Average Price: Modest
Address: 888 17th St NW
Washington, DC 20006
Phone: (202) 293-9888

#368
Brooks Brothers
Category: Men's Clothing
Average Price: Expensive
Area: Dupont Circle
Address: 1201 Connecticut Ave NW
Washington, DC 20036
Phone: (202) 659-4650

#369
Surroundings
Category: Florist
Average Price: Modest
Area: Capitol Hill, Northeast, Lincoln Park
Address: 11th St And E Capitol St SE
Washington, DC 20002
Phone: (202) 546-2125

#370
Shoe Gallery
Category: Shoe Store
Average Price: Inexpensive
Area: Georgetown
Address: 3251 M St NW
Washington, DC 20007
Phone: (202) 298-6668

#371
Alden Shoe Company
Category: Shoe Store
Average Price: Expensive
Address: 921 F St NW
Washington, DC 20004
Phone: (202) 347-2308

#372
Political Americana
Category: Hobby Shop, Flowers, Gifts
Average Price: Inexpensive
Address: 1331 Pennsylvania Ave NW
Washington, DC 20004
Phone: (202) 737-7730

#373
Gallery Plan B
Category: Art Gallery
Average Price: Modest
Area: Logan Circle
Address: 1530 14th Street, NW
Washington, DC 20005
Phone: (202) 234-2711

#374
CVS Pharmacy
Category: Drugstore
Average Price: Modest
Address: 1199 Vermont Ave NW
Washington, DC 20005
Phone: (202) 628-0720

#375
Relish
Category: Women's Clothing, Accessories
Average Price: Exclusive
Area: Georgetown
Address: 3312 Cady's Alley NW
Washington, DC 20007
Phone: (202) 333-5343

#376
Walgreens
Category: Drugstore, Cosmetics,
Beauty Supply, Convenience Store
Average Price: Modest
Area: Cleveland Park
Address: 3524 Connecticut Ave Nw
Washington, DC 20008
Phone: (202) 686-6927

#377
Legendary Beast
Category: Jewelry
Average Price: Modest
Address: 1520 U St NW
Washington, DC 20009
Phone: (202) 797-1234

#378
Lou Lou Clothing
Category: Women's Clothing
Average Price: Expensive
Area: Dupont Circle
Address: 1623 Connecticut Ave NW
Washington, DC 20009
Phone: (202) 817-3089

#379
Monarch Carnival Supply Company
Category: Toy Store
Average Price: Modest
Area: Logan Circle
Address: 1331 14th St NW
Washington, DC 20005
Phone: (202) 462-5533

#380
Sears Home Appliance Showroom
Category: Appliances, Appliances & Repair
Average Price: Modest
Area: Tenleytown
Address: 4530-A 40th Street NW
Washington, DC 20016
Phone: (202) 244-4442

#381
AT&T
Category: Mobile Phones
Average Price: Modest
Address: 1201 F St Nw, Suite B1
Washington, DC 20004
Phone: (202) 783-4999

#382
Jos. A. Bank Clothiers
Category: Men's Clothing
Average Price: Expensive
Area: Dupont Circle
Address: 1200 19th St NW
Washington, DC 20036
Phone: (202) 466-2282

#383
Skynear Designs
Category: Furniture Store,
Interior Design, Art Gallery
Average Price: Expensive
Area: Adams Morgan
Address: 2122 18th St NW
Washington, DC 20009
Phone: (202) 797-7160

#384
The Home Depot
Category: Hardware Store, Nursery,
Gardening, Appliances
Average Price: Modest
Area: Brentwood
Address: 901 Rhode Island Ave
Washington, DC 20018
Phone: (202) 526-8760

#385
Galliher & Huguely Associates
Category: Building Supplies, Hardware
Store, Door Sales/Installation
Average Price: Modest
Address: 5925 Blair Rd NW
Washington, DC 20011
Phone: (202) 723-1000

#386
America's Best Contacts
& Eyeglasses
Category: Eyewear, Opticians,
Optometrists, Ophthalmologists
Average Price: Modest
Area: Brentwood
Address: 1060 Brentwood Rd NE
Washington, DC 20018
Phone: (202) 269-5252

#387
Mobile-2-Mobile Wireless
Category: Mobile Phones
Average Price: Modest
Address: 1150 17th St NW
Washington, DC 20036
Phone: (202) 496-0690

#388
Mila's
Category: Women's Clothing
Average Price: Inexpensive
Area: U Street Corridor
Address: 2015 14th St NW
Washington, DC 20009
Phone: (202) 234-8850

#389
Cvs Pharmacy
Category: Drugstore
Average Price: Modest
Area: Brentwood
Address: 2350 Rhode Island Ave NE
Washington, DC 20019
Phone: (202) 635-8520

#390
Downtown Locker Room
Category: Sports Wear
Average Price: Modest
Area: U Street Corridor
Address: 1935 14th St NW
Washington, DC 20009
Phone: (202) 462-1500

#391
Mama Organic
Category: Cosmetics, Beauty Supply
Average Price: Expensive
Address: 1309 5th St NE
Washington, DC 20002
Phone: (571) 217-7918

#392
CVS Pharmacy
Category: Drugstore
Average Price: Inexpensive
Address: 1901 Pennsylvania Ave NW
Washington, DC 20006
Phone: (202) 331-7077

#393
Teaching For Change's Busboys And Poets Bookstore
Category: Bookstore
Average Price: Modest
Area: U Street Corridor
Address: 2021 14th St NW
Washington, DC 20009
Phone: (202) 387-7638

#394
Bouquets And More
Category: Florist
Average Price: Modest
Area: U Street Corridor
Address: 1628 U St NW
Washington, DC 20009
Phone: (202) 300-1348

#395
The Children Of The Sun
Category: Bookstore
Average Price: Modest
Address: 2810 Georgia Ave NW
Washington, DC 20001
Phone: (202) 299-0279

#396
Framesmith DC
Category: Framing
Average Price: Modest
Area: Logan Circle
Address: 1420 11th St NW
Washington, DC 20001
Phone: (202) 518-2500

#397
Chas Schwartz & Son Jewelers
Category: Jewelry, Watches
Average Price: Exclusive
Address: 1400 F St NW
Washington, DC 20004
Phone: (202) 737-4757

#398
Dressbarn
Category: Women's Clothing
Average Price: Modest
Address: 1300 F Street Nw
Washington, DC 20005
Phone: (202) 783-2627

#399
Rochester Big & Tall Clothing
Category: Men's Clothing
Average Price: Exclusive
Address: 1020 Connecticut Ave NW
Washington, DC 20036
Phone: (202) 466-3200

#400
Sprint
Category: Mobile Phones
Average Price: Modest
Area: Dupont Circle
Address: 1643 Connecticut Ave Nw 1St Fl
Washington, DC 20036
Phone: (202) 299-0694

#401
Schurman Fine Papers & Papyrus
Category: Cards, Stationery
Average Price: Expensive
Area: Georgetown
Address: 1300 Wisconsin Avenue NW
Washington, DC 20007
Phone: (202) 337-0720

#402
Beauty 360
Category: Cosmetics, Beauty Supply
Average Price: Expensive
Area: Dupont Circle
Address: 1350 Connecticut Ave
Washington, DC 20036
Phone: (202) 331-1725

#403
Morton's Care Pharmacy
Category: Drugstore
Average Price: Inexpensive
Address: 724 E Capitol St NE
Washington, DC 20001
Phone: (202) 543-1616

#404
Sophia La Belle
Category: Cosmetics,
Beauty Supply, Hair Stylists
Average Price: Expensive
Area: Georgetown
Address: 1620 Wisconsin Ave NW
Washington, DC 20007
Phone: (240) 367-4828

#405
Goodwill
Category: , Thrift Store
Average Price: Inexpensive
Area: Langdon Park, Gateway
Address: 2200 South Dakota Ave NE
Washington, DC 20018
Phone: (202) 715-2658

#406
Apex Optical Company
Category: Eyewear, Opticians
Average Price: Expensive
Area: Tenleytown
Address: 4200 Wisconsin Avenue NW
Washington, DC 20016
Phone: (202) 244-1308

#407
Capitol Hemp
Category: Tobacco Shop
Average Price: Modest
Area: Chinatown
Address: 519 H St NW
Washington, DC 20001
Phone: (202) 842-8690

#408
Major
Category: Shoe Store, Men's Clothing
Average Price: Modest
Area: Georgetown
Address: 1426 Wisconsin Ave NW
Washington, DC 20007
Phone: (202) 625-6732

#409
Verizon Wireless
Category: Mobile Phones, Electronics,
Average Price: Expensive
Address: 1736 L St NW
Washington, DC 20036
Phone: (202) 296-4400

#410
Flashpoint
Category: Performing Arts, Art Gallery
Average Price: Inexpensive
Address: 916 G St NW
Washington, DC 20001
Phone: (202) 315-1305

#411
Prince Of The Harbour
Category: Tobacco Shop, Lounge
Average Price: Modest
Area: Georgetown
Address: 1042 Wisconsin Ave NW
Washington, DC 20441
Phone: (202) 333-1500

#412
CVS Pharmacy
Category: Drugstore
Average Price: Inexpensive
Area: West End
Address: 2240 M St NW
Washington, DC 20037
Phone: (202) 296-9876

#413
The Gift Shop In The Herb Cottage
Category: Cards, Stationery, Home Decor
Average Price: Modest
Address: 3001 Wisconsin Ave NW
Washington, DC 20016
Phone: (202) 537-8982

#414
Bluemercury
Category: Cosmetics, Beauty Supply
Average Price: Expensive
Address: 1010 Wisconsin Ave NW
Washington, DC 20007
Phone: (904) 565-0003

#415
Rooms With A View
Category: Cards, Stationery, Home Decor
Average Price: Modest
Area: Georgetown
Address: 1661 Wisconsin Ave NW
Washington, DC 20007
Phone: (202) 625-0610

#416
GT Players
Category: Shoe Store
Average Price: Modest
Area: Georgetown
Address: 1328 Wisconsin Ave NW
Washington, DC 20007
Phone: (202) 333-7426

#417
Contemporaria
Category: Furniture Store
Average Price: Expensive
Area: Georgetown
Address: 3303 Cadys Ave NW
Washington, DC 20007
Phone: (202) 338-0193

#418
Dollar Star
Category: Department Store
Average Price: Expensive
Area: Mount Pleasant
Address: 3129 Mt Pleasant St NW
Washington, DC 20010
Phone: (202) 462-7900

#419
Uptown Vision
Category: Eyewear, Opticians, Optometrists
Average Price: Exclusive
Area: Cleveland Park
Address: 3424 Connecticut Ave NW
Washington, DC 20008
Phone: (202) 363-2300

#420
Ann Taylor
Category: Women's Clothing, Accessories
Average Price: Modest
Address: 600 13Th Street
Washington, DC 20005
Phone: (202) 737-0325

#421
Blink Optical
Category: Eyewear, Opticians
Average Price: Exclusive
Address: 919 18th NW
Washington, DC 20006
Phone: (202) 776-0999

#422
Radioshack
Category: Mobile Phones,
Electronics, Hobby Shop
Average Price: Modest
Address: 1830 K Street Nw
Washington, DC 20006
Phone: (202) 467-5052

#423
Riccardi Clothier
Category: Men's Clothing, Formal Wear,
Bespoke Clothing
Average Price: Expensive
Area: Dupont Circle
Address: 1300 Connecticut Ave NW
Washington, DC 20036
Phone: (202) 338-5300

#424
Jimmie Muscatello's Washington
Category: Uniforms
Average Price: Modest
Address: 900 Rhode Island Ave NE
Washington, DC 20018
Phone: (202) 393-7547

#425
Cherub Antiques Gallery
Category: Antiques, Art Gallery
Average Price: Expensive
Area: Georgetown
Address: 2918 M Street NW
Washington, DC 20007
Phone: (202) 337-2224

#426
La Belle Florist
Category: Florist
Average Price: Expensive
Area: Georgetown
Address: 3000 M St NW
Washington, DC 20007
Phone: (202) 342-8108

#427
Poltrona Frau Washington
Category: Furniture Store
Average Price: Exclusive
Address: 1010 Wisconsin Ave NW
Washington, DC 20007
Phone: (202) 333-1166

#428
T.J. Maxx & Homegoods
Category: Women's Clothing,
Department Store
Average Price: Modest
Area: Georgetown
Address: 3222 M St NW
Washington, DC 20007
Phone: (202) 333-1040

#429
Cote Jardin Antiques
Category: Antiques
Average Price: Exclusive
Area: Georgetown
Address: 3218 O Street NW
Washington, DC 20007
Phone: (202) 333-3067

#430
Susquehanna Antique Company
Category: Antiques, Art Gallery
Average Price: Expensive
Area: Georgetown
Address: 3216 O St NW
Washington, DC 20007
Phone: (202) 333-1511

#431
Boffi Studio
Category: Furniture Store
Average Price: Exclusive
Area: Georgetown
Address: 3320 M St NW
Washington, DC 20007
Phone: (202) 337-7700

#432
Andante Fine Jewelry
Category: Jewelry, Watches
Average Price: Modest
Area: Georgetown
Address: 1506 Wisconsin Ave NW
Washington, DC 20007
Phone: (202) 507-8905

#433
Sabun Home
Category: Home Decor
Average Price: Modest
Area: Georgetown
Address: 1631 Wisconsin Ave NW
Washington, DC 20007
Phone: (202) 506-6103

#434
Star Trading
Category: Electronics, Mobile Phones
Average Price: Expensive
Area: Adams Morgan
Address: 1782 Columbia Rd
Washington, DC 20009
Phone: (202) 518-8150

#435
Cvs Pharmacy
Category: Drugstore
Average Price: Modest
Address: 1025 Connecticut Ave NW
Washington, DC 20036
Phone: (202) 785-3102

#436
The Ociana Group
Category: Florist
Average Price: Modest
Area: Brentwood, Eckington
Address: 1619 Eckington Pl NE
Washington, DC 20002
Phone: (202) 269-5634

#437
Jos. A Bank Clothiers
Category: Men's Clothing
Average Price: Expensive
Area: Georgetown
Address: 1815 Wisconsin Ave NW
Washington, DC 20007
Phone: (202) 338-1392

#438
Mia Gemma
Category: Jewelry, Personal Shopping
Average Price: Expensive
Address: 933 F St NW
Washington, DC 20004
Phone: (202) 393-4367

#439
Radioshack
Category: Electronics, Hobby Shop,
Mobile Phones
Average Price: Modest
Area: Brentwood
Address: 1060 Brentwood Rd Ne
Washington, DC 20018
Phone: (202) 526-2176

#440
Biotec USA
Category: Skin Care, Cosmetics
Average Price: Expensive
Area: Foxhall
Address: 1619 45th Street NW
Washington, DC 20007
Phone: (202) 338-3391

#441
Staples
Category: Office Equipment
Average Price: Modest
Address: 1901 L St NW
Washington, DC 20036
Phone: (202) 293-4415

#442
Comfort One Shoes
Category: Shoe Store
Average Price: Expensive
Address: 716 7th St NW
Washington, DC 20001
Phone: (202) 783-1199

#443
Letterpress Light
Category: Cards, Stationery
Average Price: Expensive
Address: 3711 Macomb St NW
Washington, DC 20016
Phone: (202) 652-1556

#444
Williams-Sonoma
Category: Home Decor,
Appliances, Kitchen & Bath
Average Price: Exclusive
Area: Friendship Heights
Address: 5300 Wisconsin Ave NW
Washington, DC 20015
Phone: (202) 237-1602

#445
Byhand Invitations
Category: Cards, Stationery
Average Price: Modest
Area: Chevy Chase
Address: 5721 Western Ave NW
Washington, DC 20015
Phone: (202) 491-4729

#446
Icon & Book Service
Category: Bookstore
Average Price: Modest
Address: 1217 Quincy St NE
Washington, DC 20017
Phone: (202) 526-6061

#447
Peruvian Connection
Category: Accessories, Women's Clothing
Average Price: Expensive
Address: 950 F St NW
Washington, DC 20004
Phone: (202) 737-4405

#448
Myeyedr.
Category: Optometrists,
Eyewear, Opticians
Average Price: Expensive
Area: Capitol Hill, Southeast
Address: 233 Pennsylvania Ave SE
Washington, DC 20003
Phone: (202) 544-9220

#449
The Framing Studio
Category: Framing
Average Price: Expensive
Area: Tenleytown
Address: 4500 Wisconsin Ave NW
Washington, DC 20016
Phone: (202) 813-3602

#450
American Apparel
Category: Men's Clothing,
Women's Clothing, Accessories
Average Price: Expensive
Address: 555 11th St. N.W.
Washington, DC 20004
Phone: (202) 628-0438

#451
Center Pharmacy
Category: Drugstore
Average Price: Modest
Area: Spring Valley
Address: 4900 Massachusetts Ave NW
Washington, DC 20016
Phone: (202) 363-9240

#452
**International Art Gallery
& Custom Framing**
Category: Art Gallery, Framing
Average Price: Modest
Address: 1625 K St NW
Washington, DC 20006
Phone: (202) 466-7979

#453
Payless Shoe Source
Category: Shoe Store
Average Price: Modest
Address: 6431 Georgia Ave NW
Washington, DC 20012
Phone: (202) 723-3215

#454
Jos A Bank
Category: Men's Clothing
Average Price: Expensive
Address: 555 11th St NW
Washington, DC 20004
Phone: (202) 393-5590

#455
Classic Optical Center
Category: Optometrists, Eyewear, Opticians
Average Price: Modest
Address: 1895 L Street NW
Washington, DC 20036
Phone: (202) 659-9300

#456
Threadz
Category: Women's Clothing, Accessories
Average Price: Modest
Area: Anacostia
Address: 1345 Good Hope Rd SE
Washington, DC 20020
Phone: (202) 610-0006

#457
Gold-N-Time
Category: Jewelry, Watch Repair
Average Price: Modest
Address: 1742 Connecticut Ave NW
Washington, DC 20009
Phone: (202) 328-8700

#458
Alvear Studio Design & Imports
Category: Art Gallery, Jewelry, Furniture Store
Average Price: Expensive
Area: Capitol Hill, Southeast
Address: 705 8th St SE
Washington, DC 20003
Phone: (202) 546-8434

#459
White House Gifts
Category: Gift Shop, Art Gallery
Average Price: Modest
Address: 529 14th St NW
Washington, DC 20045
Phone: (202) 662-7280

#460
Rose Jewelers
Category: Watch Repair, Jewelry
Average Price: Modest
Area: Mount Pleasant
Address: 3159 Mt Pleasant St
Washington, DC 20010
Phone: (202) 986-7871

#461
Plaza Artist Materials & Picture Framing
Category: Art Supplies, Framing
Average Price: Modest
Address: 1990 K St NW
Washington, DC 20006
Phone: (202) 331-7090

#462
Safeway
Category: Department Store
Average Price: Modest
Area: Carver, Langston
Address: 1601 Maryland Ave NE
Washington, DC 20002
Phone: (202) 398-6903

#463
Scott's Beauty Supply
Category: Cosmetics, Beauty Supply
Average Price: Modest
Address: 2324 Pennsylvania Ave SE
Washington, DC 20020
Phone: (202) 581-1520

#464
CVS Pharmacy
Category: Drugstore
Average Price: Modest
Area: Dupont Circle
Address: 1637 P St NW
Washington, DC 20036
Phone: (202) 328-1250

#465
New Couture
Category: Bridal
Average Price: Modest
Address: 4651 Massachusetts Ave NW
Washington, DC 20016
Phone: (202) 237-1126

#466
Cvs Pharmacy
Category: Drugstore
Average Price: Modest
Area: Palisades
Address: 4859 Macarthur Blvd NW
Washington, DC 20007
Phone: (202) 965-6546

#467
Sports Zone Elite
Category: Shoe Store, Men's Clothing, Women's Clothing
Average Price: Expensive
Area: Columbia Heights
Address: 3100 14th St NW
Washington, DC 20010
Phone: (202) 234-1103

#468
Washingtonian Magazine
Category: Print Media, Newspapers & Magazines
Average Price: Modest
Address: 1828 L St NW
Washington, DC 20036
Phone: (202) 296-3600

#469
Sandy's Flowers
Category: Florist
Average Price: Exclusive
Area: Dupont Circle
Address: 1821 18th St NW
Washington, DC 20009
Phone: (202) 232-4100

#470
Lil' Thingamajigs
Category: Cards, Stationery
Average Price: Modest
Area: Georgetown
Address: 3222 M Street NW
Washington, DC 20007
Phone: (202) 944-8449

#471
Streets Of Georgetown
Category: Men's Clothing
Average Price: Exclusive
Area: Georgetown
Address: 1254 Wisconsin Ave NW
Washington, DC 20007
Phone: (202) 295-9098

#472
Jonathan Adler
Category: Home Decor
Average Price: Expensive
Area: Georgetown
Address: 1267 Wisconsin Ave NW
Washington, DC 20007
Phone: (202) 965-1416

#473
CVS Pharmacy
Category: Drugstore
Average Price: Modest
Area: Tenleytown
Address: 4555 Wisconsin Ave NW
Washington, DC 20016
Phone: (202) 537-1587

#474
Write For You
Category: Cards, Stationery
Average Price: Modest
Area: Chevy Chase
Address: 3807 Mckinley St NW
Washington, DC 20015
Phone: (202) 686-7060

#475
CVS/Pharmacy
Category: Drugstore
Average Price: Inexpensive
Address: 1117 10th St NW
Washington, DC 20001
Phone: (202) 326-1401

#476
Ann Taylor
Category: Women's Clothing, Accessories
Average Price: Modest
Address: 50 Massachusetts Ave Ne
Washington, DC 20002
Phone: (202) 371-8010

#477
Bolling Air Force Base Exchange
Category: Shopping Center
Average Price: Modest
Address: 195 Chappie James Blvd
Washington, DC 20032
Phone: (202) 562-3000

#478
Bridge Street Books
Category: Bookstore
Average Price: Modest
Area: Georgetown
Address: 2814 Pennsylvania Ave NW
Washington, DC 20007
Phone: (202) 965-5200

#479
Andrew's Ties
Category: Men's Clothing
Average Price: Modest
Address: 1155 F St NW
Washington, DC 20004
Phone: (202) 347-1002

#480
Michael Kors
Category: Accessories, Women's Clothing
Average Price: Expensive
Area: Georgetown
Address: 3105 M St NW
Washington, DC 20007
Phone: (202) 342-3103

#481
CVS/Pharmacy
Category: Drugstore,
Photography Store, Services
Average Price: Modest
Address: 1900 7th St NW
Washington, DC 20001
Phone: (202) 232-2201

#482
CVS/Pharmacy
Category: Drugstore
Average Price: Modest
Area: Georgetown
Address: 1403 Wisconsin Ave NW
Washington, DC 20007
Phone: (202) 337-4848

#483
Charles Tyrwhitt
Category: Men's Clothing
Average Price: Expensive
Address: 1000 Connecticut Ave NW
Washington, DC 20036
Phone: (202) 594-3529

#484
Picture Frame Factory
Category: Framing
Average Price: Expensive
Area: Adams Morgan
Address: 2300 18th St NW
Washington, DC 20009
Phone: (202) 265-6767

#485
Capital Discount
Category: Wholesale Store, Mattresses
Average Price: Inexpensive
Address: 1325 Rhode Island Ave NE
Washington, DC 20018
Phone: (202) 777-0137

#486
The Shops At Georgetown Park
Category: Shopping Center
Average Price: Inexpensive
Area: Georgetown
Address: 3222 M St NW
Washington, DC 20007
Phone: (202) 342-8190

#487
CVS/Pharmacy
Category: Drugstore
Average Price: Inexpensive
Area: Georgetown
Address: 2819 M St NW
Washington, DC 20007
Phone: (202) 333-1592

#488
Mattress Discounters Tenley Circle
Category: Mattresses
Average Price: Modest
Area: Tenleytown
Address: 4537 Wisconsin Avenue NW
Washington, DC 20016
Phone: (202) 244-3905

#489
Souvenir World
Category: Department Store
Average Price: Inexpensive
Address: 1004 F St NW
Washington, DC 20004
Phone: (202) 783-0388

#490
New Balance
Category: Sporting Goods, Shoe Store
Average Price: Modest
Area: Friendship Heights
Address: 5301 Wisconsin Ave NW
Washington, DC 20015
Phone: (202) 237-1840

#491
George's Place
Category: Shoe Store, Men's Clothing
Average Price: Modest
Area: H Street Corridor, Atlas District
Address: 1001 H St NE
Washington, DC 20002
Phone: (202) 397-4113

#492
Tory Burch
Category: Accessories, Shoe Store,
Women's Clothing
Average Price: Expensive
Area: Georgetown
Address: 1211 Wisconsin Ave NW
Washington, DC 20007
Phone: (202) 337-1410

#493
CVS/Pharmacy
Category: Drugstore,
Photography Store, Services
Average Price: Modest
Area: Brookland
Address: 3601 12th St NE
Washington, DC 20017
Phone: (202) 832-2064

#494
Edible Arrangements
Category: Flowers, Gifts
Average Price: Modest
Area: Capitol Hill, Southeast
Address: 600 Pennsylvania Ave SE
Washington, DC 20003
Phone: (202) 544-7273

#495
Curator's Office
Category: Art Gallery
Average Price: Expensive
Area: Logan Circle
Address: 1515 14th St NW
Washington, DC 20005
Phone: (202) 387-1008

#496
Bright Life Direct
Category: Health & Medical, Accessories
Average Price: Inexpensive
Area: Takoma
Address: 6925-D Willow St NW
Washington, DC 20012
Phone: (202) 895-6945

#497
Gospel Spreading Bible Bookstore
Category: Bookstore
Average Price: Modest
Address: 2002 Georgia Ave NW
Washington, DC 20001
Phone: (202) 745-2665

#498
Monsoon Accessorize
Category: Women's Clothing, Accessories
Average Price: Modest
Area: Georgetown
Address: 3222 M St NW
Washington, DC 20007
Phone: (202) 338-6174

#499
MyEyeDr.
Category: Optometrists,
Eyewear, Opticians
Average Price: Modest
Address: 1776 I Street NW
Washington, DC 20006
Phone: (202) 331-3931

#500
Teresa's Garden Center
Category: Nursery, Gardening
Average Price: Inexpensive
Area: Brentwood
Address: 1720 New York Ave NE
Washington, DC 20006
Phone: (202) 526-9670

TOP 500 RESTAURANTS
The Most Recommended by Locals & Trevelers
(From #1 to #500)

#1
Rose's Luxury
Cuisines: American
Average Price: Expensive
Area: Capitol Hill, Southeast
Address: 717 8th St SE
Washington, DC 20003
Phone: (202) 580-8889

#2
Founding Farmers
Cuisines: American
Average Price: Modest
Area: Foggy Bottom
Address: 1924 Pennsylvania Ave NW
Washington, DC 20006
Phone: (202) 822-8783

#3
Seasonal Pantry
Cuisines: Specialty Food
Average Price: Exclusive
Area: Shaw
Address: 1314 1/2 9th St NW
Washington, DC 20001
Phone: (202) 713-9866

#4
Basil Thyme
Cuisines: Food Stand
Average Price: Inexpensive
Address: L' Enfant Plz
Washington, DC 20024
Phone: (855) 588-7282

#5
Old Ebbitt Grill
Cuisines: Bar
Average Price: Modest
Address: 675 15th St NW
Washington, DC 20005
Phone: (202) 347-4800

#6
Dcity Smokehouse
Cuisines: Barbeque
Average Price: Modest
Address: 8 Florida Ave NW
Washington, DC 20001
Phone: (202) 733-1919

#7
Smith Public Trust
Cuisines: American
Average Price: Modest
Area: Brookland
Address: 3514 12th St NE
Washington, DC 20017
Phone: (202) 733-5834

#8
Mother Rucker's Subs
Cuisines: Sandwiches
Average Price: Inexpensive
Area: Carver, Langston
Address: 1101 Bladensburg Rd NE
Washington, DC 20002
Phone: (202) 388-1881

#9
Donburi
Cuisines: Japanese
Average Price: Modest
Area: Adams Morgan
Address: 2438 18th N W
Washington, DC 20009
Phone: (202) 629-1047

#10
Bub And Pop's
Cuisines: Sandwiches
Average Price: Modest
Area: Dupont Circle
Address: 1815 M St NW
Washington, DC 20036
Phone: (202) 457-1111

#11
The Pig
Cuisines: American
Average Price: Modest
Area: Logan Circle
Address: 1320 14th St NW
Washington, DC 20005
Phone: (202) 290-2821

#12
Amsterdam Falafelshop
Cuisines: Vegetarian
Average Price: Inexpensive
Area: Adams Morgan
Address: 2425 18th St NW
Washington, DC 20009
Phone: (202) 234-1969

#13
Keren Restaurant
Cuisines: Ethiopian
Average Price: Inexpensive
Address: 1780 Florida Ave NW
Washington, DC 20009
Phone: (202) 265-5764

#14
Komi
Cuisines: Italian
Average Price: Exclusive
Area: Dupont Circle
Address: 1509 17th St NW
Washington, DC 20050
Phone: (202) 332-9200

#15
H &Pizza
Cuisines: Pizza
Average Price: Inexpensive
Area: H Street Corridor, Atlas District
Address: 1118 H St NE
Washington, DC 20002
Phone: (202) 733-1285

#16
Cava Mezze Grill
Cuisines: Greek
Average Price: Modest
Area: Tenleytown
Address: 4237 Wisconsin Ave NW
Washington, DC 20016
Phone: (202) 695-8115

#17
City Tap House
Cuisines: Gastropub
Average Price: Modest
Address: 901 9th St NW
Washington, DC 20001
Phone: (202) 733-5333

#18
Puddin'
Cuisines: Comfort Food
Average Price: Inexpensive
Area: Capitol Hill, Southeast
Address: Eastern Market
Washington, DC 20009
Phone: (202) 725-1030

#19
Blue Duck Tavern
Cuisines: Bar
Average Price: Expensive
Area: West End
Address: 1201 24th St NW
Washington, DC 20037
Phone: (202) 419-6755

#20
Boundary Stone
Cuisines: American
Average Price: Modest
Area: Bloomingdale
Address: 116 Rhode Island Ave NW
Washington, DC 20001
Phone: (202) 621-6635

#21
Rasika
Cuisines: Indian
Average Price: Expensive
Area: Penn Quarter
Address: 633 D St NW
Washington, DC 20004
Phone: (202) 637-1222

#22
Neopol Savory Smokery
Cuisines: Bakery
Average Price: Modest
Address: 1309 5th St NE
Washington, DC 20002
Phone: (202) 543-1864

#23
Tortino
Cuisines: Italian
Average Price: Modest
Area: Logan Circle
Address: 1228 11th St NW
Washington, DC 20005
Phone: (202) 312-5570

#24
Menomale Pizza Napoletana
Cuisines: Bar
Average Price: Modest
Area: Brookland
Address: 2711 12th St NE
Washington, DC 20018
Phone: (202) 248-3946

#25
Woodland's Vegan Bistro
Cuisines: Vegan
Average Price: Modest
Area: Park View
Address: 2928 Georgia Ave NW
Washington, DC 20001
Phone: (202) 232-1700

#26
Los Hermanos
Cuisines: Dominican
Average Price: Inexpensive
Area: Columbia Heights
Address: 1426 Park Rd NW
Washington, DC 20010
Phone: (202) 483-8235

#27
Barrel
Cuisines: Bar
Average Price: Modest
Area: Capitol Hill, Southeast
Address: 613 Pennsylvania Ave SE
Washington, DC 20003
Phone: (202) 543-3622

#28
La Colombe
Cuisines: Café
Average Price: Inexpensive
Area: Shaw
Address: 1219 Blagden Alley NW
Washington, DC 20001
Phone: (202) 289-4850

#29
District Taco
Cuisines: Mexican
Average Price: Inexpensive
Address: 1309 F St NW
Washington, DC 20004
Phone: (202) 347-7359

#30
The Atlas Room
Cuisines: Bar
Average Price: Expensive
Area: H Street Corridor, Atlas District
Address: 1015 H St NE
Washington, DC 20002
Phone: (202) 388-4020

#31
Vace
Cuisines: Pizza
Average Price: Inexpensive
Address: 3315 Connecticut Ave NW
Washington, DC 20008
Phone: (202) 363-1999

#32
Right Proper Brewing Company
Cuisines: Gastropub
Average Price: Modest
Area: Shaw
Address: 624 T St NW
Washington, DC 20001
Phone: (202) 607-2337

#33
A Litteri
Cuisines: Grocery
Average Price: Inexpensive
Address: 517-519 Morse St NE
Washington, DC 20002
Phone: (202) 544-0184

#34
&Pizza
Cuisines: Pizza
Average Price: Inexpensive
Area: U Street Corridor
Address: 1250 U St NW
Washington, DC 20009
Phone: (202) 733-1286

#35
Maine Avenue Fish Market
Cuisines: Seafood Market
Average Price: Modest
Address: 1100 Maine Ave SW
Washington, DC 20024
Phone: (202) 484-2722

#36
The Red Hen
Cuisines: Italian
Average Price: Expensive
Area: Bloomingdale
Address: 1822 1st St NW
Washington, DC 20002
Phone: (202) 525-3021

#37
Toki Underground
Cuisines: Taiwanese
Average Price: Modest
Area: H Street Corridor, Atlas District
Address: 1234 H St NE
Washington, DC 20002
Phone: (202) 388-3086

#38
Zaytinya
Cuisines: Greek
Average Price: Expensive
Address: 701 9th St NW
Washington, DC 20001
Phone: (202) 638-0800

#39
Thai X-Ing
Cuisines: Thai
Average Price: Expensive
Address: 515 Florida Ave NW
Washington, DC 20001
Phone: (202) 332-4322

#40
Il Canale
Cuisines: Italian
Average Price: Modest
Area: Georgetown
Address: 1063 31st St NW
Washington, DC 20007
Phone: (202) 337-4444

#41
Simply Banh Mi
Cuisines: Vietnamese
Average Price: Inexpensive
Area: Georgetown
Address: 1624 Wisconsin Ave NW
Washington, DC 20007
Phone: (202) 333-5726

#42
Kochix
Cuisines: Korean
Average Price: Inexpensive
Address: 400 Florida Ave NW
Washington, DC 20001
Phone: (202) 232-3468

#43
Fish In The Hood
Cuisines: Seafood Market
Average Price: Modest
Area: Park View
Address: 3601 Georgia Ave NW
Washington, DC 20010
Phone: (202) 545-6974

#44
Far East Taco Grille
Cuisines: Asian Fusion
Average Price: Inexpensive
Area: Federal Triangle
Address: Federal Triangle
Washington, DC 20009
Phone: (202) 601-4346

#45
V Falafel
Cuisines: Middle Eastern
Average Price: Inexpensive
Address: 2157 P St NW
Washington, DC 20037
Phone: (202) 296-2333

#46
Matchbox Chinatown
Cuisines: Pizza
Average Price: Modest
Area: Chinatown
Address: 713 H St NW
Washington, DC 20001
Phone: (202) 289-4441

#47
Blacksalt Fish Market & Restaurant
Cuisines: Seafood
Average Price: Expensive
Area: Palisades
Address: 4883 Macarthur Blvd NW
Washington, DC 20007
Phone: (202) 342-9101

#48
Quill
Cuisines: Bar
Average Price: Expensive
Address: 1200 16th St NW
Washington, DC 20036
Phone: (202) 448-2300

#49
Figs Lebanese Cafe
Cuisines: Mediterranean
Average Price: Modest
Area: Palisades
Address: 4828 Macarthur Blvd NW
Washington, DC 20007
Phone: (202) 333-7773

#50
Corduroy
Cuisines: American
Average Price: Expensive
Address: 1122 9th St NW
Washington, DC 20001
Phone: (202) 589-0699

#51
Bistrot Du Coin
Cuisines: French
Average Price: Modest
Address: 1738 Connecticut Ave NW
Washington, DC 20009
Phone: (202) 234-6969

#52
2 Amys
Cuisines: Pizza
Average Price: Modest
Address: 3715 Macomb St NW
Washington, DC 20016
Phone: (202) 885-5700

#53
Luke's Lobster
Cuisines: Seafood
Average Price: Modest
Area: Penn Quarter
Address: 624 E St NW
Washington, DC 20004
Phone: (202) 347-3355

#54
Barcelona
Cuisines: Tapas
Average Price: Expensive
Area: Logan Circle
Address: 1622 14th St Nw
Washington, DC 20005
Phone: (202) 588-5500

#55
Le Diplomate
Cuisines: Brasseries
Average Price: Expensive
Area: Logan Circle
Address: 1601 14th Street NW
Washington, DC 20009
Phone: (202) 332-3333

#56
&Pizza
Cuisines: Pizza
Average Price: Inexpensive
Address: 1005 E St NW
Washington, DC 20004
Phone: (202) 347-5056

#57
Sunrise Caribbean Cuisine
Cuisines: Caribbean
Average Price: Inexpensive
Address: 50 Massachusetts Ave
Washington, DC 20002
Phone: (202) 291-2949

#58
Granville Moore's
Cuisines: American
Average Price: Modest
Area: H Street Corridor, Atlas District
Address: 1238 H St NE
Washington, DC 20002
Phone: (202) 399-2546

#59
Panda Gourmet
Cuisines: Szechuan
Average Price: Modest
Area: Gateway
Address: 2700 New York Ave NE
Washington, DC 20002
Phone: (202) 636-3588

#60
Indigo
Cuisines: Indian
Average Price: Modest
Area: H Street Corridor, Atlas District
Address: 243 K St NE
Washington, DC 20002
Phone: (202) 544-4777

#61
Makoto Restaurant
Cuisines: Sushi Bar
Average Price: Exclusive
Area: Palisades
Address: 4822 Macarthur Blvd NW
Washington, DC 20007
Phone: (202) 298-6866

#62
So's Your Mom
Cuisines: Deli
Average Price: Inexpensive
Area: Adams Morgan
Address: 1831 Columbia Rd NW
Washington, DC 20009
Phone: (202) 462-3666

#63
Highlands
Cuisines: Coffee, Tea
Average Price: Inexpensive
Address: 4706 14th St NW
Washington, DC 20011
Phone: (202) 829-6200

#64
MGM Roast Beef
Cuisines: Sandwiches
Average Price: Inexpensive
Area: Brentwood
Address: 905 Brentwood Rd NE
Washington, DC 20018
Phone: (202) 248-0389

#65
Churchkey
Cuisines: American
Average Price: Modest
Area: Logan Circle
Address: 1337 14th St NW
Washington, DC 20005
Phone: (202) 567-2576

#66
Mangialardo & Sons
Cuisines: Sandwiches
Average Price: Inexpensive
Area: Capitol Hill, Southeast
Address: 1317 Pennsylvania Ave SE
Washington, DC 20003
Phone: (202) 543-6212

#67
White Apron Specialty Sandwiches
Cuisines: Sandwiches
Average Price: Inexpensive
Address: 445 11th St NW
Washington, DC 20004
Phone: (202) 347-4733

#68
Salt And Pepper Grill
Cuisines: Indian
Average Price: Inexpensive
Address: 2632 Georgia Ave NW
Washington, DC 20001
Phone: (202) 588-0666

#69
Cava Mezze DC
Cuisines: Greek
Average Price: Modest
Area: Capitol Hill, Southeast
Address: 527 8th St SE
Washington, DC 20003
Phone: (202) 543-9090

#70
Hitching Post
Cuisines: Southern
Average Price: Modest
Address: 200 Upshur St Nw
Washington, DC 20011
Phone: (202) 726-1511

#71
The Capital Grille
Cuisines: American
Average Price: Exclusive
Address: 601 Pennsylvania Ave NW
Washington, DC 20004
Phone: (202) 737-6200

#72
Zenebech Injera
Cuisines: Ethiopian
Average Price: Inexpensive
Address: 608 T St NW
Washington, DC 20001
Phone: (202) 667-4700

#73
Pho Junkies
Cuisines: Street Vendor
Average Price: Inexpensive
Area: Noma
Address: Union Station
Washington, DC 20005
Phone: (202) 643-5401

#74
Rappahannock Oyster Bar
Cuisines: Seafood
Average Price: Modest
Address: 1309 5th St NE
Washington, DC 20002
Phone: (202) 544-4702

#75
Room 11
Cuisines: Wine Bar
Average Price: Modest
Area: Columbia Heights
Address: 3234 11th St NW
Washington, DC 20010
Phone: (202) 332-3234

#76
Mi Cuba Cafe
Cuisines: Cuban
Average Price: Modest
Area: Columbia Heights
Address: 1424 Park Rd NW
Washington, DC 20010
Phone: (202) 813-3489

#77
Cava Mezze Grill
Cuisines: Gluten-Free
Average Price: Inexpensive
Area: Columbia Heights
Address: 3105 14th St NW
Washington, DC 20016
Phone: (202) 695-8100

#78
West Wing Cafe
Cuisines: Deli
Average Price: Inexpensive
Address: 300 New Jersey Ave NW
Washington, DC 20001
Phone: (202) 347-5855

#79
Sakuramen
Cuisines: Asian Fusion
Average Price: Modest
Area: Adams Morgan
Address: 2441 18th St NW
Washington, DC 20009
Phone: (202) 656-5285

#80
Triple B Fresh
Cuisines: Korean
Average Price: Inexpensive
Area: Dupont Circle
Address: 1506 19th St NW
Washington, DC 20009
Phone: (202) 232-2338

#81
Fast Gourmet
Cuisines: Latin American
Average Price: Modest
Address: 1400 W St NW
Washington, DC 20009
Phone: (202) 448-9217

#82
Brookland's Finest
Cuisines: American
Average Price: Modest
Area: Brookland
Address: 3128 12th St NE
Washington, DC 20017
Phone: (202) 636-0050

#83
Tico
Cuisines: American
Average Price: Modest
Area: U Street Corridor
Address: 1926 14th St NW
Washington, DC 20009
Phone: (202) 319-1400

#84
Tabard Inn Restaurant
Cuisines: American
Average Price: Modest
Area: Dupont Circle
Address: 1739 N St NW
Washington, DC 20036
Phone: (202) 331-8528

#85
Cityzen
Cuisines: American
Average Price: Exclusive
Address: 1330 Maryland Ave SW
Washington, DC 20024
Phone: (202) 787-6006

#86
El Rinconcito Cafe
Cuisines: Latin American
Average Price: Inexpensive
Address: 1129 11th St NW
Washington, DC 20001
Phone: (202) 789-4110

#87
Ambar
Cuisines: Modern European
Average Price: Modest
Area: Capitol Hill, Southeast
Address: 523 8th St SE
Washington, DC 20003
Phone: (202) 813-3039

#88
St. Arnold's On Jefferson
Cuisines: Belgian
Average Price: Modest
Area: Dupont Circle
Address: 1827 Jefferson Pl NW
Washington, DC 20036
Phone: (202) 833-1321

#89
Pleasant Pops Farmhouse Market & Cafe
Cuisines: Ice Cream
Average Price: Inexpensive
Area: Adams Morgan
Address: 1781 Florida Ave NW
Washington, DC 20009
Phone: (202) 558-5224

#90
Mitsitam Cafe
Cuisines: American
Average Price: Modest
Address: 4th St & Independence Ave SW
Washington, DC 20560
Phone: (202) 633-1000

#91
Maple
Cuisines: Wine Bar
Average Price: Modest
Area: Columbia Heights
Address: 3418 11th St NW
Washington, DC 20010
Phone: (202) 588-7442

#92
Jetties
Cuisines: Sandwiches
Average Price: Inexpensive
Area: Foxhall
Address: 1609 Foxhall Rd NW
Washington, DC 20007
Phone: (202) 965-3663

#93
Tortilla Cafe
Cuisines: Latin American
Average Price: Inexpensive
Area: Capitol Hill, Southeast
Address: 210 7th St SE
Washington, DC 20003
Phone: (202) 547-5700

#94
Sushi Capitol
Cuisines: Japanese
Average Price: Modest
Area: Capitol Hill, Southeast
Address: 325 Pennsylvania Ave SE
Washington, DC 20003
Phone: (202) 627-0325

#95
Farmers Fishers Bakers
Cuisines: American
Average Price: Modest
Address: 3000 K St NW
Washington, DC 20007
Phone: (202) 298-8783

#96
Matchbox Capitol Hill
Cuisines: Pizza
Average Price: Modest
Area: Capitol Hill, Southeast
Address: 521 8th St SE
Washington, DC 20003
Phone: (202) 548-0369

#97
Filomena Ristorante
Cuisines: Italian
Average Price: Expensive
Area: Georgetown
Address: 1063 Wisconsin Ave NW
Washington, DC 20007
Phone: (202) 338-8800

#98
Birch & Barley
Cuisines: American
Average Price: Expensive
Area: Logan Circle
Address: 1337 14th St NW
Washington, DC 20005
Phone: (202) 567-2576

#99
China Boy
Cuisines: Chinese
Average Price: Inexpensive
Area: Chinatown
Address: 815 6th St NW
Washington, DC 20001
Phone: (202) 371-1661

#100
Carving Room
Cuisines: Deli
Average Price: Modest
Address: 300 Massachusetts Ave NW
Washington, DC 20001
Phone: (202) 525-2116

#101
Las Canteras
Cuisines: Latin American
Average Price: Modest
Area: Adams Morgan
Address: 2307 18th St NW
Washington, DC 20009
Phone: (202) 265-1780

#102
Cafe Kimchi
Cuisines: Korean
Average Price: Inexpensive
Area: Capitol Hill, Southeast
Address: 751 8th St SE
Washington, DC 20003
Phone: (202) 847-3269

#103
Red Derby
Cuisines: Dive Bar
Average Price: Inexpensive
Address: 3718 14th St NW
Washington, DC 20010
Phone: (202) 291-5000

#104
The Passenger
Cuisines: Bar
Average Price: Modest
Address: 1021 7th St NW
Washington, DC 20001
Phone: (202) 393-0220

#105
Busboys And Poets
Cuisines: Breakfast & Brunch
Average Price: Modest
Area: U Street Corridor
Address: 2021 14th St NW
Washington, DC 20009
Phone: (202) 387-7638

#106
Roti Mediterranean Grill
Cuisines: Mediterranean
Average Price: Inexpensive
Address: 1747 Pennsylvania Ave NW
Washington, DC 20006
Phone: (202) 466-7684

#107
St. Arnold's Mussel Bar
Cuisines: Bar
Average Price: Modest
Area: Cleveland Park
Address: 3433 Connecticut Ave NW
Washington, DC 20008
Phone: (202) 621-6719

#108
1789 Restaurant
Cuisines: American
Average Price: Exclusive
Area: Georgetown
Address: 1226 36th St NW
Washington, DC 20007
Phone: (202) 965-1789

#109
Joe's Seafood, Prime Steak & Stone Crab
Cuisines: Seafood
Average Price: Expensive
Address: 750 15th St NW
Washington, DC 20005
Phone: (202) 489-0140

#110
Pimento Grill
Cuisines: Caribbean
Average Price: Inexpensive
Address: 4405 Bowen Rd SE
Washington, DC 20019
Phone: (202) 582-6595

#111
Greek Deli & Catering
Cuisines: Deli
Average Price: Inexpensive
Address: 1120 19th St NW
Washington, DC 20036
Phone: (202) 296-2111

#112
Luke's Lobster
Cuisines: Seafood
Average Price: Modest
Area: Georgetown
Address: 1211 Potomac St NW
Washington, DC 20007
Phone: (202) 333-4863

#113
The Pinch
Cuisines: Dive Bar
Average Price: Modest
Area: Columbia Heights
Address: 3548 14th St NW
Washington, DC 20010
Phone: (202) 722-4440

#114
Crane & Turtle
Cuisines: Japanese
Average Price: Expensive
Area: Petworth
Address: 828 Upshur St NW
Washington, DC 20011
Phone: (202) 723-2543

#115
Thai Orchid's Kitchen
Cuisines: Thai
Average Price: Modest
Address: 2314 Pennsylvania Ave SE
Washington, DC 20020
Phone: (202) 290-3204

#116
The Brookland Cafe
Cuisines: American
Average Price: Modest
Address: 3740 12th St NE
Washington, DC 20017
Phone: (202) 635-6307

#117
Hank's Oyster Bar
Cuisines: Seafood
Average Price: Modest
Area: Dupont Circle
Address: 1624 Q St NW
Washington, DC 20009
Phone: (202) 462-4265

#118
Ted's Bulletin
Cuisines: American
Average Price: Modest
Area: Capitol Hill, Southeast
Address: 505 8th St SE
Washington, DC 20003
Phone: (202) 544-8337

#119
Mandu
Cuisines: Korean
Average Price: Modest
Address: 453 K St NW
Washington, DC 20001
Phone: (202) 289-6899

#120
&Pizza
Cuisines: Pizza
Average Price: Inexpensive
Address: 664-666 Monroe St NE
Washington, DC 20017
Phone: (202) 733-1287

#121
Tryst
Cuisines: Lounge
Average Price: Modest
Area: Adams Morgan
Address: 2459 18th St NW
Washington, DC 20009
Phone: (202) 232-5500

#122
Kafe Leopold
Cuisines: American
Average Price: Modest
Area: Georgetown
Address: 3315 Cady's Alley NW
Washington, DC 20007
Phone: (202) 965-6005

#123
Rustik Tavern
Cuisines: Mediterranean
Average Price: Modest
Area: Bloomingdale
Address: 84 T St NW
Washington, DC 20001
Phone: (202) 290-2936

#124
Roti Mediterranean Grill
Cuisines: Mediterranean
Average Price: Inexpensive
Area: Foggy Bottom
Address: 2221 I St NW
Washington, DC 20037
Phone: (202) 499-2095

#125
District Taco
Cuisines: Mexican
Average Price: Inexpensive
Area: Capitol Hill, Southeast
Address: 656 Pennsylvania Ave SE
Washington, DC 20003
Phone: (202) 735-5649

#126
Mama Ayesha's
Cuisines: Middle Eastern
Average Price: Modest
Area: Adams Morgan
Address: 1967 Calvert St NW
Washington, DC 20009
Phone: (202) 232-5431

#127
Boqueria
Cuisines: Tapas Bar
Average Price: Expensive
Address: 1837 M St NW
Washington, DC 20036
Phone: (202) 558-9545

#128
Pearl Dive Oyster Palace
Cuisines: Seafood
Average Price: Expensive
Area: Logan Circle
Address: 1612 14th St NW
Washington, DC 20009
Phone: (202) 319-1612

#129
Off The Record
Cuisines: Bar
Average Price: Expensive
Address: 800 16th St NW
Washington, DC 20006
Phone: (202) 638-6600

#130
Brasserie Beck
By Robert Wiedmaier
Cuisines: Belgian
Average Price: Expensive
Address: 1101 K St NW
Washington, DC 20005
Phone: (202) 408-1717

#131
Estadio
Cuisines: Spanish
Average Price: Expensive
Area: Logan Circle
Address: 1520 14th St NW
Washington, DC 20005
Phone: (202) 319-1404

#132
West Wing Cafe
Cuisines: Deli
Average Price: Inexpensive
Address: 1111 Pennsylvania Ave
Washington, DC 20004
Phone: (202) 628-2233

#133
Sundevich
Cuisines: Sandwiches
Average Price: Modest
Area: Shaw
Address: 1314 9th St NW
Washington, DC 20001
Phone: (202) 319-1086

#134
Blues Alley
Cuisines: Jazz, Blues
Average Price: Modest
Area: Georgetown
Address: 1073 Wisconsin Ave NW
Washington, DC 20007
Phone: (202) 337-4141

#135
Montmartre
Cuisines: French
Average Price: Modest
Area: Capitol Hill, Southeast
Address: 327 7th St SE
Washington, DC 20003
Phone: (202) 544-1244

#136
Kangaroo Boxing Club
Cuisines: American
Average Price: Modest
Area: Columbia Heights
Address: 3410 11th St NW
Washington, DC 20010
Phone: (202) 505-4522

#137
Compass Rose Bar & Kitchen
Cuisines: Mediterranean
Average Price: Modest
Address: 1346 T St NW
Washington, DC 20009
Phone: (202) 506-4765

#138
The Queen Vic
Cuisines: Pub
Average Price: Modest
Area: H Street Corridor, Atlas District
Address: 1206 H St NE
Washington, DC 20002
Phone: (202) 396-2001

#139
Nando's Peri - Peri
Cuisines: Portuguese
Average Price: Modest
Area: Dupont Circle
Address: 1210 18th St NW
Washington, DC 20036
Phone: (202) 621-8600

#140
Open City
Cuisines: Diner
Average Price: Modest
Area: Woodley Park
Address: 2331 Calvert St NW
Washington, DC 20008
Phone: (202) 332-2331

#141
Blue 44 Restaurant & Bar
Cuisines: American
Average Price: Modest
Area: Chevy Chase
Address: 5507 Connecticut Ave NW
Washington, DC 20015
Phone: (202) 362-2583

#142
Sichuan Pavilion
Cuisines: Szechuan
Average Price: Modest
Address: 1814 K St NW
Washington, DC 20006
Phone: (202) 466-7790

#143
Dumplings & Beyond
Cuisines: Chinese
Average Price: Modest
Area: Glover Park
Address: 2400 Wisconsin Ave NW
Washington, DC 20007
Phone: (202) 338-3815

#144
Kotobuki
Cuisines: Sushi Bar
Average Price: Modest
Area: Palisades
Address: 4822 Macarthur Blvd NW
Washington, DC 20007
Phone: (202) 625-9080

#145
Pho 14
Cuisines: Vietnamese
Average Price: Modest
Area: Van Ness, Forest Hills
Address: 4201 Connecticut Ave NW
Washington, DC 20008
Phone: (202) 686-6275

#146
Busboys And Poets
Cuisines: Bookstore
Average Price: Modest
Address: 1025 5th St NW
Washington, DC 20001
Phone: (202) 789-2227

#147
Proof Restaurant
Cuisines: American
Average Price: Expensive
Address: 775 G St NW
Washington, DC 20001
Phone: (202) 737-7663

#148
Tony's Breakfast
Cuisines: American
Average Price: Inexpensive
Address: 1387 H St NE
Washington, DC 20002
Phone: (202) 397-7750

#149
Food Corner Kabob House
Cuisines: Afghan
Average Price: Inexpensive
Area: Dupont Circle
Address: 2029 P St NW
Washington, DC 20036
Phone: (202) 331-3777

#150
DC Reynolds
Cuisines: American
Average Price: Modest
Area: Park View
Address: 3628 Georgia Ave NW
Washington, DC 20010
Phone: (202) 506-7178

#151
Cafe Olé
Cuisines: Mediterranean
Average Price: Modest
Area: Tenleytown
Address: 4000 Wisconsin Ave NW
Washington, DC 20016
Phone: (202) 244-1330

#152
Bayou
Cuisines: Music Venues
Average Price: Modest
Address: 2519 Pennsylvania Ave NW
Washington, DC 20037
Phone: (202) 223-6941

#153
Tash
Cuisines: Persian, Iranian
Average Price: Modest
Area: Capitol Hill, Southeast
Address: 524 8th St SE
Washington, DC 20003
Phone: (202) 733-1133

#154
Bluejacket
Cuisines: American
Average Price: Modest
Address: 300 Tingey St SE
Washington, DC 20003
Phone: (202) 524-4862

#155
Firefly
Cuisines: American
Average Price: Modest
Area: Dupont Circle
Address: 1310 New Hampshire Ave NW
Washington, DC 20036
Phone: (202) 861-1310

#156
Fogo De Chão Brazilian Steakhouse
Cuisines: Brazilian
Average Price: Expensive
Address: 1101 Pennsylvania Ave. NW
Washington, DC 20004
Phone: (202) 347-4668

#157
Julia's Empanadas
Cuisines: Latin American
Average Price: Inexpensive
Area: Dupont Circle
Address: 1221 Connecticut Ave NW
Washington, DC 20036
Phone: (202) 861-8828

#158
Urbana
Cuisines: Mediterranean
Average Price: Modest
Area: Dupont Circle
Address: 2121 P St NW
Washington, DC 20037
Phone: (202) 956-6650

#159
Wicked Waffle
Cuisines: Breakfast & Brunch
Average Price: Inexpensive
Address: 1712 I St NW
Washington, DC 20006
Phone: (202) 944-2700

#160
Unum
Cuisines: American
Average Price: Expensive
Area: Georgetown
Address: 2917 M St NW
Washington, DC 20007
Phone: (202) 621-6959

#161
Chez Billy
Cuisines: Restaurant
Average Price: Expensive
Address: 3815 Georgia Ave NW
Washington, DC 20011
Phone: (202) 506-2080

#162
Astor Mediterranean
Cuisines: Greek
Average Price: Inexpensive
Area: Adams Morgan
Address: 1829 Columbia Rd NW
Washington, DC 20009
Phone: (202) 745-7495

#163
Izakaya Seki
Cuisines: Japanese
Average Price: Expensive
Address: 1117 V St NW
Washington, DC 20009
Phone: (202) 588-5841

#164
Beau Thai - Mount Pleasant
Cuisines: Thai
Average Price: Modest
Area: Mount Pleasant
Address: 3162 Mt Pleasant St
Washington, DC 20010
Phone: (202) 450-5317

#165
Chinito's Burritos
Cuisines: Mexican
Average Price: Inexpensive
Address: 635 Florida Ave NE
Washington, DC 20002
Phone: (202) 544-4447

#166
Thally
Cuisines: American
Average Price: Expensive
Area: Shaw
Address: 1316 9th St NW
Washington, DC 20001
Phone: (202) 733-3849

#167
Fiola Mare
Cuisines: Seafood
Average Price: Exclusive
Address: 3050 K St NW
Washington, DC 20007
Phone: (202) 628-0065

#168
Pizzeria Paradiso
Cuisines: Pizza
Average Price: Modest
Area: Dupont Circle
Address: 2003 P St NW
Washington, DC 20036
Phone: (202) 223-1245

#169
Cafe Deluxe
Cuisines: Breakfast & Brunch
Average Price: Modest
Address: 3228 Wisconsin Ave Nw
Washington, DC 20016
Phone: (202) 686-2233

#170
Panas
Cuisines: Latin American
Average Price: Inexpensive
Area: Dupont Circle
Address: 2029 P St NW
Washington, DC 20036
Phone: (202) 223-2964

#171
Old Europe
Cuisines: German
Average Price: Modest
Area: Glover Park
Address: 2434 Wisconsin Ave NW
Washington, DC 20007
Phone: (202) 333-7600

#172
Eat The Rich
Cuisines: Seafood
Average Price: Modest
Area: Shaw
Address: 1839 7th St NW
Washington, DC 20001
Phone: (202) 316-9396

#173
The Greek Spot
Cuisines: Greek
Average Price: Inexpensive
Area: U Street Corridor
Address: 2017 11th St NW
Washington, DC 20001
Phone: (202) 265-3118

#174
Daily 14
Cuisines: Convenience Store
Average Price: Inexpensive
Address: 1135 14th St NW
Washington, DC 20005
Phone: (202) 289-0174

#175
Jojo Restaurant And Bar
Cuisines: American
Average Price: Modest
Area: U Street Corridor
Address: 1518 U St NW
Washington, DC 20009
Phone: (202) 319-9350

#176
Amsterdam Falafelshop
Cuisines: Falafel
Average Price: Inexpensive
Address: 1830 14th St NW
Washington, DC 20009
Phone: (202) 232-6200

#177
Ching Ching CHA
Cuisines: Tea Rooms
Average Price: Modest
Area: Georgetown
Address: 1063 Wisconsin Ave NW
Washington, DC 20007
Phone: (202) 333-8288

#178
Cornercopia
Cuisines: Deli
Average Price: Inexpensive
Address: 1000 3rd St SE
Washington, DC 20003
Phone: (202) 525-1653

#179
Duke's Grocery
Cuisines: Bar
Average Price: Modest
Area: Dupont Circle
Address: 1513 17th St NW
Washington, DC 20036
Phone: (202) 733-5623

#180
Matchbox 14th Street
Cuisines: Pizza
Average Price: Modest
Area: U Street Corridor
Address: 1901 14th St NW
Washington, DC 20009
Phone: (202) 328-0369

#181
Vinoteca
Cuisines: Wine Bar
Average Price: Modest
Area: U Street Corridor
Address: 1940 11th St NW
Washington, DC 20001
Phone: (202) 332-9463

#182
Bacio Pizzeria
Cuisines: Pizza
Average Price: Modest
Area: Bloomingdale
Address: 81 Seaton Pl NW
Washington, DC 20001
Phone: (202) 232-2246

#183
Bistro Bohem
Cuisines: Breakfast & Brunch
Average Price: Modest
Address: 600 Florida Ave NW
Washington, DC 20001
Phone: (202) 735-5895

#184
Bistro La Bonne
Cuisines: French
Average Price: Modest
Area: U Street Corridor
Address: 1340 U St NW
Washington, DC 20009
Phone: (202) 758-3413

#185
Red Toque Café
Cuisines: Mediterranean
Average Price: Inexpensive
Area: Shaw
Address: 1701 6th St NW
Washington, DC 20001
Phone: (202) 588-5516

#186
Daikaya - Ramen Shop
Cuisines: Japanese
Average Price: Modest
Address: 705 6th St NW
Washington, DC 20001
Phone: (202) 589-1600

#187
Market Lunch
Cuisines: American
Average Price: Inexpensive
Area: Capitol Hill, Southeast
Address: 225 7th St SE
Washington, DC 20003
Phone: (202) 547-8444

#188
Ninnella
Cuisines: Italian
Average Price: Expensive
Address: 106 13th St SE
Washington, DC 20003
Phone: (202) 543-0184

#189
Tacos El Chilango
Cuisines: Mexican
Average Price: Inexpensive
Address: 1119 V St NW
Washington, DC 20009
Phone: (202) 986-3030

#190
Le Grenier
Cuisines: French
Average Price: Modest
Area: H Street Corridor, Atlas District
Address: 502 H St NE
Washington, DC 20002
Phone: (202) 544-4999

#191
The Source
Cuisines: Asian Fusion
Average Price: Exclusive
Address: 575 Pennsylvania Ave NW
Washington, DC 20001
Phone: (202) 637-6100

#192
Asia 54
Cuisines: Sushi Bar
Average Price: Modest
Area: Dupont Circle
Address: 2122 P St NW
Washington, DC 20037
Phone: (202) 296-1950

#193
Cedar
Cuisines: American
Average Price: Expensive
Area: Penn Quarter
Address: 822 E St NW
Washington, DC 20004
Phone: (202) 637-0012

#194
Burger Tap & Shake
Cuisines: Burgers
Average Price: Modest
Area: Foggy Bottom
Address: 2200 Pennsylvania Ave NW
Washington, DC 20037
Phone: (202) 587-6258

#195
Breadsoda
Cuisines: Bar
Average Price: Modest
Area: Glover Park
Address: 2233 Wisconsin Ave NW
Washington, DC 20007
Phone: (202) 333-7445

#196
Bulgogi Cart
Cuisines: Korean
Average Price: Inexpensive
Address: 1400 L St
Washington, DC 20004
Phone: (703) 209-5415

#197
Ceiba
Cuisines: Latin American
Average Price: Expensive
Address: 701 14th St NW
Washington, DC 20005
Phone: (202) 393-3983

#198
Jardenea
Cuisines: American
Average Price: Expensive
Area: Foggy Bottom
Address: 2430 Pennsylvania Ave NW
Washington, DC 20037
Phone: (202) 955-6400

#199
Acadiana
Cuisines: Cajun/Creole
Average Price: Expensive
Address: 901 New York Ave NW
Washington, DC 20001
Phone: (202) 408-8848

#200
Byblos Deli
Cuisines: Middle Eastern
Average Price: Inexpensive
Area: Cleveland Park
Address: 3414 Connecticut Ave
Washington, DC 20008
Phone: (202) 364-6549

#201
Ercilia's Restaurant
Cuisines: Latin American
Average Price: Inexpensive
Area: Mount Pleasant
Address: 3070 Mt Pleasant St NW
Washington, DC 20009
Phone: (202) 387-0909

#202
Jimmy's Grill
Cuisines: American
Average Price: Modest
Address: 1100 Maine Ave SW
Washington, DC 20024
Phone: (202) 484-6008

#203
Far East Taco Grille
Cuisines: Mexican
Average Price: Inexpensive
Area: Kingman Park
Address: 409 15th St NE
Washington, DC 20002
Phone: (202) 601-4346

#204
Po Boy Jim
Cuisines: Cajun/Creole
Average Price: Modest
Area: H Street Corridor, Atlas District
Address: 709 H St NE
Washington, DC 20002
Phone: (202) 621-7071

#205
Salt And Pepper Grill II
Cuisines: Pakistani
Average Price: Modest
Address: 3925 14th St NW
Washington, DC 20011
Phone: (202) 723-0404

#206
Axian Food Factory
Cuisines: Breakfast & Brunch
Average Price: Inexpensive
Address: 1915 I St NW
Washington, DC 20006
Phone: (202) 293-1425

#207
Sweet Diablo
Cuisines: Café
Average Price: Modest
Address: 1200 19th St NW
Washington, DC 20036
Phone: (202) 450-2956

#208
Sprig And Sprout
Cuisines: Vietnamese
Average Price: Modest
Area: Glover Park
Address: 2317 Wisconsin Ave NW
Washington, DC 20007
Phone: (202) 333-2569

#209
Seventh Hill
Cuisines: Pizza
Average Price: Modest
Area: Capitol Hill, Southeast
Address: 327 7th St SE
Washington, DC 20003
Phone: (202) 544-1911

#210
Beuchert's Saloon
Cuisines: Bar
Average Price: Modest
Area: Capitol Hill, Southeast
Address: 623 Pennsylvania Ave SE
Washington, DC 20003
Phone: (202) 733-1384

#211
Stachowski Market & Deli
Cuisines: Butcher
Average Price: Modest
Area: Georgetown
Address: 1425 28th St NW
Washington, DC 20007
Phone: (202) 506-3125

#212
Toro Toro
Cuisines: Latin American
Average Price: Expensive
Address: 1300 I (Eye) Street NW
Washington, DC 20005
Phone: (202) 682-9500

#213
Taqueria Juquilita
Cuisines: Mexican
Average Price: Modest
Area: Columbia Heights
Address: 1445 Park Rd
Washington, DC 20010
Phone: (202) 265-0243

#214
Clyde's Of Georgetown
Cuisines: American
Average Price: Modest
Area: Georgetown
Address: 3236 M St NW
Washington, DC 20007
Phone: (202) 333-9180

#215
Perry's Restaurant
Cuisines: Breakfast & Brunch
Average Price: Modest
Area: Adams Morgan
Address: 1811 Columbia Rd NW
Washington, DC 20009
Phone: (202) 234-6218

#216
Moby Dick House Of Kabob
Cuisines: Middle Eastern
Average Price: Inexpensive
Area: Georgetown
Address: 1070 31st St NW
Washington, DC 20007
Phone: (202) 333-4400

#217
Co Co Sala
Cuisines: American
Average Price: Expensive
Address: 929 F St NW
Washington, DC 20004
Phone: (202) 347-4265

#218
District Commons
Cuisines: American
Average Price: Modest
Area: Foggy Bottom
Address: 2200 Pennsylvania Ave NW
Washington, DC 20037
Phone: (202) 587-8277

#219
Osteria Morini
Cuisines: Italian
Average Price: Expensive
Address: 301 Water St SE
Washington, DC 20003
Phone: (202) 484-0660

#220
The Gryphon
Cuisines: Seafood
Average Price: Modest
Area: Dupont Circle
Address: 1337 Connecticut Ave NW
Washington, DC 20036
Phone: (202) 827-8980

#221
Penn Grill
Cuisines: Sandwiches
Average Price: Inexpensive
Address: 825 20th St NW
Washington, DC 20006
Phone: (202) 296-0620

#222
Good Stuff Eatery
Cuisines: Burgers
Average Price: Modest
Area: Capitol Hill, Southeast
Address: 303 Pennsylvania Ave SE
Washington, DC 20003
Phone: (202) 543-8222

#223
Arcuri
Cuisines: American
Average Price: Modest
Area: Glover Park
Address: 2400 Wisconsin Ave NW
Washington, DC 20007
Phone: (202) 827-8745

#224
Cafe Tu-O-Tu
Cuisines: Turkish
Average Price: Inexpensive
Area: Georgetown
Address: 2816 Pennsylvania Ave NW
Washington, DC 20007
Phone: (202) 298-7777

#225
Pound The Hill
Cuisines: Coffee, Tea
Average Price: Modest
Area: Capitol Hill, Southeast
Address: 621 Pennsylvania Ave SE
Washington, DC 20003
Phone: (202) 621-6765

#226
The Regent
Cuisines: Thai
Average Price: Modest
Address: 1910 18th St NW
Washington, DC 20009
Phone: (202) 232-1781

#227
The Hamilton
Cuisines: Seafood
Average Price: Modest
Address: 600 14th St NW
Washington, DC 20005
Phone: (202) 787-1000

#228
The Fainting Goat
Cuisines: American
Average Price: Modest
Area: U Street Corridor
Address: 1330 U Street NW
Washington, DC 20009
Phone: (202) 735-0344

#229
Siam House Thai Restaurant
Cuisines: Thai
Average Price: Modest
Area: Cleveland Park
Address: 3520 Connecticut Ave NW
Washington, DC 20008
Phone: (202) 363-7802

#230
District Of Pi
Cuisines: Pizza
Average Price: Modest
Area: Penn Quarter
Address: 910 F St NW
Washington, DC 20004
Phone: (202) 393-5484

#231
Nopa Kitchen + Bar
Cuisines: American
Average Price: Expensive
Area: Penn Quarter
Address: 800 F St NW
Washington, DC 20004
Phone: (202) 347-4667

#232
Ted's Bulletin
Cuisines: Breakfast & Brunch
Average Price: Modest
Address: 1818 14th St NW
Washington, DC 20009
Phone: (202) 265-8337

#233
Southern Efficiency
Cuisines: Southern
Average Price: Modest
Area: Shaw
Address: 1841 7th St NW
Washington, DC 20004
Phone: (202) 316-9396

#234
Commissary
Cuisines: American
Average Price: Modest
Area: Logan Circle
Address: 1443 P St NW
Washington, DC 20005
Phone: (202) 299-0018

#235
Medium Rare
Cuisines: Steakhouse
Average Price: Modest
Area: Capitol Hill, Southeast
Address: 515 8th St SE
Washington, DC 20003
Phone: (202) 601-7136

#236
Carriage House
Cuisines: American
Average Price: Modest
Area: Adams Morgan
Address: 2333 18th St NW
Washington, DC 20009
Phone: (202) 817-3255

#237
Shemali's
Cuisines: Caterer
Average Price: Inexpensive
Address: 3301 New Mexico Avenue NW
Washington, DC 20016
Phone: (202) 686-7070

#238
Spicy Delight
Cuisines: Caribbean
Average Price: Modest
Area: Takoma
Address: 308 Carroll St NW
Washington, DC 20012
Phone: (202) 829-9783

#239
Boundary Road
Cuisines: American
Average Price: Expensive
Area: H Street Corridor, Atlas District
Address: 414 H St NE
Washington, DC 20002
Phone: (202) 450-3265

#240
Chix
Cuisines: Latin American
Average Price: Inexpensive
Area: U Street Corridor
Address: 2019 11th St NW
Washington, DC 20001
Phone: (202) 234-2449

#241
Hank's Oyster Bar
Cuisines: Seafood
Average Price: Modest
Area: Capitol Hill, Southeast
Address: 633 Pennsylvania Ave SE
Washington, DC 20003
Phone: (202) 733-1971

#242
Mourayo
Cuisines: Greek
Average Price: Expensive
Address: 1732 -1734 Connecticut Ave
NW Washington, DC 20009
Phone: (202) 667-2100

#243
New Course
Cuisines: Sandwiches
Average Price: Inexpensive
Address: 500 3rd St NW
Washington, DC 20001
Phone: (202) 347-7035

#244
Mintwood Place
Cuisines: American
Average Price: Expensive
Area: Adams Morgan
Address: 1813 Columbia Rd NW
Washington, DC 20009
Phone: (202) 234-6732

#245
Et Voila
Cuisines: French
Average Price: Expensive
Area: Palisades
Address: 5120 Macarthur Blvd NW
Washington, DC 20016
Phone: (202) 237-2300

#246
Booeymonger
Cuisines: Deli
Average Price: Inexpensive
Area: Georgetown
Address: 3265 Prospect St
Washington, DC 20007
Phone: (703) 524-0800

#247
Beau Thai
Cuisines: Thai
Average Price: Modest
Area: Shaw
Address: 1700 New Jersey Ave NW
Washington, DC 20001
Phone: (202) 536-5636

#248
Woodward Takeout Food
Cuisines: American
Average Price: Modest
Address: 1426 H St NW
Washington, DC 20005
Phone: (202) 347-5355

#249
CIRCA At Foggy Bottom
Cuisines: American
Average Price: Modest
Area: Foggy Bottom
Address: 2221 I St NW
Washington, DC 20037
Phone: (202) 506-5589

#250
Tune Inn
Cuisines: Dive Bar
Average Price: Inexpensive
Area: Capitol Hill, Southeast
Address: 331 Pennsylvania Ave SE
Washington, DC 20003
Phone: (202) 543-2725

#251
Sophie's Cuban Cuisine
Cuisines: Cuban
Average Price: Modest
Address: 1134 19th St NW
Washington, DC 20036
Phone: (202) 833-1005

#252
Rocklands
Cuisines: Barbeque
Average Price: Modest
Area: Glover Park
Address: 2418 Wisconsin Ave NW
Washington, DC 20007
Phone: (202) 333-2558

#253
Roti Mediterranean Grill
Cuisines: Mediterranean
Average Price: Inexpensive
Address: 50 Massachusetts Ave
Washington, DC 20002
Phone: (202) 499-5444

#254
Shake Shack
Cuisines: Burgers
Average Price: Modest
Area: Penn Quarter
Address: 800 F St NW
Washington, DC 20004
Phone: (202) 800-9930

#255
Moby Dick House Of Kabob
Cuisines: Middle Eastern
Average Price: Inexpensive
Area: Dupont Circle
Address: 1300 Connecticut Ave NW
Washington, DC 20036
Phone: (202) 833-9788

#256
Taylor Gourmet
Cuisines: Deli
Average Price: Inexpensive
Address: 485 K St NW
Washington, DC 20001
Phone: (202) 289-8001

#257
The Diner
Cuisines: Diner
Average Price: Modest
Area: Adams Morgan
Address: 2453 18th St NW
Washington, DC 20009
Phone: (202) 232-8800

#258
Julia's Empanadas
Cuisines: Latin American
Average Price: Inexpensive
Area: Adams Morgan
Address: 2452 18th St NW
Washington, DC 20009
Phone: (202) 328-6232

#259
**Mad Momos Beer Deck
And Restaurant**
Cuisines: Lounge
Average Price: Modest
Area: Columbia Heights
Address: 3605 14th St NW
Washington, DC 20010
Phone: (202) 829-1450

#260
The Pug
Cuisines: American
Average Price: Inexpensive
Area: H Street Corridor, Atlas District
Address: 1234 H St NE
Washington, DC 20002
Phone: (202) 555-1212

#261
Medium Rare
Cuisines: Steakhouse
Average Price: Modest
Area: Cleveland Park
Address: 3500 Connecticut Ave NW
Washington, DC 20008
Phone: (202) 237-1432

#262
Sweetgreen
Cuisines: American
Average Price: Inexpensive
Area: Logan Circle
Address: 1471 P St NW
Washington, DC 20005
Phone: (202) 234-7336

#263
Breadline
Cuisines: Sandwiches
Average Price: Inexpensive
Address: 1751 Pennsylvania Ave NW
Washington, DC 20006
Phone: (202) 822-8900

#264
Southern Hospitality
Cuisines: Southern
Average Price: Modest
Area: Adams Morgan
Address: 1815 Adams Mill Rd NW
Washington, DC 20009
Phone: (202) 588-0411

#265
**Andrene's Caribbean
& Soul Food Carryout**
Cuisines: Caribbean
Average Price: Modest
Address: 308 Kennedy St NW
Washington, DC 20011
Phone: (202) 291-7007

#266
Uprising Muffin Company
Cuisines: Coffee, Tea
Average Price: Inexpensive
Area: Shaw
Address: 1817 7th St NW
Washington, DC 20001
Phone: (202) 290-1196

#267
Kapnos
Cuisines: Greek
Average Price: Expensive
Address: 2201 14th St NW
Washington, DC 20009
Phone: (202) 234-5000

#268
El Chucho
Cuisines: Mexican
Average Price: Modest
Area: Columbia Heights
Address: 3313 11th St NW
Washington, DC 20010
Phone: (202) 290-3313

#269
District Taco
Cuisines: Mexican
Average Price: Inexpensive
Area: Dupont Circle
Address: 1919 M St NW
Washington, DC 20036
Phone: (202) 888-9898

#270
Protein Bar
Cuisines: Vegetarian
Average Price: Inexpensive
Area: Penn Quarter
Address: 398 7th St NW
Washington, DC 20004
Phone: (202) 621-9574

#271
Beer And Welding
Cuisines: Sandwiches
Average Price: Inexpensive
Address: 2024 P St NW
Washington, DC 20007
Phone: (202) 281-4003

#272
Lincoln
Cuisines: American
Average Price: Expensive
Address: 1110 Vermont Ave NW
Washington, DC 20005
Phone: (202) 386-9200

#273
BLT Steak
Cuisines: Steakhouse
Average Price: Exclusive
Address: 1625 I St NW
Washington, DC 20006
Phone: (202) 689-8999

#274
Café Bonaparte
Cuisines: French
Average Price: Modest
Area: Georgetown
Address: 1522 Wisconsin Ave NW
Washington, DC 20007
Phone: (202) 333-8830

#275
Mama Chuy, DC
Cuisines: Mexican
Average Price: Inexpensive
Address: 2620 Georgia Ave NW
Washington, DC 20001
Phone: (202) 667-6262

#276
Tanad Thai Cuisine
Cuisines: Thai
Average Price: Modest
Area: Tenleytown
Address: 4912 Wisconsin Ave NW
Washington, DC 20016
Phone: (202) 966-0616

#277
Macon Bistro & Larder
Cuisines: Southern
Average Price: Expensive
Area: Chevy Chase
Address: 5520 Connecticut Ave NW
Washington, DC 20015
Phone: (202) 248-7807

#278
Woodward Table
Cuisines: American
Average Price: Modest
Address: 1426 H St NW
Washington, DC 20005
Phone: (202) 347-5353

#279
Cafe Phillips
Cuisines: Breakfast & Brunch
Average Price: Inexpensive
Address: 1401 H St NW
Washington, DC 20005
Phone: (202) 408-4900

#280
Wapa Cafe Boutique
Cuisines: Coffee, Tea
Average Price: Inexpensive
Area: Brightwood
Address: 6230 Georgia Ave NW
Washington, DC 20011
Phone: (202) 291-2224

#281
Ghibellina
Cuisines: Italian
Average Price: Expensive
Area: Logan Circle
Address: 1610 14th St NW
Washington, DC 20009
Phone: (202) 803-2389

#282
Cafe Mozart
Cuisines: Deli
Average Price: Modest
Address: 1331 H St NW
Washington, DC 20005
Phone: (202) 347-5732

#283
Russia House Restaurant & Lounge
Cuisines: Lounge
Average Price: Expensive
Address: 1800 Connecticut Ave NW
Washington, DC 20009
Phone: (202) 234-9433

#284
Meridian Pint
Cuisines: Bar
Average Price: Modest
Area: Columbia Heights
Address: 3400 11th St NW
Washington, DC 20010
Phone: (202) 588-1075

#285
Pho 14
Cuisines: Vietnamese
Average Price: Modest
Area: Columbia Heights
Address: 1436 Park Rd NW
Washington, DC 20010
Phone: (202) 986-2326

#286
DC Wisey's
Cuisines: Deli
Average Price: Inexpensive
Area: Georgetown
Address: 1440 Wisconsin Nw Ave
Washington, DC 20007
Phone: (202) 333-4122

#287
Chop't Creative Salad Company
Cuisines: Sandwiches
Average Price: Inexpensive
Address: 618 12th St NW
Washington, DC 20005
Phone: (202) 783-0007

#288
Crepes On The Walk
Cuisines: Desserts
Average Price: Inexpensive
Address: 701 7th St NW
Washington, DC 20001
Phone: (202) 393-4910

#289
City Place Cafe
Cuisines: Mediterranean
Average Price: Inexpensive
Address: 1101 17th St NW
Washington, DC 20036
Phone: (202) 466-4665

#290
Lincoln's Waffle Shop
Cuisines: Breakfast & Brunch
Average Price: Inexpensive
Address: 504 10th St NW
Washington, DC 20004
Phone: (202) 638-4008

#291
Range By Bryan Voltaggio
Cuisines: American
Average Price: Expensive
Address: 5335 Wisconsin Ave NW
Washington, DC 20015
Phone: (202) 803-8020

#292
Mama's Kitchen
Cuisines: Pizza
Average Price: Inexpensive
Area: Anacostia
Address: 2028 Martin Luther King Jr Ave SE Washington, DC 20020
Phone: (202) 678-6262

#293
Muncheez Mania
Cuisines: Crêperie
Average Price: Inexpensive
Area: Georgetown
Address: 1071 Wisconsin Ave NW
Washington, DC 20007
Phone: (202) 567-3000

#294
Momiji
Cuisines: Japanese
Average Price: Modest
Area: Chinatown
Address: 505 H St NW
Washington, DC 20001
Phone: (202) 408-8110

#295
Little Red Fox
Cuisines: Café
Average Price: Modest
Area: Chevy Chase
Address: 5035 Connecticut Ave
Washington, DC 20008
Phone: (202) 248-6346

#296
Kintaro
Cuisines: Sushi Bar
Average Price: Modest
Area: Georgetown
Address: 1039 33rd St NW
Washington, DC 20007
Phone: (202) 333-4649

#297
The Codmother
Cuisines: Pub
Average Price: Inexpensive
Area: U Street Corridor
Address: 1334 U St NW
Washington, DC 20009
Phone: (202) 245-0571

#298
Kramerbooks & Afterwords Cafe
Cuisines: Bookstore
Average Price: Modest
Area: Dupont Circle
Address: 1517 Connecticut Ave NW
Washington, DC 20036
Phone: (202) 387-1400

#299
The Partisan
Cuisines: American
Average Price: Expensive
Area: Penn Quarter
Address: 709 D St NW
Washington, DC 20004
Phone: (202) 524-5322

#300
Dulcinea Bar & Grill
Cuisines: Mexican
Average Price: Modest
Address: 2618 Georgia Ave NW
Washington, DC 20001
Phone: (202) 265-0868

#301
Masa 14
Cuisines: Asian Fusion
Average Price: Expensive
Address: 1825 14th St NW
Washington, DC 20009
Phone: (202) 328-1414

#302
Umi Japanese Cuisine
Cuisines: Sushi Bar
Average Price: Modest
Area: Woodley Park
Address: 2625 Connecticut Ave NW
Washington, DC 20008
Phone: (202) 332-3636

#303
Shake Shack
Cuisines: Burgers
Average Price: Modest
Area: Dupont Circle
Address: 1216 18th St NW
Washington, DC 20036
Phone: (202) 683-9922

#304
The Grist Mill
Cuisines: Southern
Average Price: Modest
Address: 815 14th St NW
Washington, DC 20005
Phone: (202) 783-7800

#305
The Tombs
Cuisines: Pub
Average Price: Modest
Area: Georgetown
Address: 1226 36th St NW
Washington, DC 20007
Phone: (202) 337-6668

#306
Restaurant Judy
Cuisines: Latin American
Average Price: Modest
Address: 2212 14th St NW
Washington, DC 20009
Phone: (202) 265-2519

#307
Shophouse Southeast Asian Kitchen
Cuisines: Asian Fusion
Average Price: Inexpensive
Area: Georgetown
Address: 2805 M St NW
Washington, DC 20007
Phone: (202) 627-1958

#308
Potbelly Sandwich Shop
Cuisines: Sandwiches
Average Price: Inexpensive
Area: Penn Quarter
Address: 637 Indiana NW
Washington, DC 20004
Phone: (202) 347-2353

#309
Nando's Peri-Peri
Cuisines: Portuguese
Average Price: Modest
Area: Chinatown
Address: 819 7th St NW
Washington, DC 20001
Phone: (202) 898-1225

#310
Dupont Market
Cuisines: Specialty Food
Average Price: Inexpensive
Area: Dupont Circle
Address: 1807 18th St NW
Washington, DC 20009
Phone: (202) 797-0222

#311
Suki Asia
Cuisines: Asian Fusion
Average Price: Inexpensive
Address: 1730 Rhode Island Ave NW
Washington, DC 20036
Phone: (202) 223-1337

#312
Capitol City Brewing Company
Cuisines: Brewerie
Average Price: Modest
Address: 1100 New York Ave NW
Washington, DC 20005
Phone: (202) 628-2222

#313
Mr. P's Ribs And Fish
Cuisines: Barbeque
Average Price: Modest
Area: Shaw
Address: 514 Rhode Island Ave NE
Washington, DC 20002
Phone: (202) 438-3215

#314
Little Ricky's
Cuisines: Southern
Average Price: Modest
Area: Brookland
Address: 3522 12th St NE
Washington, DC 20017
Phone: (202) 525-2120

#315
Table
Cuisines: Modern European
Average Price: Expensive
Area: Shaw
Address: 903 N St NW
Washington, DC 20001
Phone: (202) 588-5200

#316
Georgia Brown's Restaurant
Cuisines: Southern
Average Price: Expensive
Address: 950 15th St NW
Washington, DC 20005
Phone: (202) 393-4499

#317
Döner Bistro
Cuisines: German
Average Price: Inexpensive
Address: 1654 Columbia Rd NW
Washington, DC 20009
Phone: (202) 462-8355

#318
Sixth Engine
Cuisines: American
Average Price: Modest
Address: 438 Massachusetts Ave NW
Washington, DC 20001
Phone: (202) 506-2455

#319
Justin's Cafe
Cuisines: American
Average Price: Modest
Address: 1025 1st St SE
Washington, DC 20003
Phone: (202) 652-1009

#320
Casa Luca
Cuisines: Italian
Average Price: Expensive
Address: 1099 New York Ave NW
Washington, DC 20001
Phone: (202) 628-1099

#321
Patisserie Poupon
Cuisines: Bakery
Average Price: Modest
Area: Georgetown
Address: 1645 Wisconsin Ave Nw
Washington, DC 20007
Phone: (202) 342-3248

#322
Ben's Chili Bowl
Cuisines: Hot Dogs
Average Price: Inexpensive
Area: U Street Corridor
Address: 1213 U St NW
Washington, DC 20009
Phone: (202) 667-0909

#323
Stoney's Bar And Grill
Cuisines: Bar
Average Price: Modest
Area: Logan Circle
Address: 1433 P St NW
Washington, DC 20005
Phone: (202) 234-1818

#324
Super Tacos & Bakery
Cuisines: Mexican
Average Price: Inexpensive
Area: Adams Morgan
Address: 1762 Columbia Rd NW
Washington, DC 20009
Phone: (202) 232-7121

#325
Etto
Cuisines: Bar
Average Price: Modest
Area: Logan Circle
Address: 1541 14th St NW
Washington, DC 20005
Phone: (202) 232-0920

#326
The Rye Bar
Cuisines: American
Average Price: Modest
Area: Georgetown
Address: 1050 31st NW
Washington, DC 20007
Phone: (202) 617-2400

#327
Mari Vanna
Cuisines: Russian
Average Price: Expensive
Address: 1141 Connecticut Ave Nw
Washington, DC 20036
Phone: (202) 783-7777

#328
Roti Mediterranean Grill
Cuisines: Mediterranean
Average Price: Inexpensive
Address: 1275 First St NE
Washington, DC 20002
Phone: (202) 618-6969

#329
Chix
Cuisines: Latin American
Average Price: Inexpensive
Address: 1121 14th St NW
Washington, DC 20005
Phone: (202) 682-2449

#330
Bodega
Cuisines: Tapas Bar
Average Price: Modest
Area: Georgetown
Address: 3116 M St NW
Washington, DC 20007
Phone: (202) 333-4733

#331
Pica Taco
Cuisines: Mexican
Average Price: Inexpensive
Address: 1406 Florida Ave NW
Washington, DC 20009
Phone: (202) 518-6820

#332
Smoke & Barrel
Cuisines: Bar
Average Price: Modest
Area: Adams Morgan
Address: 2471 18th St NW
Washington, DC 20009
Phone: (202) 319-9353

#333
Sip Of Seattle
Cuisines: Restaurant
Average Price: Inexpensive
Address: 1120 G St NW
Washington, DC 20001
Phone: (202) 393-5058

#334
Harmony Café
Cuisines: Chinese
Average Price: Inexpensive
Area: Georgetown
Address: 3287 M St NW
Washington, DC 20007
Phone: (202) 338-3881

#335
Mothership
Cuisines: American
Average Price: Modest
Area: Park View
Address: 3301 Georgia Ave NW
Washington, DC 20010
Phone: (202) 629-3034

#336
GW Delicatessen
Cuisines: Deli
Average Price: Inexpensive
Area: Foggy Bottom
Address: 2133 G St NW
Washington, DC 20037
Phone: (202) 331-9391

#337
El Rinconcito II
Cuisines: Latin American
Average Price: Inexpensive
Area: Columbia Heights
Address: 1326 Park Rd
Washington, DC 20009
Phone: (202) 299-1076

#338
Goshen
Cuisines: Juice Bar
Average Price: Modest
Address: 1309 5th St, NE
Washington, DC 20002
Phone: (202) 704-2600

#339
Art And Soul
Cuisines: Soul Food
Average Price: Expensive
Address: 415 New Jersey Ave NW
Washington, DC 20001
Phone: (202) 393-7777

#340
Stevens Sandwich Shoppe
Cuisines: Sandwiches
Average Price: Inexpensive
Address: 1250 I Street NW
Washington, DC 20005
Phone: (202) 682-0434

#341
Clyde's Of Gallery Place
Cuisines: American
Average Price: Modest
Address: 707 7th St NW
Washington, DC 20001
Phone: (202) 349-3700

#342
Dino's Grotto
Cuisines: Farmers Market
Average Price: Modest
Area: U Street Corridor
Address: 1914 9th St NW
Washington, DC 20001
Phone: (202) 686-2966

#343
Rasika West End
Cuisines: Indian
Average Price: Expensive
Area: West End
Address: 1190 New Hampshire Ave NW
Washington, DC 20037
Phone: (202) 466-2500

#344
**Pete's New Haven
Style Apizza**
Cuisines: Pizza
Average Price: Modest
Area: Columbia Heights
Address: 1400 Irving St NW
Washington, DC 20009
Phone: (202) 332-7383

#345
Good Stuff Eatery
Cuisines: American
Average Price: Modest
Area: Georgetown
Address: 3291 M St NW
Washington, DC 20007
Phone: (202) 337-4663

#346
Potbelly Sandwich Shop
Cuisines: Sandwiches
Average Price: Inexpensive
Address: 1701 Pennsylvania Ave NW
Washington, DC 20006
Phone: (202) 775-1450

#347
Jam Doung Style Cuisine
Cuisines: Caribbean
Average Price: Inexpensive
Area: Bloomingdale
Address: 1726 N Capitol St NW
Washington, DC 20002
Phone: (202) 483-2445

#348
Chicken And Rice
Cuisines: Indian
Average Price: Modest
Area: H Street Corridor, Atlas District
Address: 819 H St NE
Washington, DC 20002
Phone: (202) 544-0000

#349
I-Thai Restaurant & Sushi Bar
Cuisines: Thai
Average Price: Modest
Area: Georgetown
Address: 3003 M St NW
Washington, DC 20007
Phone: (202) 580-8852

#350
Level One
Cuisines: American
Average Price: Modest
Area: Dupont Circle
Address: 1639 R St NW
Washington, DC 20009
Phone: (202) 745-0025

#351
Teddy's Roti Shop
Cuisines: Caribbean
Average Price: Modest
Address: 7304 Georgia Ave NW
Washington, DC 20012
Phone: (202) 882-6488

#352
Chupacabra Latin Kitchen & Taqueria
Cuisines: Latin American
Average Price: Inexpensive
Area: H Street Corridor, Atlas District
Address: 822 H St NE
Washington, DC 20002
Phone: (202) 505-4628

#353
Crepeaway
Cuisines: Crêperie
Average Price: Inexpensive
Address: 2001 L St NW
Washington, DC 20036
Phone: (202) 973-0404

#354
The Bottom Line
Cuisines: American
Average Price: Inexpensive
Address: 1716 I St NW
Washington, DC 20006
Phone: (202) 298-8488

#355
Cashion's Eat Place
Cuisines: American
Average Price: Expensive
Area: Adams Morgan
Address: 1819 Columbia Rd NW
Washington, DC 20009
Phone: (202) 797-1819

#356
Marvin
Cuisines: Lounge
Average Price: Modest
Area: U Street Corridor
Address: 2007 14th St NW
Washington, DC 20009
Phone: (202) 797-7171

#357
Askale Cafe
Cuisines: Ethiopian
Average Price: Modest
Address: 3629 12th St NE
Washington, DC 20017
Phone: (202) 758-0077

#358
Agora Restaurant
Cuisines: Mediterranean
Average Price: Modest
Area: Dupont Circle
Address: 1527 17th St NW
Washington, DC 20036
Phone: (202) 332-6767

#359
Oohh's & Aahh's
Cuisines: Soul Food
Average Price: Modest
Area: U Street Corridor
Address: 1005 U St NW
Washington, DC 20005
Phone: (202) 667-7142

#360
Pizzeria Paradiso
Cuisines: Pizza
Average Price: Modest
Area: Georgetown
Address: 3282 M St NW
Washington, DC 20007
Phone: (202) 337-1245

#361
Flavors Of India
Cuisines: Indian
Average Price: Modest
Area: Foggy Bottom
Address: 2524 L St NW
Washington, DC 20037
Phone: (202) 333-1155

#362
Surfside
Cuisines: Mexican
Average Price: Modest
Area: Glover Park
Address: 2444 Wisconsin Ave NW
Washington, DC 20007
Phone: (202) 337-0004

#363
G Sandwich
Cuisines: Sandwiches
Average Price: Modest
Address: 2201 14th St NW
Washington, DC 20009
Phone: (202) 234-5015

#364
Libertine
Cuisines: Lounge
Average Price: Modest
Area: Adams Morgan
Address: 2435 18th St
Washington, DC 20009
Phone: (202) 450-3106

#365
Stoney's On L
Cuisines: American
Average Price: Modest
Address: 2101 L St NW
Washington, DC 20037
Phone: (202) 721-0019

#366
Chadwicks
Cuisines: American
Average Price: Modest
Address: 3205 K St NW
Washington, DC 20007
Phone: (202) 333-2565

#367
Argonaut Tavern
Cuisines: Bar
Average Price: Modest
Address: 1433 H St NE
Washington, DC 20002
Phone: (202) 250-3660

#368
Cafe Carvy
Cuisines: Café
Average Price: Inexpensive
Address: 1020 19th St NW
Washington, DC 20036
Phone: (202) 223-1981

#369
Del Frisco's Grille
Cuisines: Steakhouse
Average Price: Expensive
Address: 1201 Pennsylvania Ave NW
Washington, DC 20004
Phone: (202) 450-4686

#370
Pedro And Vinny's
Cuisines: Food Stand
Average Price: Inexpensive
Address: 1500 K St NW
Washington, DC 20005
Phone: (571) 237-1875

#371
Cafe Grande
Cuisines: Café
Average Price: Inexpensive
Address: 1775 K St NW
Washington, DC 20036
Phone: (202) 223-3636

#372
Mai Thai
Cuisines: Thai
Average Price: Modest
Area: Dupont Circle
Address: 1200 19th St NW
Washington, DC 20036
Phone: (202) 452-6870

#373
Scion Restaurant
Cuisines: American
Average Price: Modest
Area: Dupont Circle
Address: 2100 P St Nw
Washington, DC 20037
Phone: (202) 833-8899

#374
Rosemary's Thyme Bistro
Cuisines: Greek
Average Price: Modest
Area: Dupont Circle
Address: 1801 18th St NW
Washington, DC 20009
Phone: (202) 332-3200

#375
Food Corner Kabob & Rotisserie
Cuisines: Pakistani
Average Price: Inexpensive
Area: Pleasant Plains
Address: 2301 Georgia Ave NW
Washington, DC 20001
Phone: (202) 588-5046

#376
Hot N Juicy Crawfish
Cuisines: Seafood
Average Price: Modest
Area: Woodley Park
Address: 2651 Connecticut Ave NW
Washington, DC 20008
Phone: (202) 299-9448

#377
La Granja De Oro
Cuisines: Latin American
Average Price: Inexpensive
Area: Adams Morgan
Address: 1832 Columbia Rd NW
Washington, DC 20009
Phone: (202) 232-8888

#378
Eatonville
Cuisines: Cajun/Creole
Average Price: Modest
Address: 2121 14th St NW
Washington, DC 20009
Phone: (202) 332-9672

#379
Shophouse
Cuisines: Asian Fusion
Average Price: Inexpensive
Area: Dupont Circle
Address: 1516 Connecticut Ave NW
Washington, DC 20009
Phone: (202) 232-4141

#380
Iron Gate
Cuisines: American
Average Price: Exclusive
Area: Dupont Circle
Address: 1734 N St NW
Washington, DC 20001
Phone: (202) 524-5202

#381
Marcel's By Robert Wiedmaier
Cuisines: French
Average Price: Exclusive
Address: 2401 Pennsylvania Ave NW
Washington, DC 20037
Phone: (202) 296-1166

#382
Vapiano
Cuisines: Italian
Average Price: Modest
Address: 1800 M St NW
Washington, DC 20036
Phone: (202) 640-1868

#383
Micho's Lebanese Grill
Cuisines: Lebanese
Average Price: Inexpensive
Area: H Street Corridor, Atlas District
Address: 500 H Street NE
Washington, DC 20002
Phone: (202) 450-4533

#384
Shanghai Lounge
Cuisines: Chinese
Average Price: Modest
Area: Georgetown
Address: 1734 Wisconsin Ave NW
Washington, DC 20007
Phone: (202) 338-1588

#385
Laliguras
Cuisines: Indian
Average Price: Modest
Area: Van Ness, Forest Hills
Address: 4221-B Connecticut Ave NW
Washington, DC 20008
Phone: (202) 735-5097

#386
Kitty O'Shea's DC
Cuisines: Pub
Average Price: Modest
Area: Tenleytown
Address: 4624 Wisconsin Ave NW
Washington, DC 20016
Phone: (202) 450-5077

#387
Thunder Burger & Bar
Cuisines: Burgers
Average Price: Modest
Area: Georgetown
Address: 3056 M St NW
Washington, DC 20007
Phone: (202) 333-2888

#388
Silvestre Cafe
Cuisines: Mexican
Average Price: Inexpensive
Area: Brookland
Address: 3000 12th St NE
Washington, DC 20017
Phone: (202) 526-3119

#389
Bourbon
Cuisines: Bar
Average Price: Modest
Area: Adams Morgan
Address: 2321 18th St NW
Washington, DC 20009
Phone: (202) 332-0800

#390
The Mediterranean Spot
Cuisines: Mediterranean
Average Price: Inexpensive
Area: U Street Corridor
Address: 1501 U St NW
Washington, DC 20009
Phone: (202) 232-7108

#391
Floriana
Cuisines: Italian
Average Price: Modest
Area: Dupont Circle
Address: 1602 17th St NW
Washington, DC 20009
Phone: (202) 667-5937

#392
Bistro Cacao
Cuisines: French
Average Price: Expensive
Area: Capitol Hill, Northeast
Address: 320 Massachusetts Ave NE
Washington, DC 20002
Phone: (202) 546-4737

#393
Deli City Restaurant
Cuisines: Sandwiches
Average Price: Inexpensive
Area: Langdon Park
Address: 2200 Bladensburg Rd NE
Washington, DC 20018
Phone: (202) 526-1800

#394
Teaism
Cuisines: Coffee, Tea
Average Price: Modest
Area: Penn Quarter
Address: 400 8th St NW
Washington, DC 20004
Phone: (202) 638-6010

#395
Zorbas Cafe
Cuisines: Greek
Average Price: Modest
Area: Dupont Circle
Address: 1612 20th St NW
Washington, DC 20009
Phone: (202) 387-8555

#396
Taqueria Distrito Federal
Cuisines: Mexican
Average Price: Inexpensive
Area: Columbia Heights
Address: 3463 14th St NW
Washington, DC 20010
Phone: (202) 276-7331

#397
Mandu
Cuisines: Korean
Average Price: Modest
Area: Dupont Circle
Address: 1805 18th St NW
Washington, DC 20009
Phone: (202) 588-1540

#398
Circa At Dupont
Cuisines: Café
Average Price: Modest
Area: Dupont Circle
Address: 1601 Connecticut Ave NW
Washington, DC 20009
Phone: (202) 667-1601

#399
My Little Bistro
Cuisines: Vegan
Average Price: Inexpensive
Area: Takoma
Address: 353 Cedar St NW
Washington, DC 20012
Phone: (202) 722-4787

#400
Stan's Restaurant & Bar
Cuisines: Lounge
Average Price: Modest
Address: 1029 Vermont Ave NW
Washington, DC 20005
Phone: (202) 347-4488

#401
District Chophouse & Brewery
Cuisines: Steakhouse
Average Price: Expensive
Area: Penn Quarter
Address: 509 7th St NW
Washington, DC 20004
Phone: (202) 347-3434

#402
Ripple
Cuisines: Wine Bar
Average Price: Expensive
Area: Cleveland Park
Address: 3417 Connecticut Ave NW
Washington, DC 20008
Phone: (202) 244-7995

#403
Nage
Cuisines: American
Average Price: Modest
Area: Dupont Circle
Address: 1600 Rhode Island Ave NW
Washington, DC 20036
Phone: (202) 448-8005

#404
Cafe Phillips
Cuisines: Deli
Average Price: Inexpensive
Address: 650 Massachusetts Ave NW
Washington, DC 20001
Phone: (202) 408-0417

#405
Belga Cafe
Cuisines: Belgian
Average Price: Modest
Area: Capitol Hill, Southeast
Address: 514 8th St SE
Washington, DC 20003
Phone: (202) 544-0100

#406
Raku
Cuisines: Asian Fusion
Average Price: Modest
Area: Dupont Circle
Address: 1900 Q St NW
Washington, DC 20009
Phone: (202) 265-7258

#407
Paul Bakery & Café
Cuisines: Bakery
Average Price: Modest
Address: 801 Pennsylvania Ave NW
Washington, DC 20004
Phone: (202) 524-4500

#408
**Osman & Joe's
Steak 'N Egg Kitchen**
Cuisines: Breakfast & Brunch
Average Price: Inexpensive
Area: Tenleytown
Address: 4700 Wisconsin Ave NW
Washington, DC 20016
Phone: (202) 686-1201

#409
Le Caprice DC
Cuisines: Café
Average Price: Inexpensive
Area: Columbia Heights
Address: 3460 14th St NW
Washington, DC 20010
Phone: (202) 290-3109

#410
The Big Board
Cuisines: Burgers
Average Price: Modest
Area: H Street Corridor, Atlas District
Address: 421 H St NE
Washington, DC 20002
Phone: (202) 543-3630

#411
Willie T's Lobster Shack
Cuisines: Seafood
Average Price: Modest
Area: Dupont Circle
Address: 1511 Connecticut Ave NW
Washington, DC 20009
Phone: (202) 332-3690

#412
Smith Commons
Cuisines: American
Average Price: Modest
Area: H Street Corridor, Atlas District
Address: 1245 H St NE
Washington, DC 20002
Phone: (202) 396-0038

#413
The Grill From Ipanema
Cuisines: Brazilian
Average Price: Modest
Area: Adams Morgan
Address: 1858 Columbia Rd NW
Washington, DC 20009
Phone: (202) 986-0757

#414
Zest Bistro
Cuisines: American
Average Price: Modest
Area: Capitol Hill, Southeast
Address: 735 8th St SE
Washington, DC 20003
Phone: (202) 544-7171

#415
Five Guys Burgers & Fries
Cuisines: Burgers
Average Price: Inexpensive
Address: 1400 I St
Washington, DC 20005
Phone: (202) 450-3412

#416
1905 Bistro
Cuisines: American
Average Price: Modest
Address: 1905 9th St NW
Washington, DC 20001
Phone: (202) 332-1905

#417
Biergarten Haus
Cuisines: German
Average Price: Modest
Address: 1355 H St NE
Washington, DC 20002
Phone: (202) 388-4053

#418
Pizza Mart
Cuisines: Pizza
Average Price: Inexpensive
Area: Adams Morgan
Address: 2445 18th St NW
Washington, DC 20009
Phone: (202) 234-9700

#419
Policy
Cuisines: American
Average Price: Modest
Area: U Street Corridor
Address: 1904 14th St NW
Washington, DC 20009
Phone: (202) 387-7654

#420
Meat In A Box
Cuisines: Persian, Iranian
Average Price: Inexpensive
Address: 2005 18th St NW
Washington, DC 20009
Phone: (202) 986-4646

#421
Carmine's
Cuisines: Italian
Average Price: Modest
Area: Penn Quarter
Address: 425 7th St NW
Washington, DC 20004
Phone: (202) 737-7770

#422
El Centro DF
Cuisines: Mexican
Average Price: Modest
Address: 1819 14th St NW
Washington, DC 20009
Phone: (202) 328-3131

#423
Lebanese Taverna
Cuisines: Lebanese
Average Price: Modest
Area: Woodley Park
Address: 2641 Connecticut Ave NW
Washington, DC 20008
Phone: (202) 265-8681

#424
The Black Squirrel
Cuisines: American
Average Price: Modest
Area: Adams Morgan
Address: 2427 18th St NW
Washington, DC 20009
Phone: (202) 232-1011

#425
Bukom Cafe
Cuisines: African
Average Price: Modest
Area: Adams Morgan
Address: 2442 18th St NW
Washington, DC 20441
Phone: (202) 265-4600

#426
The District Fishwife
Cuisines: Seafood
Average Price: Modest
Address: 1309 5th St NE
Washington, DC 20002
Phone: (202) 543-2592

#427
Wingo's
Cuisines: American
Average Price: Inexpensive
Area: Georgetown
Address: 3207 O St NW
Washington, DC 20007
Phone: (202) 338-2478

#428
Potbelly Sandwich Shop
Cuisines: Sandwiches
Average Price: Inexpensive
Address: 718 14th St NW
Washington, DC 20005
Phone: (202) 628-9500

#429
Oyamel
Cuisines: Mexican
Average Price: Expensive
Area: Penn Quarter
Address: 401 7th St NW
Washington, DC 20004
Phone: (202) 628-1005

#430
Eddie's
Cuisines: American
Average Price: Inexpensive
Address: 1251 Bladensburg Rd NE
Washington, DC 20002
Phone: (202) 399-1725

#431
Silo
Cuisines: American
Average Price: Modest
Address: 919 5th St NW
Washington, DC 20001
Phone: (202) 290-2233

#432
DC Noodles
Cuisines: Thai
Average Price: Modest
Area: U Street Corridor
Address: 1412 U St NW
Washington, DC 20009
Phone: (202) 232-8424

#433
Captain White's Seafood City
Cuisines: Seafood
Average Price: Modest
Address: 1100 Maine Ave SW
Washington, DC 20024
Phone: (202) 484-2722

#434
Tackle Box
Cuisines: Seafood
Average Price: Modest
Area: Georgetown
Address: 3245 M St NW
Washington, DC 20007
Phone: (202) 337-8269

#435
Z-Burger
Cuisines: Burgers
Average Price: Inexpensive
Address: 1101 4th St SW
Washington, DC 20024
Phone: (202) 599-0400

#436
Shelly's Back Room
Cuisines: Lounge
Average Price: Modest
Address: 1331 F St NW
Washington, DC 20004
Phone: (202) 737-3003

#437
Town Hall
Cuisines: American
Average Price: Modest
Area: Glover Park
Address: 2340 Wisconsin Ave NW
Washington, DC 20007
Phone: (202) 333-5640

#438
Cafe Berlin
Cuisines: German
Average Price: Modest
Area: Capitol Hill, Northeast
Address: 322 Massachusetts Ave NE
Washington, DC 20002
Phone: (202) 543-7656

#439
Peacock Cafe
Cuisines: American
Average Price: Modest
Area: Georgetown
Address: 3251 Prospect St NW
Washington, DC 20007
Phone: (202) 625-2740

#440
El Fuego
Cuisines: Food Truck
Average Price: Inexpensive
Address: Maryland Ave SW
Washington, DC 20597
Phone: (703) 459-7931

#441
Daikaya Izakaya
Cuisines: Japanese
Average Price: Modest
Address: 705 6th St NW
Washington, DC 20001
Phone: (202) 589-1600

#442
The Wonderland Ballroom
Cuisines: Dance Club
Average Price: Modest
Area: Columbia Heights
Address: 1101 Kenyon St NW
Washington, DC 20009
Phone: (202) 232-5263

#443
Beacon Bar And Grill
Cuisines: Bar
Average Price: Modest
Area: Dupont Circle
Address: 1615 Rhode Island Ave NW
Washington, DC 20036
Phone: (202) 872-1126

#444
Fat Pete's Barbeque
Cuisines: Barbeque
Average Price: Modest
Area: Cleveland Park
Address: 3407 Connecticut Ave NW
Washington, DC 20008
Phone: (202) 362-7777

#445
Quick Pita
Cuisines: Middle Eastern
Average Price: Inexpensive
Area: Georgetown
Address: 1210 Potomac St NW
Washington, DC 20007
Phone: (202) 338-7482

#446
Maddy's Taproom
Cuisines: American
Average Price: Modest
Address: 1100 13th St NW
Washington, DC 20005
Phone: (202) 408-5500

#447
Cafe Phillips
Cuisines: Café
Average Price: Modest
Address: 425 3rd St SW
Washington, DC 20472
Phone: (202) 479-3958

#448
Grillfish
Cuisines: Seafood
Average Price: Modest
Address: 1200 New Hampshire Ave NW
Washington, DC 20036
Phone: (202) 331-7310

#449
El Centro DF
Cuisines: Bar
Average Price: Modest
Area: Georgetown
Address: 1218 Wisconsin Ave NW
Washington, DC 20007
Phone: (202) 333-4100

#450
Otello
Cuisines: Italian
Average Price: Modest
Area: Dupont Circle
Address: 1329 Connecticut Ave NW
Washington, DC 20036
Phone: (202) 429-0209

#451
Bourbon
Cuisines: American
Average Price: Modest
Area: Glover Park
Address: 2348 Wisconsin Ave NW
Washington, DC 20007
Phone: (202) 625-7770

#452
Steel Plate
Cuisines: Cocktail Bar
Average Price: Modest
Area: Brookland
Address: 3523 12th St NE
Washington, DC 20017
Phone: (202) 290-2310

#453
Petworth Citizen
Cuisines: Bar
Average Price: Modest
Area: Petworth
Address: 829 Upshur St NW
Washington, DC 20011
Phone: (202) 722-2939

#454
Chef Geoff's
Cuisines: American
Average Price: Modest
Address: 3201 New Mexico Ave NW
Washington, DC 20016
Phone: (202) 237-7800

#455
Lauriol Plaza
Cuisines: Mexican
Average Price: Modest
Area: Dupont Circle
Address: 1835 18th St NW
Washington, DC 20050
Phone: (202) 387-0035

#456
Pete's New Haven Style Apizza
Cuisines: Pizza
Average Price: Modest
Address: 4940 Wisconsin Ave NW
Washington, DC 20016
Phone: (202) 237-7383

#457
Lavagna
Cuisines: Italian
Average Price: Modest
Area: Capitol Hill, Southeast
Address: 539 8th St SE
Washington, DC 20003
Phone: (202) 546-5006

#458
Pharmacy Bar
Cuisines: Restaurant
Average Price: Inexpensive
Area: Adams Morgan
Address: 2337 18th St NW
Washington, DC 20009
Phone: (202) 483-1200

#459
Murasaki Japanese Restaurant
Cuisines: Japanese
Average Price: Modest
Area: Tenleytown
Address: 4620 Wisconsin Ave NW
Washington, DC 20016
Phone: (202) 966-0023

#460
Campono
Cuisines: Pizza
Average Price: Modest
Area: Foggy Bottom
Address: 600 New Hampshire Ave NW
Washington, DC 20037
Phone: (202) 505-4000

#461
The Coupe
Cuisines: Diner
Average Price: Modest
Area: Columbia Heights
Address: 3415 11th St NW
Washington, DC 20010
Phone: (202) 290-3342

#462
Luna Grill & Diner
Cuisines: Diner
Average Price: Modest
Area: Dupont Circle
Address: 1301 Connecticut Ave NW
Washington, DC 20036
Phone: (202) 835-2280

#463
Cantina Marina
Cuisines: Cajun/Creole
Average Price: Modest
Address: 600 Water St SW
Washington, DC 20024
Phone: (202) 554-8396

#464
Bistro Bis
Cuisines: French
Average Price: Expensive
Address: 15 E St NW
Washington, DC 20001
Phone: (202) 661-2700

#465
Bar-Cöde
Cuisines: American
Average Price: Modest
Address: 1101 17th St NW
Washington, DC 20036
Phone: (202) 955-9001

#466
Ben's Next Door
Cuisines: Bar
Average Price: Modest
Area: U Street Corridor
Address: 1211 U St NW
Washington, DC 20009
Phone: (202) 667-8880

#467
Cafe Tu-O-Tu Express
Cuisines: Café
Average Price: Modest
Area: Georgetown
Address: 3421 M St
Washington, DC 20007
Phone: (202) 337-4455

#468
Momoyama
Cuisines: Japanese
Average Price: Modest
Address: 231 2nd St NW
Washington, DC 20001
Phone: (202) 737-0397

#469
Tel'Veh Cafe & Wine Bar
Cuisines: Wine Bar
Average Price: Modest
Address: 401 Massachusetts Ave NW
Washington, DC 20001
Phone: (202) 758-2929

#470
Doi Moi
Cuisines: Vietnamese
Average Price: Expensive
Address: 1800 14th St NW
Washington, DC 20009
Phone: (202) 733-5131

#471
Shaw's Tavern
Cuisines: Gastropub
Average Price: Modest
Address: 520 Florida Ave NW
Washington, DC 20001
Phone: (202) 518-4092

#472
Senart's Oyster Bar & Chop House
Cuisines: Seafood
Average Price: Expensive
Area: Capitol Hill, Southeast
Address: 520 8th St SE
Washington, DC 20003
Phone: (202) 544-1168

#473
Cure Bar And Bistro
Cuisines: American
Average Price: Modest
Address: 1000 H St NW
Washington, DC 20001
Phone: (202) 637-4906

#474
Sweet Mango Cafe
Cuisines: Caribbean
Average Price: Modest
Address: 3701 New Hampshire Ave NW
Washington, DC 20010
Phone: (202) 726-2646

#475
Georgetown Dinette
Cuisines: Diner
Average Price: Modest
Area: Georgetown
Address: 3206 O St NW
Washington, DC 20007
Phone: (202) 337-3649

#476
Terasol
Cuisines: French
Average Price: Modest
Area: Chevy Chase
Address: 5010 Connecticut Ave NW
Washington, DC 20008
Phone: (202) 237-5555

#477
Florida Avenue Grill
Cuisines: Diner
Average Price: Inexpensive
Address: 1100 Florida Ave NW
Washington, DC 20009
Phone: (202) 265-1586

#478
Station 4
Cuisines: American
Average Price: Modest
Address: 1101 4th St SW
Washington, DC 20024
Phone: (202) 488-0987

#479
Menu- Market, Bistrobar, Kitchen
Cuisines: Restaurant
Average Price: Expensive
Area: Penn Quarter
Address: 405 8th St NW
Washington, DC 20004
Phone: (202) 347-7491

#480
Asian Spice
Cuisines: Asian Fusion
Average Price: Modest
Area: Chinatown
Address: 717 H St NW
Washington, DC 20001
Phone: (202) 589-0900

#481
Afghan Grill
Cuisines: Middle Eastern
Average Price: Modest
Area: Woodley Park
Address: 2309 Calvert St NW
Washington, DC 20008
Phone: (202) 234-5095

#482
Sweetgreen
Cuisines: American
Average Price: Inexpensive
Area: Georgetown
Address: 3333 M St NW
Washington, DC 20007
Phone: (202) 337-9338

#483
Graffiato
Cuisines: Pizza
Average Price: Expensive
Address: 707 6th St NW
Washington, DC 20001
Phone: (202) 289-3600

#484
Annie's Paramount Steak House
Cuisines: Steakhouse
Average Price: Modest
Area: Dupont Circle
Address: 1609 17th St NW
Washington, DC 20009
Phone: (202) 232-0395

#485
24 Seven Plus
Cuisines: Greek
Average Price: Inexpensive
Area: U Street Corridor
Address: 1408 U St NW
Washington, DC 20009
Phone: (202) 232-7108

#486
Panache Restaurant
Cuisines: Tapas Bar
Average Price: Modest
Address: 1725 Desales St NW
Washington, DC 20036
Phone: (202) 293-7760

#487
The Heights
Cuisines: American
Average Price: Modest
Area: Columbia Heights
Address: 3115 14th St NW
Washington, DC 20010
Phone: (202) 797-7227

#488
Drafting Table
Cuisines: Gastropub
Average Price: Modest
Area: Logan Circle
Address: 1529 14th St NW
Washington, DC 20005
Phone: (202) 621-7475

#489
Ri Ra Irish Pub: Georgetown
Cuisines: Irish
Average Price: Modest
Area: Georgetown
Address: 3125 M St Nw
Washington, DC 20007
Phone: (202) 751-2111

#490
The Dubliner
Cuisines: Pub
Average Price: Modest
Address: 520 N Capitol St NW
Washington, DC 20001
Phone: (202) 737-3773

#491
Fobogro
Cuisines: Deli
Average Price: Inexpensive
Area: Foggy Bottom
Address: 2140 F St NW
Washington, DC 20037
Phone: (202) 296-0125

#492
Bar Pilar
Cuisines: American
Average Price: Modest
Address: 1833 14th St NW
Washington, DC 20009
Phone: (202) 265-1751

#493
3 Salsas
Cuisines: Mexican
Average Price: Inexpensive
Area: Columbia Heights
Address: 3439 14th St NW
Washington, DC 20010
Phone: (202) 733-5821

#494
El Pollo Sabroso
Cuisines: Latin American
Average Price: Inexpensive
Area: Columbia Heights
Address: 1434 Park Rd NW
Washington, DC 20010
Phone: (202) 986-0022

#495
Saint's Paradise Cafeteria
Cuisines: Soul Food
Average Price: Modest
Address: 601 M St NW
Washington, DC 20001
Phone: (202) 789-2289

#496
Healthy Bites
Cuisines: Food Delivery Services
Average Price: Inexpensive
Address: 5329 Georgia Ave NW
Washington, DC 20012
Phone: (202) 882-1969

#497
Roti Mediterranean Grill
Cuisines: Mediterranean
Average Price: Inexpensive
Address: 1311 F St NW
Washington, DC 20004
Phone: (202) 499-4145

#498
Nooshi
Cuisines: Sushi Bar
Average Price: Modest
Address: 1120 19th St NW
Washington, DC 20036
Phone: (202) 293-3138

#499
Diego
Cuisines: Mexican
Average Price: Modest
Area: U Street Corridor
Address: 2100 14th St NW
Washington, DC 20009
Phone: (202) 758-3376

#500
Degrees Bar & Lounge
Cuisines: American
Average Price: Expensive
Area: Georgetown
Address: 3100 S St NW
Washington, DC 20007
Phone: (202) 912-4100

TOP 500
ARTS & ENTERTAINMENT
The Most Recommended by Locals & Trevelers
(From #1 to #500)

#1
National Gallery Of Art
Category: Museum
Address: 6th St & Constitution Ave NW
Washington, DC 20001
Phone: (202) 737-4215

#2
Newseum
Category: Museum
Address: 555 Pennsylvania Ave NW
Washington, DC 20001
Phone: (888) 639-7386

#3
Screen On The Green
Category: Local Flavor, Festival
Address: The National Mall
Washington, DC 56901
Phone: (617) 335-2185

#4
**Smithsonian American
Art Museum**
Category: Landmark/Historical, Museum
Address: 8th St & F St NW
Washington, DC 20560
Phone: (202) 357-1300

#5
United States Botanic Garden
Category: Botanical Garden
Address: 245 1st St SW
Washington, DC 20024
Phone: (202) 225-8333

#6
**National Geographic Museum
And Live Events**
Category: Museum, Performing Arts
Address: 1145 17th St NW
Washington, DC 20036
Phone: (202) 857-7700

#7
**National Museum
Of Natural History**
Category: Museum
Address: 10th St & Constitution Ave Nw
Washington, DC 20560
Phone: (202) 633-1000

#8
National Arboretum
Category: Botanical Garden, Park
Address: 3501 New York Ave NE
Washington, DC 20002
Phone: (202) 245-2726

#9
**John F. Kennedy Center
For The Performing Arts**
Category: Performing Arts
Address: Foggy Bottom 2700 F St NW
Washington, DC 20566
Phone: (202) 467-4600

#10
Ford's Theatre
Category: Performing Arts,
Landmark/Historical, Museum
Address: 511 10Th St NW
Washington, DC 20004
Phone: (202) 347-4833

#11
**Smithsonian National
Zoological Park**
Category: Zoo, Museum
Address: Woodley Park 3001 Connecticut
Ave NW Washington, DC 20008
Phone: (202) 633-4888

#12
Artjamz
Category: Art Gallery
Address: 1728 Connecticut Ave NW
Washington, DC 20009
Phone: (202) 709-8096

#13
9:30 Club
Category: Music Venues, Dance Club, Bar
Address: 815 V St NW
Washington, DC 20001
Phone: (202) 265-0930

#14
**Hirshhorn Museum
& Sculpture Garden**
Category: Museum, Art Gallery
Address: 7th St & Independence Ave SW
Washington, DC 20560
Phone: (202) 633-4674

#15
The Phillips Collection
Category: Museum, Art Gallery
Address: Dupont Circle 1600 21st St NW
Washington, DC 20009
Phone: (202) 387-2151

#16
National Gallery Of Art Sculpture Garden & Ice Rink
Category: Skating Rinks, Art Gallery, Landmark/Historical
Address: 700 Constitution Ave NW Washington, DC 20565
Phone: (202) 289-3360

#17
National Air And Space Museum
Category: Museum
Address: Independence Ave And 6th St SW Washington, DC 20560
Phone: (202) 633-1000

#18
National Archives And Records Administration
Category: Landmark/Historical, Museum
Address: Federal Triangle 700 Pennsylvania Ave NW Washington, DC 20408

#19
Dumbarton House
Category: Venues, Event Space, Museum
Address: Georgetown 2715 Q St NW Washington, DC 20007
Phone: (202) 337-2288

#20
Avalon Theatre
Category: Cinema
Address: Chevy Chase 5612 Connecticut Ave NW Washington, DC 20015
Phone: (202) 966-6000

#21
Blues Alley
Category: Jazz, Blues, Cajun/Creole
Address: Georgetown 1073 Wisconsin Ave NW Washington, DC 20007
Phone: (202) 337-4141

#22
Bloombars
Category: Art Gallery, Festival
Address: Columbia Heights 3222 11th St NW Washington, DC 20010
Phone: (202) 567-7713

#23
National Museum Of Crime & Punishment
Category: Museum
Address: Penn Quarter 575 7th St NW Washington, DC 20004
Phone: (202) 393-1099

#24
U Street Music Hall
Category: Music Venues, Dance Club
Address: U Street Corridor 1115 U St NW Washington, DC 20009
Phone: (202) 588-1880

#25
AMC Loews Uptown 1
Category: Cinema
Address: Cleveland Park 3426 Connecticut Ave NW Washington, DC 20008
Phone: (202) 966-5401

#26
National Museum Of American History
Category: Museum
Address: 1400 Constitution Ave NW Washington, DC 20004
Phone: (202) 357-1300

#27
U.S. Capitol Visitor Center
Category: Museum, Landmark/Historical
Address: East Capitol St, NE And 1st St, NE Washington, DC 20004
Phone: (202) 226-8000

#28
Speakeasydc
Category: Performing Arts
Address: Columbia Heights Washington, DC 20010
Phone: (240) 888-9751

#29
National Postal Museum
Category: Landmark/Historical, Museum, Art Gallery
Address: Noma 2 Massachusetts Ave NE Washington, DC 20001
Phone: (202) 357-1300

#30
Hillwood Museum And Gardens
Category: Museum, Tours
Address: 4155 Linnean Ave NW Washington, DC 20008
Phone: (202) 686-5807

#31
The Smithsonian Institution
Category: Landmark/Historical, Museum, Art Gallery
Address: 1000 Jefferson Dr SW Washington, DC 20560
Phone: (202) 357-1300

#32
International Spy Museum
Category: Museum
Address: Penn Quarter 800 F St NW
Washington, DC 20004
Phone: (202) 393-7798

#33
Gypsy Sally's
Category: Music Venues, Bar
Address: Georgetown 3401 K St NW
Washington, DC 20007
Phone: (202) 333-7700

#34
National Cherry Blossom Festival
Category: Festival, Park
Address: Tidal Basin
Washington, DC 20050

#35
Anderson House
Category: Museum, Landmark/Historical
Address: Dupont Circle 2118 Massachusetts
Ave NW Washington, DC 20008
Phone: (202) 785-2040

#36
Madam's Organ
Category: Jazz, Blues, Music Venues
Address: Adams Morgan 2461 18th St NW
Washington, DC 20009
Phone: (202) 667-5370

#37
Studio Theatre
Category: Performing Arts
Address: Logan Circle 1501 14th St NW
Washington, DC 20005
Phone: (202) 332-3300

#38
The Kreeger Museum
Category: Museum
Address: Foxhall 2401 Foxhall Rd NW
Washington, DC 20007
Phone: (202) 337-3050

#39
Insect Zoo At National
Museum Of Natural History
Category: Museum
Address: 10th St And Constitution Ave NW
Washington, DC 20560
Phone: (202) 357-1729

#40
West End Cinema
Category: Cinema
Address: West End 2301 M St NW
Washington, DC 20037
Phone: (202) 419-3456

#41
Nationals Park
Category: Stadium/Arena, Venues,
Event Space, Tours
Address: 1500 S Capitol St SE
Washington, DC 20003
Phone: (888) 632-6287

#42
Bohemian Caverns
Category: Jazz, Blues, American
Address: U Street Corridor 2003 11th St NW
Washington, DC 20001
Phone: (202) 299-0800

#43
Renwick Gallery
Category: Landmark/Historical, Museum
Address: 1661 Pennsylvania Ave NW
Washington, DC 20006
Phone: (202) 357-1300

#44
Black Cat
Category: Music Venues, Bar
Address: 1811 14th St NW
Washington, DC 20009
Phone: (202) 667-4490

#45
Atlas Performing Arts Center
Category: Performing Arts
Address: H Street Corridor/Atlas
District/Near Northeast 1333 H St NE
Washington, DC 20002
Phone: (202) 399-7993

#46
Josh Norris' Mind Reading
And Magic Show
Category: Magicians, Performing Arts
Address: Logan Circle 1430 Rhode Island
Ave NW Washington, DC 20005

#47
The Pinch
Category: Dive Bar,
Music Venues, American
Address: Columbia Heights 3548 14th St
NW Washington, DC 20010
Phone: (202) 722-4440

#48
The Great Zucchini
Category: Performing Arts,
Address: Chevy Chase 5402
Connecticut Ave NW
Washington, DC 20015
Phone: (202) 271-3108

#49
HR-57
Category: Jazz, Blues, Music Venues
Address: H Street Corridor/Atlas
District/Near Northeast 1007 H St NE
Washington, DC 20002
Phone: (202) 253-0044

#50
Atlas Arcade
Category: Arcade
Address: H Street Corridor/Atlas
District/Near Northeast 1236 H St NE
Washington, DC 20002
Phone: (202) 399-2323

#51
The Mansion On O Street
Category: Hotel, Museum, Venues,
Event Space
Address: Dupont Circle 2020 O St NW
Washington, DC 20037
Phone: (202) 496-2020

#52
Folger Shakespeare Library
Folger Theatre
Category: Performing Arts,
Museum, Libraries
Address: 201 E Capitol St SE
Washington, DC 20003
Phone: (202) 544-7077

#53
Lincoln Theatre
Category: Performing Arts
Address: U Street Corridor 1215 U St NW
Washington, DC 20009
Phone: (202) 888-0050

#54
Smithsonian Kite Festival
Category: Arts, Entertainment, Local Flavor
Address: Washington Monument
Washington, DC 20050

#55
Landmark's E Street Cinema
Category: Cinema
Address: 555 11th St NW
Washington, DC 20004
Phone: (202) 783-9494

#56
The Black Squirrel
Category: American, Bar, Music Venues
Address: Adams Morgan 2427 18th St NW
Washington, DC 20009
Phone: (202) 232-1011

#57
Carter Barron Amphitheatre
Category: Music Venues
Address: 4850 Colorado Ave, N.W.
Washington, DC 20011
Phone: (202) 426-0486

#58
National Building Museum
Category: Museum
Address: 401 F Street NW
Washington, DC 20001
Phone: (202) 272-2448

#59
United States Holocaust
Memorial Museum
Category: Museum
Address: 100 Raoul Wallenberg Pl SW
Washington, DC 20024
Phone: (202) 488-0400

#60
The Smithsonian Folklife Festival
Category: Local Flavor, Festival
Address: National Mall
Washington, DC 20050
Phone: (202) 633-6440

#61
The Fridge
Category: Art Gallery, Venues,
Event Space
Address: 516 1/2 8th St SE
Washington, DC 20003
Phone: (202) 664-4151

#62
Artomatic
Category: Performing Arts, Art Gallery,
Music Venues
Address: 55 M St SE
Washington, DC 20003

#63
National Museum
Of The American Indian
Category: Museum, Cultural Center
Address: 4th St & Independence Ave SW
Washington, DC 20560
Phone: (202) 633-1000

#64
Crafty Bastards Arts & Crafts Fair
Category: Art Gallery, Arts, Crafts
Address: 1309 5th St NE
Washington, DC 20002
Phone: (202) 332-2100

#65
District Of Columbia Arts Center
Category: Performing Arts,
Cinema, Art Gallery
Address: Adams Morgan 2438 18th St NW
Washington, DC 20009
Phone: (202) 462-7833

#66
Chief Ike's Mambo Room
Category: Dive Bar, Sports Bar,
Music Venues
Address: Adams Morgan 1725 Columbia Rd
NW Washington, DC 20009
Phone: (202) 332-2211

#67
**Frederick Douglass
National Historic Site**
Category: Museum
Address: Anacostia 1411 W St SE
Washington, DC 20020
Phone: (202) 426-5961

#68
Echostage
Category: Music Venues, Dance Club
Address: Langdon Park 2135 Queens
Chapel Rd NE Washington, DC 20018
Phone: (202) 503-2330

#69
National Portrait Gallery
Category: Landmark/Historical, Museum
Address: Penn Quarter 8th St & F St NW
Washington, DC 20560
Phone: (202) 357-1300

#70
Cirque Du Soleil
Category: Performing Arts
Address: 1300 H St. NW
Washington, DC 20050

#71
**National Museum
Of Women In The Arts**
Category: Museum
Address: 1250 New York Ave NW
Washington, DC 20005
Phone: (202) 783-5000

#72
Christian Heurich House Museum
Category: Museum
Address: Dupont Circle 1307 New
Hampshire Ave NW
Washington, DC 20036
Phone: (202) 429-1894

#73
Army & Navy Club
Category: Social Club
Address: 901 17th St NW
Washington, DC 20006
Phone: (202) 628-8401

#74
AMC Loews Georgetown 14
Category: Cinema
Address: 3111 K Street N.W.
Washington, DC 20007
Phone: (202) 342-6033

#75
Columbia Station
Category: Jazz, Blues, American
Address: Adams Morgan 2325 18th St NW
Washington, DC 20009
Phone: (202) 462-6040

#76
Adams Morgan Day Festival
Category: Festival
Address: 1780 Florida Ave NW
Washington, DC 20009

#77
Petersen's Boarding House
Category: Local Flavor, Museum
Address: 516 10th St NW
Washington, DC 20004
Phone: (202) 426-6924

#78
The B Spot
Category: Art Gallery, Juice Bar
Address: Capitol Hill/Southeast 1123 B
Pennsylvania Ave SE
Washington, DC 20003
Phone: (202) 546-7186

#79
Textile Museum
Category: Museum
Address: Foggy Bottom 701 21st St NW
Washington, DC 20052
Phone: (202) 667-0441

#80
Vegas Lounge
Category: Jazz, Blues, Lounge
Address: Logan Circle 1415 P St NW
Washington, DC 20005
Phone: (202) 483-3971

#81
Japan Information
And Culture Center
Category: Embassy, Cultural Center
Address: 1150 18th St NW
Washington, DC 20036
Phone: (202) 238-6900

#82
The Lab DC
Category: Dance Studio, Performing Arts
Address: Takoma 6925 Willow St
Washington, DC 20012
Phone: (202) 882-5221

#83
Britishink Tattoo Studio
And Gallery
Category: Tattoo, Art Gallery
Address: H Street Corridor/Atlas
District/Near Northeast 508 H St NE
Washington, DC 20002
Phone: (202) 302-1669

#84
The Corcoran Gallery Of Art
Category: Museum,
Address: Foggy Bottom 500 17Th St Nw
Washington, DC 20006
Phone: (202) 639-1700

#85
Jojo Restaurant And Bar
Category: American, Jazz, Blues, Lounge
Address: U Street Corridor 1518 U St NW
Washington, DC 20009
Phone: (202) 319-9350

#86
AMC Mazza Gallerie
Category: Cinema
Address: Friendship Heights 5300 Wisconsin
Ave. NW Washington, DC 20015
Phone: (202) 537-9551

#87
Zogsports
Category: Sports Club,
Amateur Sports Team, Social Club
Address: Capitol Hill/Southeast
Washington, DC 20003
Phone: (202) 461-3399

#88
Marine Barracks
Category: Arts, Entertainment
Address: Capitol Hill/Southeast 8th And I St
SE Washington, DC 20390
Phone: (202) 433-6682

#89
Theater J
Category: Performing Arts
Address: 1529 16th St NW
Washington, DC 20036
Phone: (202) 777-3210

#90
Velvet Lounge
Category: Music Venues
Address: U Street Corridor 915 U St NW
Washington, DC 20001
Phone: (202) 462-3213

#91
African American Civil War
Memorial Freedom Foundation
Category: Landmark/Historical, Museum
Address: U Street Corridor 1925 Vermont
Ave Washington, DC 20001
Phone: (202) 667-2667

#92
Dance Place
Category: Performing Arts
Address: Brookland 3225 8th St NE
Washington, DC 20017
Phone: (202) 269-1600

#93
National Conservatory
Of Dramatic Arts
Category: Performing Arts,
Address: Georgetown 1556 Wisconsin Ave
NW Washington, DC 20007
Phone: (202) 333-2202

#94
Laogai Museum
Category: Museum
Address: Dupont Circle 1734 20th St NW
Washington, DC 20009
Phone: (202) 730-9308

#95
Better Off Bowling
Category: Social Club, Bowling
Address: 701 7th St NW
Washington, DC 20001
Phone: (617) 299-0862

#96
Twins Jazz
Category: Jazz, Blues, American, Breakfast & Brunch
Address: U Street Corridor 1344 U St NW Washington, DC 20009
Phone: (202) 234-0072

#97
Terasol
Category: French, Art Gallery, Café
Address: Chevy Chase 5010 Connecticut Ave NW Washington, DC 20008
Phone: (202) 237-5555

#98
Islamic Mosque And Cultural Center
Category: Cultural Center, Mosques
Address: 2551 Massachusetts Ave NW Washington, DC 20008

#99
Madame Tussauds
Category: Museum, Art Gallery
Address: 1001 F St NW Washington, DC 20004
Phone: (866) 823-9565

#100
S. Dillon Ripley Center
Category: Museum
Address: 1100 Jefferson Dr SW Washington, DC 20560
Phone: (202) 633-1000

#101
National Gallery Of Art - Friday Jazz In The Garden Series
Category: Jazz, Blues, Performing Arts
Address: Federal Triangle 700 Constitution Ave NW Washington, DC 20004
Phone: (202) 289-3360

#102
DC9 Nightclub
Category: Bar, Music Venues, Burgers
Address: 1940 9th St NW Washington, DC 20001
Phone: (202) 483-5000

#103
Metropolitan Club-DC
Category: Social Club
Address: 1700 H St NW Washington, DC 20006
Phone: (202) 835-2500

#104
Chevy Chase Ballroom And Dance Sport Center
Category: Performing Arts, Dance Studio
Address: Friendship Heights 5207 Wisconsin Ave NW Washington, DC 20015
Phone: (202) 363-8344

#105
Meridian House
Category: Landmark/Historical, Venues, Event Space, Art Gallery
Address: 1630 Crescent Pl NW Washington, DC 20009
Phone: (202) 667-6800

#106
Lockheed Martin IMAX Theater
Category: Cinema
Address: 6th St & Independence Ave SW Washington, DC 20560
Phone: (866) 868-7774

#107
Washington Improv Theater
Category: Performing Arts, Comedy Club
Address: 1835 14th St NW Washington, DC 20009
Phone: (202) 204-7770

#108
DC Asian Pacific American Film Festival
Category: Cinema, Festival
Address: Columbia Heights Washington, DC 20010

#109
Vitaminwater Uncapped Live
Category: Art Gallery, Music Venues, Dance Club
Address: 2217 14th St NW Washington, DC 20009
Phone: (707) 726-2246

#110
Dc Armory
Category: Stadium/Arena
Address: 2001 East Capital Street Washington, DC 20003
Phone: (202) 547-9077

#111
Church Street Theater
Category: Performing Arts
Address: Dupont Circle 1742 Church St NW Washington, DC 20036
Phone: (202) 265-3767

#112
Art Enables
Category: Art Gallery,
Address: 2204 Rhode Island Ave NE
Washington, DC 20018
Phone: (202) 554-9455

#113
Taste Of Georgetown
Category: Festival
Address: Georgetown Wisconsin Ave
Between M And K
Washington, DC

#114
Capital Fringe Festival
Category: Festival
Address: 607 New York Ave NW
Washington, DC 20001
Phone: (866) 811-4111

#115
The Bier Baron Tavern
Category: Pub, Jazz, Blues
Address: 1523 22nd St NW
Washington, DC 20037
Phone: (202) 293-1887

#116
DC Bocce League
Category: Social Club, Amateur Sports
Team, Sports Club
Address: Columbia Heights
Washington, DC 20010
Phone: (202) 422-2106

#117
American Social Sports
Category: Social Club, Sports Club
Address: 300 Massachusetts Ave NW
Washington, DC 20001
Phone: (703) 239-4756

#118
Matthew J Viator- Studio V
Category: Performing Arts, Private Tutor,
Musical Instruments
Address: 350 G St SW 309 N
Washington, DC 20024
Phone: (202) 803-2493

#119
**Washington Nationals
Baseball Club**
Category: Professional Sports Team
Address: 1500 S Capitol St SE
Washington, DC 20003
Phone: (202) 675-5100

#120
Veracruz
Category: Art Gallery
Address: 2100 Vermont Ave
Washington, DC 20001
Phone: (202) 906-9209

#121
Turkish Festival
Category: Performing Arts
Address: 12-14th St, Pennsylvannia Ave
Washington, DC

#122
The Tulip Library
Category: Botanical Garden, Park
Address: Near The North Side Of The Tidal
Basin Washington, DC 20024

#123
The Washington Auto Show
Category: Festival
Address: 801 Mount Vernon Pl NW
Washington, DC 20001
Phone: (202) 237-7200

#124
Museum Of Censored Art
Category: Museum
Address: Penn Quarter 799 F St NW
Washington, DC 20001

#125
Sahara Dance
Category: Performing Arts, Dance School
Address: Tenleytown 4433 Wisconsin Ave
NW Washington, DC 20016
Phone: (202) 362-4400

#126
Arts Club Of Washington
Category: Landmark/Historical, Art Gallery
Address: 2017 I St NW
Washington, DC 20006
Phone: (202) 331-7282

#127
H Street Playhouse
Category: Performing Arts
Address: 1365 H St NE
Washington, DC 20002
Phone: (202) 396-2125

#128
Art Museum Of The Americas
Category: Museum
Address: Foggy Bottom 201 18th St NW
Washington, DC 20006
Phone: (202) 370-0147

#129
Toolbox
Category: Pilates, Art Gallery,
Venues, Event Space
Address: Dupont Circle 1627 R Connecticut
Ave NW Washington, DC 20009
Phone: (202) 664-3808

#130
Half Street Fairgrounds
Category: Festival
Address: 20 M St SE
Washington, DC 20003

#131
Saint Sophia Greek Festival
Category: Festival
Address: 2815 36th St
Washington, DC 20007
Phone: (202) 333-4730

#132
Tango At Eastern Market
Category: Local Flavor, Arts,
Entertainment, Fitness & Instruction
Address: Capitol Hill/Southeast 7th St And N
Carolina Ave NE Washington, DC 20003
Phone: (240) 372-5134

#133
All2Dance
Category: Performing Arts, Dance Studio
Address: Foxhall 4380 Macarthur Blvd NW
Washington, DC 20007
Phone: (202) 422-6250

#134
Sakura Matsuri Japanese
Street Festival
Category: Festival
Address: Federal Triangle 12th St And
Pennsylvania Ave NW
Washington, DC 20004
Phone: (202) 833-2210

#135
The Sewall Belmont
House & Museum
Category: Museum
Address: Capitol Hill/Northeast 144
Constitution Ave NE
Washington, DC 20002
Phone: (202) 546-1210

#136
Constitution Gardens
Category: Park, Botanical Garden,
Landmark/Historical
Address: 1836-1898 Constitution Ave NW
Washington, DC 20245

#137
Marian Koshland Science Museum
Category: Museum
Address: Penn Quarter 525 E St NW
Washington, DC 20001
Phone: (202) 334-1201

#138
Batala Women's Drum Corps
Category: Dance Studio, Arts, Entertainment
Address: Foggy Bottom Faragut Square
Washington, DC 20006
Phone: (202) 361-8993

#139
Luft Und Raumfahrtsmuseum
Category: Museum
Address: Independence Avenue
Washington, DC 20597

#140
Foundry Gallery
Category: Art Gallery
Address: Dupont Circle 1314 18th Street,
NW Washington, DC 20036
Phone: (202) 463-0203

#141
Octagon House
Category: Museum
Address: Foggy Bottom 1799 New York Ave
NW Washington, DC 20006

#142
The Anacostia Community Museum
Category: Museum
Address: 1901 Fort Place SE
Washington, DC 20020
Phone: (202) 633-4820

#143
The Washington Ballet At THEARC
Category: Performing Arts, Dance School
Address: 1901 Mississippi Ave SE
Washington, DC 20020
Phone: (202) 889-8150

#144
**American University Museum
At The Katzen Arts Center**
Category: Museum, Art Gallery
Address: 4400 Massachusetts Ave NW
Washington, DC 20016
Phone: (202) 885-1300

#145
Washington Wizards
Category: Professional Sports Team
Address: 601 F St NW
Washington, DC 20004
Phone: (202) 661-5050

#146
Sage String Quartet
Category: Performing Arts
Address: Capitol Hill/Southeast Capitol Hill
SE Washington, DC 20003
Phone: (202) 642-5612

#147
**Washington DC International
Wine & Food Festival**
Category: Festival
Address: Federal Triangle 1300
Pennsylvania Ave NW
Washington, DC 20004

#148
Howard Theatre
Category: Music Venues, American
Address: Shaw 620 T St NW
Washington, DC 20001
Phone: (202) 803-2899

#149
**Tudor Place Historic
House & Garden**
Category: Museum, Venues,
Event Space, Botanical Garden
Address: Georgetown 1644 31st Street, NW
Washington, DC 20007
Phone: (202) 965-0400

#150
**Monty Python's Spamalot
At The National Theatre**
Category: Performing Arts
Address: Penn Quarter 1321 Pennsylvania
Ave Washington, DC 20004
Phone: (202) 628-6161

#151
Wohlfarth Galleries
Category: Art Gallery
Address: Brookland 3418 9th St NE
Washington, DC 20017
Phone: (202) 526-8022

#152
Tango At Freedom Plaza
Category: Local Flavor, Arts,
Entertainment, Active Life
Address: 14th St NW And Pennsylvania Ave
NW Washington, DC 20004

#153
**Historical Society
Of Washington, DC**
Category: Museum,
Landmark/Historical, Libraries
Address: Mount Vernon Square 801 K St
NW Washington, DC 20001
Phone: (202) 249-3955

#154
Keegan Theatre
Category: Performing Arts
Address: Dupont Circle 1742 Church St NW
Washington, DC 20036
Phone: (703) 892-0202

#155
One World Studios
Category: Performing Arts,
Address: Shaw 905 N St NW
Washington, DC 20001
Phone: (202) 234-2771

#156
The House Where Lincoln Died
Category: Museum
Address: Shaw 516 10th St NW
Washington, DC 20001
Phone: (202) 347-4833

#157
**Woodrow Wilson International
Center For Scholars**
Category: Museum
Address: Shaw 1300 Pennsylvania Avenue
NW Washington, DC 20001
Phone: (202) 691-4000

#158
**Newman Gallery
And Custom Frames**
Category: Framing, Art Gallery
Address: Capitol Hill/Southeast 513 11th St
SE Washington, DC 20003
Phone: (202) 544-7577

#159
Source
Category: Performing Arts
Address: 1835 14th St NW
Washington, DC 20009
Phone: (202) 204-7800

#160
DC Beer Festival
Category: Festival
Address: 1500 S Capitol St SE
Washington, DC 20020

#161
Green Festival
Category: Arts, Entertainment
Address: Mount Vernon Square 801 Mt
Vernon Pl NW
Washington, DC 20001

#162
Goethe-Institut
Category: Cinema, Art Gallery,
Language School
Address: Chinatown 812 7th St NW
Washington, DC 20001
Phone: (202) 289-1200

#163
Ghost Story Tour Of Washington
Category: Arts, Entertainment
Address: St. John's Church
Washington, DC 20005
Phone: (301) 588-9255

#164
Shakespeare Theatre Company
Category: Performing Arts
Address: Penn Quarter 450 7th St NW
Washington, DC 20004
Phone: (202) 547-1122

#165
Angelika Pop-Up At Union Market
Category: Cinema
Address: 550 Penn St NE
Washington, DC 20002
Phone: (571) 512-3313

#166
RFK Stadium
Category: Stadium/Arena
Address: 2400 E Capitol St SE
Washington, DC 20003
Phone: (202) 547-9077

#167
Shear Madness
Category: Performing Arts
Address: Foggy Bottom 2700 F St NW
Washington, DC 20001
Phone: (202) 467-4600

#168
Hamiltonian Gallery
Category: Art Gallery
Address: U Street Corridor 1353 U Street,
NW Washington, DC 20009
Phone: (202) 332-1116

#169
Taste Of DC
Category: Festival
Address: 1201 Pennsylvania Ave NW
Washington, DC 20004

#170
**Woolly Mammoth
Theatre Company**
Category: Performing Arts
Address: Penn Quarter 641 D St NW
Washington, DC 20004
Phone: (202) 393-3939

#171
Alvear Studio Design & Imports
Category: Art Gallery, Jewelry,
Furniture Store
Address: Capitol Hill/Southeast 705 8th St
SE Washington, DC 20003
Phone: (202) 546-8434

#172
The Corner Store
Category: Art Gallery, Performing Arts,
Music Venues
Address: Capitol Hill/Southeast 900 S
Carolina Ave SE Washington, DC 20003
Phone: (202) 544-5807

#173
**Arts & Industries Building
Smithsonian Institution**
Category: Landmark/Historical, Museum
Address: 900 Jefferson Dr SW
Washington, DC 20560
Phone: (202) 357-1300

#174
National Guard Memorial Museum
Category: Museum
Address: One Massachusetts Avenue NW
Washington, DC 20001
Phone: (202) 408-5887

#175
DC Jazz Festival 2011
Category: Festival, Jazz, Blues
Address: 2700 F Street, NW
Washington, DC 20566

#176
Artist's Proof Gallery
Category: Venues, Art Gallery
Address: Georgetown 3320 Cady's Alley NW
Washington, DC 20007
Phone: (202) 803-2782

#177
Arena Stage
Category: Performing Arts
Address: 1101 6th St SW
Washington, DC 20024
Phone: (202) 554-9066

#178
National Symphony Orchestra
Category: Performing Arts
Address: Foggy Bottom 2700 F St NW
Washington, DC 20566
Phone: (202) 467-4600

#179
H St Festival 2012
Category: Festival
Address: H Street Corridor/Atlas
District/Near Northeast H St NE
Washington, DC

#180
German-American Heritage Museum
Category: Museum
Address: 719 6th St NW
Washington, DC 20001
Phone: (202) 467-5000

#181
Tivoli Theatre
Category: Performing Arts
Address: Columbia Heights 3333 14th St
NW Washington, DC 20010
Phone: (202) 234-7174

#182
Samuel C Johnson IMAX Theater
Category: Cinema
Address: Federal Triangle National
Museum Of Natural History
Washington, DC 20560
Phone: (866) 868-7774

#183
Montserrat House
Category: Music Venues,
Performing Arts, Art Gallery
Address: 2016 9th St NW
Washington, DC 20001

#184
Constellation Theatre Company
Category: Performing Arts
Address: 1835 14th Street NW
Washington, DC 20009
Phone: (202) 204-7741

#185
National Museum
of American History
Category: Museum
Address: Shaw Const Avenue Bet 12
Washington, DC 20001
Phone: (202) 357-1300

#186
Mirrors
Category: Restaurant, Music Venues
Address: 33 New York Avenue NE
Washington, DC 20002
Phone: (202) 326-0774

#187
Naval Heritage Center
Category: Venues, Event Space, Museum
Address: Penn Quarter 701 Pennsylvania
Ave NW Washington, DC 20004
Phone: (202) 380-0710

#188
Savor
Category: Beer, Wine, Spirits, Festival
Address: 401 F St NW
Washington, DC 20001
Phone: (202) 272-2448

#189
Noma Summer Screen
Category: Festival
Address: 1041 2nd St NE
Washington, DC 20002
Phone: (202) 289-0111

#190
Capital Pride Parade
Category: Festival
Address: Dupont Circle 1527 17th St NW
Washington, DC 20036

#191
George Washington Lisner
Auditorium
Category: Arts, Entertainment
Address: Foggy Bottom 730 21st St NW
Washington, DC 20052
Phone: (202) 994-6800

#192
Corcoran School Of Art
Category: Museum,
Address: Shaw 17th Ny Ave NW
Washington, DC 20001
Phone: (202) 639-1800

#193
D. C. United
Category: Stadium/Arena
Address: Trinidad 2400 E Capitol St
Washington, DC 20003
Phone: (202) 587-5000

#194
The Lodge At Redrocks
Category: Music Venues
Address: 1348 H St NE
Washington, DC 20002
Phone: (202) 621-7300

#195
Conner Contemporary Art
Category: Art Gallery
Address: 1358 Florida Ave NE
Washington, DC 20002
Phone: (202) 588-8750

#196
Capital Fringe Festival
Category: Stadium/Arena
Address: 507 7th St NW
Washington, DC 20050
Phone: (866) 811-4111

#197
International Visions
Category: Art Gallery
Address: Woodley Park 2629 Connecticut
Ave NW Washington, DC 20008
Phone: (202) 234-5112

#198
Anacostia Arts Center
Category: Art Gallery
Address: Anacostia 1231 Good Hope Rd SE
Washington, DC 20020
Phone: (202) 631-6291

#199
Smith Center
Category: Stadium/Arena
Address: Foggy Bottom 600 22Nd St. N.W.
Washington, DC 20052
Phone: (202) 994-6650

#200
Washington Coliseum
Category: Stadium/Arena
Address: H Street Corridor/Atlas
District/Near Northeast 3rd & M St NE
Washington, DC 20005
Phone: (202) 669-7229

#201
Cirque Du Soleil
Michael Jackson The Immortal
Category: Arts, Entertainment
Address: Penn Quarter 601 F St NW
Washington, DC 20004
Phone: (202) 628-3200

#202
Gravensteen Haunted Productions
Category: Performing Arts
Address: 50 Florida Ave NE
Washington, DC 20001
Phone: (888) 681-4713

#203
Dar Constitution Hall
Category: Performing Arts, Venues
Address: West End 1776 St NW
Washington, DC 20006
Phone: (202) 628-4780

#204
SAVOR
Category: Festival
Address: 401 F St NW
Washington, DC 20001
Phone: (303) 447-0816

#205
Dumbarton Concert Series
Category: Music Venues, Jazz, Blues
Address: Georgetown 3133 Dumbarton St
NW Washington, DC 20007
Phone: (202) 965-2000

#206
The DC Bachata Congress
Category: Festival
Address: Van Ness/Forest Hills
Washington, DC 20008
Phone: (703) 599-3018

#207
US Government Printing Office
Category: Landmark/Historical, Museum
Address: Noma 732 North Capitol St NW
Washington, DC 20401
Phone: (202) 512-1957

#208
Alliance Francaise De Washington
Category: Adult Education, Cultural Center
Address: Penn Quarter 421 7th St NW
Washington, DC 20004
Phone: (202) 234-7911

#209
Honfleur Gallery
Category: Art Gallery
Address: Anacostia 1241 Good Hope Rd SE
Washington, DC 20020
Phone: (202) 536-8994

#210
Lem Design
Category: Art Gallery, Interior Design
Address: 1843 14th St NW
Washington, DC 20009
Phone: (202) 288-1391

#211
Tree House Lounge
Category: Lounge, Jazz, Blues,
Music Venues
Address: 1006 Florida Ave NE
Washington, DC 20002
Phone: (202) 398-7700

#212
Rorschach Theatre
Category: Performing Arts
Address: H Street Corridor/Atlas
District/Near Northeast 1333 H St NE
Washington, DC 20002
Phone: (202) 452-5538

#213
Live! On Woodrow Wilson Plaza
Category: Festival
Address: Federal Triangle
Washington, DC

#214
Capital Children's Museum
Category: Museum
Address: H Street Corridor/Atlas
District/Near Northeast 800 3rd St NE
Washington, DC 20002
Phone: (202) 675-4120

#215
National Christmas Tree
Category: Festival
Address: 1201 Eye St
Washington, DC 20005

#216
The Blue Parka
Category: Jazz, Blues,
Address: Columbia Heights Parkwood Pl
NW Washington, DC 20010

#217
Avodah House
Category: Social Club
Address: 1532 Spring Pl NW
Washington, DC 20010
Phone: (202) 723-0046

#218
DC Casineros
Category: Performing Arts, Dance School
Address: Brookland 3225 8th St NE
Washington, DC 20017
Phone: (571) 213-9109

#219
Washingtonian Living
Social Best Of Party
Category: Festival
Address: 401 F St NW
Washington, DC 20001

#220
National Book Festival
Category: Local Flavor, Festival
Address: 7th Street & Constitution NW
Washington, DC 20050
Phone: (888) 714-4696

#221
In Series
Category: Performing Arts
Address: 1835 14th St. NW
Washington, DC 20009
Phone: (202) 518-0152

#222
Takoma Station Tavern
Category: Music Venues, American
Address: Takoma 6914 4th St NW
Washington, DC 20012
Phone: (202) 829-1999

#223
The Legends
Category: Performing Arts
Address: 1321 Pennsylvania Ave
Washington, DC 20050

#224
Politicsprosepurl Knitting Circle
Category: Arts, Crafts, Social Club
Address: Chevy Chase 5015 Connecticut
Ave NW Washington, DC 20008

#225
Kathrine Dulin Folger Rose Garden
Category: Botanical Garden
Address: 900 Jefferson Drive SW
Washington, DC 20560

#226
Miss Representation Screening
Category: Cinema
Address: Columbia Heights 3333 14th St
NW Washington, DC 20010

#227
The Women Of Brewster Place
Category: Performing Arts
Address: 1101 6th St SW
Washington, DC 20050
Phone: (202) 488-3300

#228
Letelier Theater
Category: Cinema, Performing Arts
Address: Georgetown 3251 Prospect St NW
Washington, DC 20007
Phone: (202) 338-5835

#229
Anchorman The Exhibit
At The Newseum
Category: Museum
Address: 555 Pennsylvania Ave NW
Washington, DC 20001
Phone: (888) 639-7386

#230
One In Ten
Category: Arts, Entertainment
Address: 2201 P Street NW
Washington, DC 20037
Phone: (202) 986-1119

#231
Shamrock Fest
Category: Festival
Address: Capitol Hill/Southeast RFK
Stadium Washington, DC 20003

#232
Messiah Sing Along
Category: Arts, Entertainment
Address: Shaw Kennedy Center For The
Performing Arts Washington, DC 20001
Phone: (800) 444-1324

#233
The Guitar Gallery
Category: Musical Instruments,
Arts, Entertainment
Address: 3400 Connecticut Ave NW
Washington, DC 20008
Phone: (202) 244-4200

#234
Howard University Burr Gymnasium
Category: Amateur Sports Team,
Stadium/Arena
Address: Pleasant Plains 6th & Girard
Streets NW Washington, DC 20001

#235
Bound
Category: Dance Club, Music Venues
Address: 411 New York Ave NE
Washington, DC 20002
Phone: (703) 303-9470

#236
20s/30s Fun Asians
Category: Social Club
Address: 1600 Pennsylvania Avenue NW
Washington, DC 20500

#237
College Republican National
Committee
Category: Social Club
Address: 1500 K St NW
Washington, DC 20005
Phone: (202) 608-1411

#238
Twelfth Annual Film Festival
Category: Festival
Address: Freer Gallery
Washington, DC 20050

#239
The Loft At 600 F
Category: Venues, Event Space,
Music Venues
Address: Penn Quarter 600 F St NW
Washington, DC 20004
Phone: (202) 431-8516

#240
Chefs For Equality
Category: Festival
Address: West End 1150 22nd St NW
Washington, DC 20037
Phone: (202) 835-0500

#241
DC Bike Party
Category: Social Club
Address: Dupont Circle 1 Dupont Cir NW
Washington, DC 20036

#242
Jewish Film Festival
Category: Festival
Address: Logan Circle 1529 16th St NW
Washington, DC 20036

#243
DC Dragonboat Festival
Category: Festival, Rafting/Kayaking
Address: 2900 Virginia Ave NW
Washington, DC 20037
Phone: (202) 333-9543

#244
The Incubator
Category: Social Club
Address: 1324 S St NW
Washington, DC 20009
Phone: (202) 525-6770

#245
Cherub Antiques Gallery
Category: Antiques, Art Gallery
Address: Georgetown 2918 M Street NW
Washington, DC 20007
Phone: (202) 337-2224

#246
Hoi Thanh Nien Sinh Vien Vietnam
Category: Social Club
Address: Kalorama 2251 R St NW
Washington, DC 20008

#247
A Drag X-Mas
Category: Performing Arts, Adult
Entertainment
Address: Shaw 620 T St NW
Washington, DC 20001
Phone: (202) 803-2899

#248
Rock & Roll Hotel
Category: Music Venues
Address: 1353 H St NE
Washington, DC 20002
Phone: (202) 388-7625

#249
Imani Temple
Category: Arts, Entertainment,
Address: Capitol Hill/Northeast 609
Maryland Ave NE
Washington, DC 20002
Phone: (202) 388-8155

#250
The Performing Arts
Training Studio
Category: Performing Arts,
Address: Columbia Heights 733 Euclid St
NW Washington, DC 20001
Phone: (202) 321-0779

#251
Pleasant Plains Workshop
Category: Art Gallery, Arts, Crafts
Address: 2608 Georgia Ave NW
Washington, DC 20001

#252
Holiday Inn Georgetown
Magical Events
Category: Magicians, Performing Arts
Address: 2101 Wisconsin Ave NW
Washington, DC 20007
Phone: (202) 338-2903

#253
Marine Barracks - NCO Club
Category: Social Club
Address: 8th & I St
Washington, DC 20003
Phone: (202) 433-3266

#254
Lansburgh Theatre
Category: Performing Arts
Address: Penn Quarter 450 7th St NW
Washington, DC 20004
Phone: (202) 547-1122

#255
Scena Theatre
Category: Performing Arts
Address: Trinidad 1365 H Street NE
Washington, DC 20002
Phone: (703) 683-2824

#256
Clavekazi Dance Studio
Category: Performing Arts, Dance School
Address: Trinidad 411 New York Ave NE
Washington, DC 20002

#257
Yuri's Night At Anacostia Arts Center
Category: Festival
Address: Anacostia 1231 Good Hope Rd SE
Washington, DC 20020

#258
Arabian Lounge
Category: Jazz, Blues, Music Venues
Address: 2001 Benning Road NE
Washington, DC 20002

#259
Catholic University's Hartke Theatre
Category: Performing Arts
Address: 620 Michigan Ave NE
Washington, DC 20064
Phone: (202) 319-4000

#260
The Washington Ballet
Category: Performing Arts
Address: 3515 Wisconsin Ave NW
Washington, DC 20016
Phone: (202) 362-3606

#261
Regal Gallery Place Stadium 14
Category: Cinema, Performing Arts
Address: 707 7th St NW
Washington, DC 20001
Phone: (202) 393-2121

#262
Words Of Elixir
Category: Performing Arts
Address: 16th Street Heights
Washington, DC 20011
Phone: (301) 887-3531

#263
Fiesta Asia Street Fair
Category: Arts, Entertainment
Address: Fort Totten Pennsylvania Ave, Nw
Between 3rd & 6th St
Washington, DC 20017
Phone: (202) 470-0899

#264
Pass Gallery
Category: Art Gallery
Address: 1617 S St NW
Washington, DC 20009
Phone: (202) 745-0796

#265
Fort Fringe
Category: Performing Arts, Venues, Event Space
Address: 607 New York Ave NW
Washington, DC 20001

#266
Chinatown Community & Cultural Center
Category: Social Club, Cultural Center
Address: Chinatown 616 H St NW
Washington, DC 20001
Phone: (202) 628-1688

#267
Smithsonian Folk Life Festival
Category: Festival
Address: 1000 Jefferson Dr SW
Washington, DC 20560
Phone: (202) 633-1000

#268
Snallygaster DC
Category: Festival
Address: 300 Water St SE
Washington, DC 20003
Phone: (202) 567-2576

#269
Blue Penetrable BBL
Category: Art Gallery
Address: 7th St & Independence Ave SW
Washington, DC 20553
Phone: (202) 633-1000

#270
Prisons Gallery Of Art
Category: Art Gallery
Address: 1600 K Street , NW
Washington, DC 20005
Phone: (202) 393-1511

#271
Govinda Gallery
Category: Art Gallery
Address: Georgetown 1227 34th St NW
Washington, DC 20007
Phone: (202) 333-1180

#272
The Art Gallery At The Washington Design Center
Category: Art Gallery, Framing
Address: 300 D St SW
Washington, DC 20024
Phone: (202) 479-7242

#273
G Fine Art
Category: Art Gallery
Address: Trinidad 1350 Florida Ave NE
Washington, DC 20002
Phone: (202) 462-1601

#274
Organization Of American States
Category: Landmark/Historical, Art Gallery
Address: Foggy Bottom 201 18th Street NW
Washington, DC 20006
Phone: (202) 458-6016

#275
Mid City Artists
Category: Art Gallery
Address: Logan Circle Dupont & Logan Cir
Washington, DC 20036
Phone: (202) 669-4226

#276
Maruka Gallery
Category: Jewelry, Art Gallery
Address: Shaw 1300 9th St NW
Washington, DC 20001
Phone: (202) 745-1881

#277
DAR Museum
Category: Museum
Address: Foggy Bottom 1776 D St NW
Washington, DC 20006
Phone: (202) 628-1776

#278
White House Gifts
Category: Gift Shop, Art Gallery
Address: 529 14th St NW
Washington, DC 20045
Phone: (202) 662-7280

#279
The DC Whiskey Walk
Category: Pub, Arts, Entertainment
Address: Dupont Circle 1 Dupont Cir NW
Washington, DC 20036
Phone: (202) 905-2903

#280
Burton Marinkovich Fine Art
Category: Art Gallery
Address: Dupont Circle 1506 21st St NW
Washington, DC 20036
Phone: (202) 296-6563

#281
GALA Hispanic Theatre
Category: Performing Arts, Music Venues
Address: Columbia Heights 3333 14th St
NW Washington, DC 20010
Phone: (202) 234-7174

#282
Livingsocial's Craft Beer + Food Truck Festival
Category: Festival
Address: 800 Water St SW
Washington, DC 20024
Phone: (877) 521-4191

#283
Cirque Dreams Holidaze
Category: Performing Arts
Address: West End 2700 F St
Washington, DC 20037
Phone: (954) 975-9525

#284
Addison/Ripley Fine Art
Category: Art Gallery
Address: Georgetown 1670 Wisconsin
Avenue, NW Washington, DC 20007
Phone: (202) 338-5180

#285
Spanish Ambassador's Former Residence
Category: Nightlife, Museum
Address: 2801 16th St NW
Washington, DC 20009

#286
DC Mariachi
Category: Performing Arts, Djs
Address: Columbia Heights
Washington, DC 20010
Phone: (202) 510-0469

#287
Brookland Poetry
Category: Performing Arts
Address: Brookland 3420 9th Street, NE
Washington, DC 20017
Phone: (202) 526-1632

#288
Quidam
Category: Performing Arts
Address: Pleasant Plains 601 F St NW
Washington, DC 20059

#289
Naked Boys Singing
Category: Performing Arts, Local Flavor
Address: Logan Circle 1409 Playbill Cafe
Washington, DC 20005

#290
D.C. United
Category: Professional Sports Team
Address: Trinidad 2400 E Capitol St SE
Washington, DC 20002
Phone: (202) 587-5000

#291
Washington Home
And Garden Show
Category: Arts, Entertainment
Address: 801 Mt Vernon Place NW
Washington, DC 20001
Phone: (202) 249-4056

#292
Rally To Restore Sanity
And/Or Fear
Category: Local Flavor, Arts, Entertainment
Address: National Mall
Washington, DC 20560

#293
The Frederick Douglass
Museum On Capitol Hill
Category: Museum
Address: Capitol Hill/Northeast 320 A St NE
Washington, DC 20002
Phone: (202) 544-6130

#294
Pridon Goisashvili
At Eastern Market
Category: Art Gallery
Address: Capitol Hill/Southeast 225 7th St
SE Washington, DC 20003
Phone: (240) 485-6488

#295
Baird Auditorium
Museum Of Natural History
Category: Cultural Center
Address: 10th & Constitution Ave NW
Washington, DC 20530

#296
International Gallery Of Art
Category: Art Gallery
Address: 1100 Jefferson Dr SW
Washington, DC 20024

#297
Discovery Theater
Category: Performing Arts, Museum
Address: 900 Jefferson Dr SW
Washington, DC 20560
Phone: (202) 357-1500

#298
USA Science
& Engineering Festival
Category: Festival
Address: Mount Vernon Square 801 Mt
Vernon Pl NW Washington, DC 20001

#299
Living Aloha Hawaii Festival
Category: Festival
Address: 317-349 Maryland Ave SW
Washington, DC 20024

#300
Lillian & Albert Small
Jewish Museum
Category: Museum
Address: 701 3rd St NW
Washington, DC 20001
Phone: (202) 789-0900

#301
National Museum Of American
Jewish Military History
Category: Museum
Address: Dupont Circle 1811 R St NW
Washington, DC 20009
Phone: (202) 265-6280

#302
Story League
Category: Arts, Entertainment
Address: U Street Corridor 2021 14th St NW
Washington, DC 20009

#303
Lost City Art
Category: Art Gallery
Address: 50 Massachusetts Ave NE
Washington, DC 20002
Phone: (202) 589-1870

#304
Sound Bites - A Festival Of Music,
Food And Change
Category: Festival
Address: 815 V St NW
Washington, DC 20001

#305
Ralls Collection
Category: Art Gallery
Address: Georgetown 1516 31st St
NW Washington, DC 20007
Phone: (202) 342-1298

#306
White-Meyer House
Category: Art Gallery
Address: 1624 Crescent Place NW
Washington, DC 20001
Phone: (202) 667-6670

#307
Noa Gallery
Category: Art Gallery
Address: Bloomingdale 132
Rhode Island Avenue NW
Washington, DC 20001
Phone: (202) 483-7328

#308
Dabbling In DC
Category: Social Club
Address: Georgetown Georgetown
Washington, DC 20007

#309
The DC Scoop
Category: Festival, Ice Cream
Address: 1309 5th St
Washington, DC 20002

#310
Step Afrika!
Category: Performing Arts
Address: H Street Corridor/Atlas
District/Near Northeast 1333 H St NE
Washington, DC 20002
Phone: (202) 399-7993

#311
Folklore Society
Of Greater Washington
Category: Performing Arts
Address: Capitol Hill/Southeast
Washington, DC 20003

#312
DC Vegfest
Category: Festival
Address: 355 Water St SE
Washington, DC 20003

#313
7th Annual Open-Air
French Market
Category: Festival
Address: Wisconsin Ave
Washington, DC

#314
Shamrock Festival 2010
Category: Festival
Address: 2400 E Capitol St NE
Washington, DC 20003

#315
America's Islamic
Heritage Museum
Category: Museum
Address: 2524 Elvans Rd SE
Washington, DC 20020
Phone: (202) 610-0586

#316
Sensorium
Category: Performing Arts, Specialty Food
Address: 10 Water St
Washington, DC 20003
Phone: (202) 573-8197

#317
THEARC Theater
Category: Cultural Center, Performing Arts,
Recreation Center
Address: 1901 Mississippi Ave SE
Washington, DC 20032

#318
Doonya
Category: Dance Studio, Performing Arts
Address: Dupont Circle
Washington, DC 20036
Phone: (703) 828-4319

#319
Emerge Art Fair
Category: Arts, Entertainment
Address: 10 I St SW
Washington, DC 20024

#320
NAKID Social Sports
Category: Amateur Sports Team,
Social Club, Sports Club
Address: 235 2nd St NW
Washington, DC 20001
Phone: (855) 466-2543

#321
611 Florida
Category: Music Venues
Address: 611 Florida Avenue, NW
Washington, DC 20001
Phone: (202) 360-9739

#322
Cosmos Club
Category: Bar, American, Social Club
Address: Dupont Circle 2121 Massachusetts
Ave NW Washington, DC 20008
Phone: (202) 387-7783

#323
Axum's Level X Lounge
Category: Music Venues, Lounge
Address: U Street Corridor 1934 9th St NW
Washington, DC 20001
Phone: (202) 387-0765

#324
Sulgrave Club
Category: American, Social Club
Address: Dupont Circle 1801 Massachusetts
Ave NW
Washington, DC 20036
Phone: (202) 462-5800

#325
Eight At Eight Dinner Club
Category: Social Club,
Address: Penn Quarter 413 St NW
Washington, DC 20001
Phone: (202) 584-8848

#326
Transformer Gallery
Category: Art Gallery
Address: Logan Circle 1404 P St NW
Washington, DC 20005
Phone: (202) 483-1102

#327
AMC
Category: Cinema
Address: 1200 H St NW
Washington, DC 20005
Phone: (202) 789-2262

#328
**National Society Daughters
Of The American Revolution**
Category: Museum, Libraries
Address: Foggy Bottom 1776 D St NW
Washington, DC 20006
Phone: (202) 628-1776

#329
Washington School Of Ballet
Category: Performing Arts, Dance School
Address: 3515 Wisconsin Ave NW
Washington, DC 20016
Phone: (202) 362-3606

#330
Rock And Roll Marathon Series
Category: Festival
Address: 1400 Constitution Ave NW
Washington, DC 20227

#331
Downtown Countdown
Category: Social Club
Address: 1919 Connecticut Ave NW
Washington, DC 20009

#332
Margarita March
Category: Festival
Address: U Street Corridor Dupont Cir
Washington, DC

#333
**Washington Area Bicyclist
Association**
Category: Social Club
Address: Adams Morgan 2599 Ontario Rd
NW Washington, DC 20009
Phone: (202) 518-0524

#334
Adamson Gallery
Category: Art Gallery
Address: Logan Circle 1515 14th St NW
Washington, DC 20001
Phone: (202) 232-0707

#335
**Grease The Musical
At National Theater**
Category: Performing Arts
Address: 1321 Pennsylvania Ave NW
Washington, DC 20004
Phone: (202) 628-6161

#336
**National Cherry Blossom
Festival Parade**
Category: Festival
Address: 1200 Constitution Ave NW
Washington, DC 20002
Phone: (877) 442-5666

#337
America, Oh Yes!
Category: Art Gallery
Address: 1350 Connecticut Ave NW
Washington, DC 56901
Phone: (202) 721-0043

#338
Young Benefactors Of The Smithsonian Institution
Category: Museum, Social Club
Address: PO Box 23293
Washington, DC 20026
Phone: (202) 633-3030

#339
L. Ron Hubbard House
Category: Museum
Address: Dupont Circle 1812 19th St NW
Washington, DC 20009
Phone: (202) 234-7490

#340
National Museum Of African Art
Category: Museum
Address: 950 Independence Ave SW
Washington, DC 20560
Phone: (202) 357-1300

#341
Funky Fresh Foodie Festival
Category: Festival
Address: 1201-1299 Half St SE
Washington, DC 20003

#342
Livingsocial's Craft Beer + Food Truck Festival
Category: Festival
Address: 1299 Half St SE
Washington, DC 20003
Phone: (877) 521-4191

#343
Smile Project Street Carnival
Category: Festival
Address: 620 M St SE
Washington, DC 20003

#344
The Bead Studio
Category: Arts, Entertainment
Address: Tenleytown 4450 Wisconsin Ave NW Washington, DC 20016

#345
Warehouse Theater
Category: Performing Arts, Cinema
Address: 1021 7th St NW
Washington, DC 20001
Phone: (202) 783-3933

#346
El Mundo De Luchadores
Category: Festival
Address: 1/2 St SE
Washington, DC 20002

#347
Minnesota Liquors
Category: Winery
Address: 2237 Minnesota Ave SE
Washington, DC 20020
Phone: (202) 584-6363

#348
American Painting
Category: Art Gallery
Address: Palisades 5118 Macarthur Boulevard NW
Washington, DC 20016
Phone: (202) 244-3244

#349
11th Wine And Food Festival
Category: Festival
Address: Penn Quarter 1300 Pennsylvania Ave NW Washington, DC 20004

#350
DC Africa Festival
Category: Festival
Address: 300 Van Buren St NW
Washington, DC 20012
Phone: (202) 727-5634

#351
AFI Silver Theatre And Cultural Center
Category: Cinema
Address: 8633 Colesville Rd
Silver Spring, MD 20910
Phone: (301) 495-6700

#352
Hinckley Pottery
Category: Art Gallery
Address: Adams Morgan 1707 Kalorama Rd NW Washington, DC 20009
Phone: (202) 745-7055

#353
Chinese New Year Parade
Category: Local Flavor
Address: H St NW
Washington, DC 20001

#354
Susquehanna Antique Company
Category: Antiques, Art Gallery
Address: Georgetown 3216 O St NW
Washington, DC 20007
Phone: (202) 333-1511

#355
Washington Sinfonietta
Category: Performing Arts
Address: Logan Circle 5 Thomas Cir NW
Washington, DC 20005
Phone: (202) 580-6535

#356
Burka's Wine & Liquor Store
Category: Beer, Wine, Spirits, Winery
Address: 3500 Wisconsin Avenue NW
Washington, DC 20016
Phone: (202) 966-7676

#357
H Street Festival 2011
Category: Festival
Address: H Street Corridor/Atlas
District/Near Northeast 1245 H St NE
Washington, DC 20002

#358
Capital Pride
Category: Arts, Entertainment
Address: Pennsylvania Ave NW &
Constitution Ave
Washington, DC 20004

#359
**701 Pennsylvania Avenue
Restaurant & Bar**
Category: American, Jazz, Blues
Address: Penn Quarter 701 Pennsylvania
Ave NW Washington, DC 20004
Phone: (202) 393-0701

#360
Young Playwrights' Theater
Category: Performing Arts
Address: Columbia Heights 2437 15th St
NW Washington, DC 20009
Phone: (202) 387-9173

#361
1776 Ford's Theatre
Category: Museum
Address: 511 10th St NW
Washington, DC 20004
Phone: (202) 347-4833

#362
**Anne Truitt: Perception And
Reflection At The Hirshhorn
Museum**
Category: Museum
Address: Capitol Hill/Southeast
Independence Avenue At Seventh Street SW
Washington, DC 20001
Phone: (202) 633-1000

#363
**Orange Arrow
Anti-Restaurant Club**
Category: Social Club
Address: Trinidad
Washington, DC 20002

#364
**Electric Maid
Community Exchange**
Category: Performing Arts, Music Venues
Address: Takoma 268 Carroll St NW
Washington, DC 20012
Phone: (202) 545-3980

#365
Studio H Gallery And Workshop
Category: Art Gallery
Address: H Street Corridor/Atlas
District/Near Northeast 408a H St NE
Washington, DC 20002
Phone: (202) 468-5277

#366
Redrum
Category: Performing Arts
Address: Shaw 612 L St NW
Washington, DC 20001

#367
Gala
Category: Art Gallery
Address: Georgetown 1671 Wisconsin Ave
NW Washington, DC 20007
Phone: (202) 333-1337

#368
Skynear Designs
Category: Furniture Store, Art Gallery
Address: Adams Morgan 2122 18th St NW
Washington, DC 20009
Phone: (202) 797-7160

#369
Artisphere
Category: Art Gallery
Address: Rosslyn 1101 Wilson Blvd
Arlington, VA 22209
Phone: (703) 875-1100

#370
Torpedo Factory Art Center
Category: Art Gallery, Jewelry
Address: Old Town Alexandria 105 N Union
St Alexandria, VA 22314
Phone: (703) 838-4565

#371
Capitol Hill Club
Category: Social Club
Address: Capitol Hill/Southeast 300 1st St
SE Washington, DC 20003
Phone: (202) 484-4590

#372
US House Of Representatives
Category: Arts, Entertainment
Address: 200 D Street SW
Washington, DC 20001
Phone: (202) 554-4672

#373
**Angelika Film Center
& Cafe At Mosaic**
Category: Cinema, Café
Address: Mosaic, Merrifield 2911 District
Avefairfax, VA 22031
Phone: (571) 512-3301

#374
Be With Me Playseum
Category: Playground, Arts, Entertainment
Address: Capitol Hill/Southeast 545 8th St
SE Washington, DC 20003
Phone: (202) 999-0510

#375
Holiday Party At Newseum
Category: Social Club, Nightlife
Address: 555 Pennsylvania Ave NW
Washington, DC 20001

#376
**Recording Industry
Association Of America**
Category: Arts, Entertainment
Address: 1025 F St NW
Washington, DC 20004
Phone: (202) 775-0101

#377
Lisner Auditorium
Category: Performing Arts, Music Venues
Address: Foggy Bottom George Washington
University
Washington, DC 20052
Phone: (202) 994-6800

#378
Neon Tuxedo Party At The Huxley
Category: Music Venues
Address: 1730 M St NW
Washington, DC 20036
Phone: (202) 670-1730

#379
Mike Mitchell
Category: Art Gallery
Address: Dupont Circle 1754B T St NW
Washington, DC 20009
Phone: (202) 234-6400

#380
AMC Courthouse Plaza 8
Category: Cinema
Address: Court House 2150 Clarendon Blvd.
Arlington, VA 22201
Phone: (703) 243-4950

#381
Arlington Cinema & Drafthouse
Category: Cinema, Restaurant, Bar,
Performing Arts
Address: Columbia Heights 2903 Columbia
Pike Arlington, VA 22204
Phone: (703) 486-2345

#382
**The Smithsonian Associates -
Resident Associate Program**
Category: Museum, Adult Education
Address: 1100 Jefferson Dr SW
Washington, DC 20024
Phone: (202) 633-3030

#383
Phillips Collection
Category: Museum, Art Gallery
Address: Shaw 21 Q St NW
Washington, DC 20001
Phone: (202) 387-2151

#384
Davis Center The
Category: Performing Arts
Address: 6133 Georgia Ave NW Apt 1
Washington, DC 20011
Phone: (202) 726-7146

#385
Acebass Productions
Category: Arts, Entertainment,
Musical Instruments
Address: Michigan Park 4427 13th St NE
Washington, DC 20017
Phone: (202) 635-2875

#386
**Harvey Star Washington Fashion
Show Producer**
Category: Arts, Entertainment
Address: Brightwood 1364 Underwood
Street NW Washington, DC 20012
Phone: (212) 333-4422

#387
Pure Lounge
Category: Lounge, Music Venues,
Social Club
Address: U Street Corridor 1326 U St NW
Washington, DC 20009
Phone: (202) 290-7058

#388
Greenberg Theatre
Category: Performing Arts
Address: Tenleytown 4200 Wisconsin Ave
NW Washington, DC 20016
Phone: (202) 885-2787

#389
DTR Modern Galleries
Category: Art Gallery
Address: Georgetown 2820 Pennsylvania
Ave NW Washington, DC 20007
Phone: (202) 338-0625

#390
Washington Studio School
Category: Art Gallery
Address: Kalorama 2129 S St NW
Washington, DC 20008
Phone: (202) 234-3030

#391
Unique Art And Framing
Category: Art Gallery, Framing
Address: U Street Corridor 1628 U St NW
Washington, DC 02009
Phone: (202) 802-8645

#392
Kollaboration DC
Category: Festival
Address: West End
Washington, DC 20037
Phone: (703) 507-4375

#393
Music Center At Strathmore
Category: Art Gallery, Music Venues,
Performing Arts
Address: 5301 Tuckerman Lanen
Bethesda, MD 20852
Phone: (301) 581-5100

#394
Prada Gallery
Category: Art Gallery
Address: Georgetown 1030 Wisconsin
Avenue NW Washington, DC 20007
Phone: (202) 342-0067

#395
Alex Galleries
Category: Art Gallery, Venues,
Event Space
Address: 2106 R St NW
Washington, DC 20008
Phone: (202) 667-2599

#396
Winter Palace Studio
Category: Interior Design, Art Gallery,
Address: Serving
Washington, DC And The Surrounding Area
Phone: (301) 263-0000

#397
**John F Kennedy Center
For The Performing Arts**
Category: Performing Arts
Address: Foggy Bottom 2700 F St NW
Washington, DC 20037
Phone: (202) 416-8340

#398
Gallery Nk
Category: Art Gallery
Address: H Street Corridor/Atlas
District/Near Northeast 321 K St NE
Washington, DC 20002
Phone: (240) 486-0261

#399
Signature Theatre
Category: Performing Arts
Address: Shirlington 4200 Campbell Ave
Arlington, VA 22206
Phone: (703) 820-9771

#400
Smithsonian Institution
Category: Museum
Address: Capitol Hill/Southeast 750 9th St
SE Washington, DC 20003
Phone: (202) 357-1300

#401
Randallscottprojects
Category: Art Gallery
Address: 1326 H St NE
Washington, DC 20002
Phone: (202) 396-0300

#402
Solly's Tavern
Category: Music Venues, Bar
Address: U Street Corridor 1942 11th St NW
Washington, DC 20001
Phone: (202) 232-6590

#403
Galaxy Hut
Category: Dive Bar, Vegetarian,
Music Venues
Address: 2711 Wilson Blvd
Arlington, VA 22201
Phone: (703) 525-8646

#404
Friday Morning Music Club
Category: Performing Arts
Address: Mount Vernon Square 801 K St
NW Washington, DC 20001
Phone: (202) 333-2075

#405
DAR Constitution Hall
Category: Performing Arts, Music Venues
Address: 18Th & C Streets N.W.
Washington, DC 20006
Phone: (202) 347-1581

#406
Gallery Plan B
Category: Art Gallery
Address: Logan Circle 1530 14th Street, NW
Washington, DC 20005
Phone: (202) 234-2711

#407
AFL Studio LLC
Category: Musical Instruments, Private
Tutor, Cultural Center
Address: Trinidad
Washington, DC 20002
Phone: (703) 362-9041

#408
Crinkle
Category: Arts, Entertainment
Address: Petworth Petworth
Washington, DC 20011
Phone: (484) 538-7675

#409
Artfully Chocolate
Category: Chocolate Shop, Art Gallery
Address: Del Ray 2003A Mt. Vernon Ave
Alexandria, VA 22301
Phone: (703) 635-7917

#410
Knock On Wood Tap Studio
Category: Performing Arts, Dance School
Address: Takoma 6925 Willow St NW
Washington, DC 20012
Phone: (202) 722-1625

#411
Nihal Art
Category: Art Gallery
Address: H Street Corridor/Atlas
District/Near Northeast 321 K St NE
Washington, DC 20002
Phone: (240) 486-0261

#412
Littleton Maurine & Gallery
Category: Art Gallery
Address: Georgetown 1667 Wisconsin
Avenue NW Washington, DC 20007
Phone: (202) 333-9307

#413
**Live Band Karaoke
W/Northeast Corridor**
Category: Arts, Entertainment
Address: Adams Morgan 1725 Columbia Rd
NW Washington, DC 20009
Phone: (202) 332-2211

#414
Ovo Cirque Du Soleil
Category: Performing Arts
Address: Harborview Ave
Oxon Hill, MD 20745

#415
Bethesda Row Cinema
Category: Cinema
Address: 7235 Woodmont Ave
Bethesda, MD 20814
Phone: (301) 652-7273

#416
Medieval Madness
Category: Performing Arts, American
Address: Old Town Alexandria 710 King St
Alexandria, VA 22314
Phone: (703) 329-3075

#417
Arlington's David M. Brown Planetarium
Category: Museum
Address: 1426 N Quincy St
Arlington, VA 22201

#418
Mary Livingston Ripley Garden
Category: Botanical Garden
Address: 900 Jefferson Dr. SW
Washington, DC 20560

#419
Oby Lee
Category: Winery, Gluten-Free
Address: Clarendon 3000 N Washington
Blvd Arlington, VA 22201
Phone: (571) 257-5054

#420
Kastles Stadium At The Wharf
Category: Stadium/Arena
Address: 800 Water St SW
Washington, DC 20024

#421
IOTA Club & Cafe
Category: Music Venues, Bar, American
Address: Clarendon 2832 Wilson Blvd
Arlington, VA 22201
Phone: (703) 522-8340

#422
Zoo Lights
Category: Festival, Zoo
Address: Olmstead Walk
Washington, DC 20008

#423
Art Walk
Category: Art Gallery
Address: 909 H St NW
Washington, DC 20001

#424
Imagination Stage
Category: Performing Arts, Education
Address: 4908 Auburn Ave
Bethesda, MD 20814
Phone: (301) 961-6060

#425
Verizon Center
Category: Stadium/Arena,
Address: 601 F Street NW
Washington, DC 20004
Phone: (202) 628-3200

#426
Art-O-Matic 2012
Category: Art Gallery
Address: Crystal City 1851 S Bell St
Arlington, VA 22202

#427
Professionals In The City
Category: Social Club, Jazz, Blues
Address: Shaw
Washington, DC 20001
Phone: (202) 686-5990

#428
DC Shorts Film Festival
Category: Local Flavor, Festival
Address: 1317 F Street, NW, Suite 920
Washington, DC 20004
Phone: (202) 393-4266

#429
H Street Festival
Category: Festival, Street Vendor
Address: H Street Corridor/Atlas
District/Near Northeast 1000 H St NE
Washington, DC 20002

#430
Birchmere
Category: Music Venues
Address: 3701 Mt. Vernon Ave
Alexandria, VA 22305
Phone: (703) 549-7500

#431
Totem Cirque Du Soleil
Category: Performing Arts
Address: 156 Waterfront St
Oxon Hill, MD 20745

#432
The Hamilton
Category: Seafood, American,
Music Venues
Address: 600 14th St NW
Washington, DC 20005
Phone: (202) 787-1000

#433
Galerie Myrtis
Category: Art Gallery
Address: Capitol Hill/Southeast 500 9th St
SE Washington, DC 20003
Phone: (202) 548-7575

#434
The George Washington Masonic National Memorial
Category: Museum
Address: 101 Callahan Drive
Alexandria, VA 22301
Phone: (703) 683-2007

#435
International Art Gallery & Custom Framing
Category: Art Gallery, Framing
Address: 1625 K St NW
Washington, DC 20006
Phone: (202) 466-7979

#436
Cirque Du Soleil's Amaluna
Category: Performing Arts
Address: 300 Waterfront St
Oxon Hill, MD 20745
Phone: (877) 628-5427

#437
Basin Street Lounge
Category: Lounge, Jazz, Blues, Cajun/Creole
Address: Old Town Alexandria 219 King St
Alexandria, VA 22314
Phone: (703) 549-1141

#438
River Farm
Category: Venues, Event Space, Botanical Garden
Address: 7931 E Blvd Dr
Alexandria, VA 22308
Phone: (703) 768-5700

#439
Woman's National Democratic Club, WNDC
Category: Social Club, Venues, Event Space
Address: Dupont Circle 1526 New Hampshire Ave NW
Washington, DC 20036
Phone: (202) 232-7363

#440
The National Theatre
Category: Performing Arts
Address: 1321 Pennsylvania Ave NW
Washington, DC 20004
Phone: (202) 628-6161

#441
Arlington House
Category: Landmark/Historical, Museum
Address: Arlington National Cemetery
Arlington, VA 22211
Phone: (703) 607-8000

#442
Pier 7 Restaurant
Category: Seafood, Music Venues
Address: 650 Water St SW
Washington, DC 20024
Phone: (202) 554-2500

#443
The Fillmore
Category: Music Venues
Address: 8656 Colesville Rd
Silver Spring, MD 20910
Phone: (301) 960-9999

#444
The State Theatre
Category: Venues, Event Space, Music Venues
Address: Falls Church City 220 N Washington St Falls Church, VA 22046
Phone: (703) 237-0300

#445
Empress Lounge
Category: Jazz, Blues
Address: 1330 Maryland Ave Sw
Washington, DC 20024
Phone: (202) 787-6042

#446
Little Theatre Of Alexandria
Category: Performing Arts
Address: 600 Wolfe St
Alexandria, VA 22314
Phone: (703) 683-0496

#447
Synetic Theater
Category: Performing Arts
Address: Pentagon City 1800 S Bell St
Arlington, VA 22206
Phone: (703) 824-8060

#448
Max Major - Mind Reading And Magic Show
Category: Performing Arts, Magicians
Address: 718 7th St NW
Washington, DC 20004
Phone: (888) 406-7571

#449
**Glen Echo Park Partnership
For Arts & Culture**
Category: Arts, Entertainment,
Dance School,
Address: 7300 Macarthur Blvd
Glen Echo, MD 20812
Phone: (301) 634-2222

#450
**Stabler-Leadbeater
Apothecary Museum**
Category: Museum
Address: Old Town Alexandria 105-107 S
Fairfax St Alexandria, VA 22314
Phone: (703) 838-3852

#451
The Carlyle Club
Category: American, Venues, Event Space,
Performing Arts
Address: 411 John Carlyle Street
Alexandria, VA 22314
Phone: (703) 548-5953

#452
Artful Gallery
Category: Art Gallery
Address: H Street Corridor/Atlas
District/Near Northeast 1349 Maryland Ave
NE Washington, DC 20002
Phone: (301) 270-2427

#453
Superstartickets
Category: Performing Arts,
Address: Court House 2305 Wilson Blvd
Arlington, VA 22201
Phone: (703) 553-8500

#454
**The National Capital
Barbecue Battle**
Category: Local Flavor, Jazz, Blues, Food
Address: Federal Triangle 9th Street NW
And Pennsylvania Ave NW
Washington, DC 20005
Phone: (202) 828-3099

#455
Crystal Screen - Outdoor Movies
Category: Cinema
Address: Crystal City 1851 S Bell St
Arlington, VA 22202

#456
**Kenilworth Park
And Aquatic Gardens**
Category: Park, Botanical Garden
Address: 1550 Anacostia Ave NE
Washington, DC 20019
Phone: (202) 426-6905

#457
Westover Beer Garden & Haus
Category: Dive Bar, Music Venues
Address: 5863 N Washington Blvd
Arlington, VA 22205
Phone: (703) 536-5040

#458
College Park Aviation Museum
Category: Museum
Address: 1985 Corporal Frank Scott Dr
College Park, MD 20740
Phone: (301) 864-6029

#459
Washington Revels
Category: Performing Arts
Address: 531 Dale Dr
Silver Spring, MD 20910
Phone: (301) 587-3835

#460
Shadowland Laser Adventures
Category: Amusement Park,
Arcade, Karaoke
Address: 5508 Franconia Rd
Alexandria, VA 22310
Phone: (703) 921-1004

#461
**Allen Custom Frame
& Biscarr Fine Art**
Category: Art Gallery, Framing
Address: Tenleytown 4620 Wisconsin Ave
NW Washington, DC 20016
Phone: (202) 628-1389

#462
Hallow Inc
Category: Arts, Entertainment
Address: 11840 Rockville Pike
Rockville, MD 20852
Phone: (240) 292-9473

#463
Cowboy Cafe
Category: Burgers, American,
Music Venues
Address: 4792 Lee Hwy
Arlington, VA 22207
Phone: (703) 243-8010

#464
Wags N' Whiskers
Category: Festival
Address: Shirlington 2700 S Quincy St
Arlington, VA 22206
Phone: (703) 887-5514

#465
National Museum
Of The US Navy
Category: Museum
Address: 805 Kidder Breese St SE
Washington Navy Yard, DC 20374
Phone: (202) 433-4882

#466
Gallery 10 Ltd
Category: Art Gallery
Address: Dupont Circle 1519 Connecticut
Ave NW Washington, DC 20036
Phone: (202) 232-3326

#467
AMC Tysons Corner 16
Category: Cinema
Address: Tysons Corner 7850 Tysons
Corner Center Mclean, VA 22102
Phone: (703) 734-6212

#468
Lioudmila's Dance Studio
Category: Arts, Entertainment,
Dance Studio
Address: 18 Roth St
Alexandria, VA 22314
Phone: (703) 751-8868

#469
City Museum Of Washington DC
Category: Museum
Address: Mount Vernon Square 801 K St
NW Washington, DC 20001
Phone: (202) 383-1800

#470
Wine Pro Tours
Category: Tours, Winery
Address: Arlington, VA 22204
Phone: (703) 209-7139

#471
AMC Hoffman Center 22
Category: Cinema
Address: 206 Swamp Fox Rd.
Alexandria, VA 22314
Phone: (703) 236-1083

#472
Laugh Riot At The Hyatt
Category: Arts, Entertainment,
Comedy Club
Address: 7400 Wisconsin Ave
Bethesda, MD 20814
Phone: (301) 946-1102

#473
Totem Cirque Du Soleil
Category: Performing Arts
Address: 165 Waterfront Stfort
Washington, MD 20744

#474
National Museum
Of Health And Medicine
Category: Museum
Address: 2500 Linden Ln
Silver Spring, MD 20910
Phone: (301) 319-3300

#475
AMC Loews Shirlington 7
Category: Cinema
Address: Shirlington 2772 South Randolph
St. Arlington, VA 22206
Phone: (703) 671-0978

#476
Bobby Mckey's Dueling Piano Bar
Category: Bar, Music Venues
Address: 172 Fleet St
National Harbor, MD 20745
Phone: (301) 602-2209

#477
DEA Museum And Visitor Center
Category: Museum
Address: Pentagon City 700 Navy Army
Drive Arlington, VA 22202
Phone: (202) 307-3463

#478
Regal Kingstowne 16
Category: Cinema
Address: 5910 Kingstowne Towne Ctr
Alexandria, VA 22315
Phone: (703) 822-4956

#479
Zenith Gallery
Category: Art Gallery
Address: Shepherd Park 1429 Iris St NW
Washington, DC 20012
Phone: (202) 783-2963

#480
1st Stage
Category: Performing Arts
Address: 1524 Spring Hill Rd
Tysons, VA 22102
Phone: (703) 854-1856

#481
Art Soiree's Grand Launch
Fine Art Series
Category: Art Gallery
Address: Georgetown 3100 S St NW
Washington, DC 20007
Phone: (202) 841-6441

#482
Old Town Theater
Category: Cinema, Performing Arts,
Music Venues
Address: Old Town Alexandria 815 1/2 King
St Alexandria, VA 22314
Phone: (703) 549-1025

#483
Silver Spring Jazz Festival
Category: Festival
Address: Veterans Plaza
Silver Spring, MD 20910
Phone: (240) 777-5300

#484
Taste Of Bethesda
Category: Festival
Address: Norfolk, Fairmont, St. Elmo Cordell
Avenues Bethesda, MD 20814
Phone: (301) 215-6666

#485
Dance Factory
Category: Performing Arts, Dance School
Address: Arlington, VA 22201

#486
Nanny O'Brien's Irish Pub
Category: Pub, Music Venues, Irish
Address: 3319 Connecticut Ave NW
Washington, DC 20008
Phone: (202) 686-9189

#487
Arlington Arts Center
Category: Art Gallery, Venues,
Event Space
Address: Virginia Square 3550 Wilson Blvd
Arlington, VA 22204
Phone: (703) 248-6800

#488
Capitol Hill Arts Workshop
Category: Art Gallery, Performing Arts
Address: Capitol Hill/Southeast 545 7th St
SE Washington, DC 20003
Phone: (202) 547-6839

#489
Toro Mata
Category: Art Gallery, Arts, Crafts
Address: Adams Morgan 2410 18th St NW
Washington, DC 20009
Phone: (202) 232-3890

#490
Project 4 Gallery
Category: Art Gallery
Address: 1353 U St NW
Washington, DC 20009
Phone: (202) 232-4340

#491
Regal Majestic Stadium 20
Category: Cinema
Address: 900 Ellsworth Dr
Silver Spring, MD 20910
Phone: (301) 565-8884

#492
DJ Sharkey
Category: Performing Arts, Djs
Address: 1234 Evergreen Terrace
Arlington, VA 22205

#493
Royale 14 Cinemas
Category: Cinema
Address: 6505 America Blvd
Hyattsville, MD 20782
Phone: (301) 864-3456

#494
Alexandria Arts Festival
Category: Festival
Address: Old Town Alexandria 480 King St
Alexandria, VA 22314

#495
Barry Taylor Magician
Category: Performing Arts
Address: 5544-A Nicholson Ln
Kensington, MD 20895
Phone: (301) 744-8545

#496
Metropolitan School Of The Arts
Category: Performing Arts
Address: 5775 Barclay Dr
Alexandria, VA 22315
Phone: (703) 339-0444

#497
The Bethesda Theatre
Category: Performing Arts
Address: 7719 Wisconsin Ave
Bethesda, MD 20814
Phone: (301) 657-7827

#498
ICE! At The Gaylord National
Category: Performing Arts
Address: 201 Waterfront Street
National Harbor, MD 20745
Phone: (877) 352-3629

#499
The Jerk Pit
Category: Caribbean, Music Venues
Address: 9070 Baltimore Ave
College Park, MD 20740
Phone: (301) 982-5375

#500
219 Restaurant
Category: Jazz, Blues, Southern
Address: Old Town Alexandria 219 King St
Alexandria, VA 22314
Phone: (703) 549-1141

TOP 500 NIGHTLIFE

The Most Recommended by Locals & Trevelers

(From #1 to #500)

#1
Columbia Room
Category: Bar
Average Price: Expensive
Address: 1021 7th St NW
Washington, DC 20001
Phone: (202) 393-0336

#2
Blues Alley
Category: Jazz, Blues
Average Price: Modest
Address: 1073 Wisconsin Ave NW
Washington, DC 20007
Phone: (202) 337-4141

#3
HR-57
Category: Jazz, Blues
Average Price: Inexpensive
Address: 1007 H St NE
Washington, DC 20002
Phone: (202) 253-0044

#4
U Street Music Hall
Category: Music Venues
Average Price: Modest
Address: 1115 U St NW
Washington, DC 20009
Phone: (202) 588-1880

#5
Minibar
Category: American
Average Price: Exclusive
Address: 855 E St NW
Washington, DC 20004
Phone: (202) 393-0812

#6
9:30 Club
Category: Music Venues
Average Price: Modest
Address: 815 V St NW
Washington, DC 20001
Phone: (202) 265-0930

#7
Harold Black
Category: Lounge
Average Price: Expensive
Address: 212 7th St SE
Washington, DC 20003
Phone: (202) 540-0459

#8
Red Derby
Category: Dive Bar
Average Price: Inexpensive
Address: 3718 14th St NW
Washington, DC 20010
Phone: (202) 291-5000

#9
Blue Duck Tavern
Category: Bar
Average Price: Expensive
Address: 1201 24th St NW
Washington, DC 20037
Phone: (202) 419-6755

#10
Boundary Stone
Category: American
Average Price: Modest
Address: 116 Rhode Island Ave NW
Washington, DC 20001
Phone: (202) 621-6635

#11
Gypsy Sally's
Category: Music Venues
Average Price: Modest
Address: 3401 K St NW
Washington, DC 20007
Phone: (202) 333-7700

#12
Tryst
Category: Lounge
Average Price: Modest
Address: 2459 18th St NW
Washington, DC 20009
Phone: (202) 232-5500

#13
City Tap House
Category: Gastropub
Average Price: Modest
Address: 901 9th St NW
Washington, DC 20001
Phone: (202) 733-5333

#14
The Gibson
Category: Lounge
Average Price: Expensive
Address: 2009 14th St NW
Washington, DC 20003
Phone: (202) 232-2156

#15
Churchkey
Category: American
Average Price: Modest
Address: 1337 14th St NW
Washington, DC 20005
Phone: (202) 567-2576

#16
Madam's Organ
Category: Jazz, Blues
Average Price: Modest
Address: 2461 18th St NW
Washington, DC 20009
Phone: (202) 667-5370

#17
Eighteenth Street Lounge
Category: Lounge
Average Price: Modest
Address: 1212 18th St N W
Washington, DC 20036
Phone: (202) 466-3922

#18
Barmini
Category: American
Average Price: Expensive
Address: 855 E St NW
Washington, DC 20004
Phone: (202) 393-4451

#19
Black Jack
Category: Lounge
Average Price: Modest
Address: 1612 14th St NW
Washington, DC 20009
Phone: (202) 319-1612

#20
The Passenger
Category: Bar
Average Price: Modest
Address: 1021 7th St NW
Washington, DC 20001
Phone: (202) 393-0220

#21
Darnell's Bar
Category: Lounge
Average Price: Modest
Address: 944 Florida Ave NW
Washington, DC 20001
Phone: (202) 290-2865

#22
Off The Record
Category: Bar
Average Price: Expensive
Address: 800 16th St NW
Washington, DC 20006
Phone: (202) 638-6600

#23
Patty Boom Boom
Category: Caribbean
Average Price: Inexpensive
Address: 1359 U St NW
Washington, DC 20009
Phone: (202) 629-1712

#24
Quill
Category: Bar
Average Price: Expensive
Address: 1200 16th St NW
Washington, DC 20036
Phone: (202) 448-2300

#25
A&D Bar
Category: Dive Bar
Average Price: Modest
Address: 1314 9th St NW
Washington, DC 20001
Phone: (202) 290-1804

#26
Wisdom
Category: Lounge
Average Price: Modest
Address: 1432 Pennsylvania Ave SE
Washington, DC 20003
Phone: (202) 543-2323

#27
Dacha Beer Garden
Category: Bar
Average Price: Modest
Address: 1600 7th St NW
Washington, DC 20001
Phone: (202) 524-8790

#28
Degrees Bar & Lounge
Category: American
Average Price: Expensive
Address: 3100 S St NW
Washington, DC 20007
Phone: (202) 912-4100

#29
Pharmacy Bar
Category: Restaurant
Average Price: Inexpensive
Address: 2337 18th St NW
Washington, DC 20009
Phone: (202) 483-1200

#30
Dan's Cafe
Category: Restaurant
Average Price: Inexpensive
Address: 2315 18th St NW
Washington, DC 20009
Phone: (202) 265-0299

#31
Co Co Sala
Category: American
Average Price: Expensive
Address: 929 F St NW
Washington, DC 20004
Phone: (202) 347-4265

#32
The Jam Cellar
Category: Dance Club
Average Price: Inexpensive
Address: 2437 15th St NW
Washington, DC 20009
Phone: (202) 569-8329

#33
KABIN
Category: Dance Club
Average Price: Modest
Address: 1337 Connecticut Ave NW
Washington, DC 20036
Phone: (202) 810-2770

#34
Board Room
Category: Sports Bar
Average Price: Inexpensive
Address: 1737 Connecticut Ave NW
Washington, DC 20009
Phone: (202) 518-7666

#35
The Saloon
Category: Pub
Average Price: Modest
Address: 1205 U St NW
Washington, DC 20009
Phone: (202) 462-2640

#36
Jackpot
Category: Bar
Average Price: Modest
Address: 726 7th St NW
Washington, DC 20001
Phone: (202) 628-5225

#37
Barcelona
Category: Tapas
Average Price: Expensive
Address: 1622 14th St Nw
Washington, DC 20005
Phone: (202) 588-5500

#38
HEIST
Category: Champagne Bar
Average Price: Expensive
Address: 1802 Jefferson Pl NW
Washington, DC 20036
Phone: (202) 450-2126

#39
Matchbox Chinatown
Category: Pizza
Average Price: Modest
Address: 713 H St NW
Washington, DC 20001
Phone: (202) 289-4441

#40
DC Improv
Category: Comedy Club
Average Price: Modest
Address: 1140 Connecticut Ave NW
Washington, DC 20036
Phone: (202) 296-7008

#41
Thomas Foolery
Category: Bar
Average Price: Inexpensive
Address: 2029 P St NW
Washington, DC 20036
Phone: (202) 822-6200

#42
Jojo Restaurant And Bar
Category: American
Average Price: Modest
Address: 1518 U St NW
Washington, DC 20009
Phone: (202) 319-9350

#43
Bohemian Caverns
Category: Jazz, Blues
Average Price: Modest
Address: 2003 11th St NW
Washington, DC 20001
Phone: (202) 299-0800

#44
Dodge City
Category: Bar
Average Price: Modest
Address: 917 U St
Washington, DC 20001
Phone: (202) 588-9080

#45
Breadsoda
Category: Bar
Average Price: Modest
Address: 2233 Wisconsin Ave NW
Washington, DC 20007
Phone: (202) 333-7445

#46
Kostume Karaoke
Category: Karaoke
Average Price: Inexpensive
Address: 1942 11th St NW
Washington, DC 20001
Phone: (202) 232-6590

#47
Bravo Bar
Category: Bar
Average Price: Inexpensive
Address: 2917 Georgia Ave NW
Washington, DC 20001
Phone: (202) 629-2583

#48
The Wonderland Ballroom
Category: Dance Club
Average Price: Modest
Address: 1101 Kenyon St NW
Washington, DC 20009
Phone: (202) 232-5263

#49
Tune Inn
Category: Dive Bar
Average Price: Inexpensive
Address: 331 Pennsylvania Ave SE
Washington, DC 20003
Phone: (202) 543-2725

#50
Barrel
Category: Bar
Average Price: Modest
Address: 613 Pennsylvania Ave SE
Washington, DC 20003
Phone: (202) 543-3622

#51
Le Bar
Category: Bar
Average Price: Expensive
Address: 806 15th St NW
Washington, DC 20005
Phone: (202) 737-8800

#52
Mockingbird Hill
Category: Wine Bar
Average Price: Modest
Address: 1843 7th St NW
Washington, DC 20001
Phone: (202) 316-9396

#53
DC Reynolds
Category: American
Average Price: Modest
Address: 3628 Georgia Ave NW
Washington, DC 20010
Phone: (202) 506-7178

#54
The Rye Bar
Category: American
Average Price: Modest
Address: 1050 31st NW
Washington, DC 20007
Phone: (202) 617-2400

#55
Iron Horse Tap Room
Category: Bar
Average Price: Modest
Address: 507 7th St NW
Washington, DC 20004
Phone: (202) 347-7665

#56
Trusty's Full-Serve Bar
Category: Dive Bar
Average Price: Inexpensive
Address: 1420 Pennsylvania Ave SE
Washington, DC 20003
Phone: (202) 547-1010

#57
The Pug
Category: American
Average Price: Inexpensive
Address: 1234 H St NE
Washington, DC 20002
Phone: (202) 555-1212

#58
Room 11
Category: Wine Bar
Average Price: Modest
Address: 3234 11th St NW
Washington, DC 20010
Phone: (202) 332-3234

#59
The Pinch
Category: Dive Bar
Average Price: Modest
Address: 3548 14th St NW
Washington, DC 20010
Phone: (202) 722-4440

#60
Meridian Pint
Category: Bar
Average Price: Modest
Address: 3400 11th St NW
Washington, DC 20010
Phone: (202) 588-1075

#61
The Raven Grill
Category: Dive Bar
Average Price: Inexpensive
Address: 3125 Mt Pleasant Ave NW
Washington, DC 20010
Phone: (202) 387-8411

#62
Four Seasons Garden Terrace
Category: Wine Bar
Average Price: Expensive
Address: 2800 Pennsylvania Ave NW
Washington, DC 20037
Phone: (202) 944-2026

#63
DC9 Nightclub
Category: Bar
Average Price: Modest
Address: 1940 9th St NW
Washington, DC 20001
Phone: (202) 483-5000

#64
Atomic Billiards
Category: Pool Hall
Average Price: Inexpensive
Address: 3427 Connecticut Ave NW
Washington, DC 20008
Phone: (202) 363-7665

#65
Echostage
Category: Music Venues
Average Price: Modest
Address: 2135 Queens Chapel Rd NE
Washington, DC 20018
Phone: (202) 503-2330

#66
Bar-Cöde
Category: American
Average Price: Modest
Address: 1101 17th St NW
Washington, DC 20036
Phone: (202) 955-9001

#67
Zeba
Category: Bar
Average Price: Modest
Address: 3423 14th St NW
Washington, DC 20010
Phone: (202) 506-4603

#68
Black Cat
Category: Music Venues
Average Price: Modest
Address: 1811 14th St NW
Washington, DC 20009
Phone: (202) 667-4490

#69
Firefly
Category: American
Average Price: Modest
Address: 1310 New Hampshire Ave NW
Washington, DC 20036
Phone: (202) 861-1310

#70
**Mad Momos Beer Deck
And Restaurant**
Category: Lounge
Average Price: Modest
Address: 3605 14th St NW
Washington, DC 20010
Phone: (202) 829-1450

#71
All Souls Bar
Category: Bar
Average Price: Modest
Address: 725 T St NW
Washington, DC 20001
Phone: (202) 733-5929

#72
The Bottom Line
Category: American
Average Price: Inexpensive
Address: 1716 I St NW
Washington, DC 20006
Phone: (202) 298-8488

#73
Timehri International
Category: Dance Club
Average Price: Modest
Address: 2439 18th St NW
Washington, DC 20009
Phone: (202) 518-2626

#74
Rock & Roll Hotel
Category: Music Venues
Average Price: Modest
Address: 1353 H St NE
Washington, DC 20002
Phone: (202) 388-7625

#75
Open City
Category: Diner
Average Price: Modest
Address: 2331 Calvert St NW
Washington, DC 20008
Phone: (202) 332-2331

#76
Indulj
Category: American
Average Price: Modest
Address: 1208 U St NW
Washington, DC 20009
Phone: (202) 986-9400

#77
Tropicalia
Category: Dance Club
Average Price: Modest
Address: 2001 14th St NW
Washington, DC 20009
Phone: (202) 629-4535

#78
Chief Ike's Mambo Room
Category: Dive Bar
Average Price: Inexpensive
Address: 1725 Columbia Rd NW
Washington, DC 20009
Phone: (202) 332-2211

#79
Bar Pilar
Category: American
Average Price: Modest
Address: 1833 14th St NW
Washington, DC 20009
Phone: (202) 265-1751

#80
Beuchert's Saloon
Category: Bar
Average Price: Modest
Address: 623 Pennsylvania Ave SE
Washington, DC 20003
Phone: (202) 733-1384

#81
Bourbon
Category: Bar
Average Price: Modest
Address: 2321 18th St NW
Washington, DC 20009
Phone: (202) 332-0800

#82
Flash
Category: Dance Club
Average Price: Modest
Address: 645 Florida Ave NW
Washington, DC 20001
Phone: (202) 827-8791

#83
The Black Squirrel
Category: American
Average Price: Modest
Address: 2427 18th St NW
Washington, DC 20009
Phone: (202) 232-1011

#84
Kangaroo Boxing Club
Category: American
Average Price: Modest
Address: 3410 11th St NW
Washington, DC 20010
Phone: (202) 505-4522

#85
Old Ebbitt Grill
Category: Bar
Average Price: Modest
Address: 675 15th St NW
Washington, DC 20005
Phone: (202) 347-4800

#86
Civil Cigar Lounge
Category: Tobacco Shop
Average Price: Expensive
Address: 5335 Wisconsin Ave NW
Washington, DC 20015
Phone: (202) 364-0800

#87
SAX
Category: French
Average Price: Expensive
Address: 734 11th St NW
Washington, DC 20001
Phone: (202) 737-0101

#88
Café Citron
Category: Latin American
Average Price: Modest
Address: 1343 Connecticut Ave NW
Washington, DC 20036
Phone: (202) 530-8844

#89
Looking Glass Lounge
Category: Lounge
Average Price: Modest
Address: 3634 Georgia Ave NW
Washington, DC 20010
Phone: (202) 722-7669

#90
Nomad
Category: Hookah Bar
Average Price: Modest
Address: 1200 H St NE
Washington, DC 20002
Phone: (202) 326-6623

#91
Pound The Hill
Category: Coffee, Tea
Average Price: Modest
Address: 621 Pennsylvania Ave SE
Washington, DC 20003
Phone: (202) 621-6765

#92
The Hamilton
Category: Seafood
Average Price: Modest
Address: 600 14th St NW
Washington, DC 20005
Phone: (202) 787-1000

#93
Science Club
Category: Lounge
Average Price: Modest
Address: 1136 19th St NW
Washington, DC 20036
Phone: (202) 775-0747

#94
Smith Public Trust
Category: American
Average Price: Modest
Address: 3514 12th St NE
Washington, DC 20017
Phone: (202) 733-5834

#95
Bourbon
Category: American
Average Price: Modest
Address: 2348 Wisconsin Ave NW
Washington, DC 20007
Phone: (202) 625-7770

#96
Shelly's Back Room
Category: Lounge
Average Price: Modest
Address: 1331 F St NW
Washington, DC 20004
Phone: (202) 737-3003

#97
Green Lantern
Category: Gay Bar
Average Price: Inexpensive
Address: 1335 Green Ct NW
Washington, DC 20005
Phone: (202) 347-4533

#98
L2 Lounge
Category: Lounge
Average Price: Expensive
Address: 3315 Cady's Alley NW
Washington, DC 20007
Phone: (202) 965-2001

#99
A BAR + Kitchen
Category: Lounge
Average Price: Modest
Address: 2500 Pennsylvania Ave
Washington, DC 20037
Phone: (202) 464-5610

#100
The Park At Fourteenth
Category: American
Average Price: Modest
Address: 920 14th St NW
Washington, DC 20005
Phone: (202) 737-7275

#101
Habana Village
Category: Cuban
Average Price: Modest
Address: 1834 Columbia Rd NW
Washington, DC 20009
Phone: (202) 462-6310

#102
Smoke & Barrel
Category: Bar
Average Price: Modest
Address: 2471 18th St NW
Washington, DC 20009
Phone: (202) 319-9353

#103
Fado Irish Pub & Restaurant
Category: Pub
Average Price: Modest
Address: 808 7th St NW
Washington, DC 20001
Phone: (202) 789-0066

#104
Stan's Restaurant & Bar
Category: Lounge
Average Price: Modest
Address: 1029 Vermont Ave NW
Washington, DC 20005
Phone: (202) 347-4488

#105
District Nightclub
Category: Dance Club
Average Price: Modest
Address: 2473 18th St NW
Washington, DC 20009
Phone: (202) 518-9820

#106
Modern
Category: Lounge
Average Price: Modest
Address: 3287 M St NW
Washington, DC 20007
Phone: (202) 540-0635

#107
Ben's Next Door
Category: Bar
Average Price: Modest
Address: 1211 U St NW
Washington, DC 20009
Phone: (202) 667-8880

#108
Ivy & Coney
Category: Dive Bar
Average Price: Inexpensive
Address: 1537 7th St NW
Washington, DC 20001
Phone: (202) 670-9489

#109
Dickson Wine Bar
Category: Wine Bar
Average Price: Modest
Address: 903 U St NW
Washington, DC 20001
Phone: (202) 332-1779

#110
Cobalt
Category: Gay Bar
Average Price: Modest
Address: 1639 R St NW
Washington, DC 20009
Phone: (202) 232-4416

#111
Avery's Bar And Lounge
Category: Pub
Average Price: Inexpensive
Address: 1370 H St NE
Washington, DC 20002
Phone: (202) 525-2827

#112
St. Arnold's Mussel Bar
Category: Bar
Average Price: Modest
Address: 3433 Connecticut Ave NW
Washington, DC 20008
Phone: (202) 621-6719

#113
Town Hall
Category: American
Average Price: Modest
Address: 2340 Wisconsin Ave NW
Washington, DC 20007
Phone: (202) 333-5640

#114
The Big Hunt
Category: Pub
Average Price: Inexpensive
Address: 1345 Connecticut Ave NW
Washington, DC 20036
Phone: (202) 785-2333

#115
Kitty O'Shea's DC
Category: Pub
Average Price: Modest
Address: 4624 Wisconsin Ave NW
Washington, DC 20016
Phone: (202) 450-5077

#116
POV Roof Terrace And Lounge
Category: Lounge
Average Price: Expensive
Address: 515 15th St NW
Washington, DC 20004
Phone: (202) 661-2400

#117
Jake's Boiler Room
Category: American
Average Price: Modest
Address: 5018 Connecticut Ave NW
Washington, DC 20008
Phone: (202) 966-5253

#118
Biergarten Haus
Category: German
Average Price: Modest
Address: 1355 H St NE
Washington, DC 20002
Phone: (202) 388-4053

#119
Fox And Hounds Lounge
Category: Dive Bar
Average Price: Inexpensive
Address: 1537 17th St NW
Washington, DC 20036
Phone: (202) 232-6307

#120
The 201 Bar
Category: Bar
Average Price: Modest
Address: 201 Massachusetts Ave NE
Washington, DC 20002
Phone: (202) 544-5201

#121
Brookland's Finest
Category: American
Average Price: Modest
Address: 3128 12th St NE
Washington, DC 20017
Phone: (202) 636-0050

#122
Bardeo Wine Bar
Category: Wine Bar
Average Price: Modest
Address: 3309 Connecticut Ave NW
Washington, DC 20008
Phone: (202) 244-6550

#123
Sona Creamery
Category: Wine Bar
Average Price: Modest
Address: 660 Pennsylvania Ave SE
Washington, DC 20003
Phone: (202) 758-3556

#124
Den Of Thieves
Category: Dance Club
Average Price: Modest
Address: 2005 14th St NW
Washington, DC 20009
Phone: (202) 747-2377

#125
The Ugly Mug
Category: American
Average Price: Modest
Address: 723 8th St SE
Washington, DC 20003
Phone: (202) 547-8459

#126
Cork Wine Bar
Category: Wine Bar
Average Price: Modest
Address: 1720 14th St NW
Washington, DC 20009
Phone: (202) 265-2675

#127
Libertine
Category: Lounge
Average Price: Modest
Address: 2435 18th St
Washington, DC 20009
Phone: (202) 450-3106

#128
The Partisan
Category: American
Average Price: Expensive
Address: 709 D St NW
Washington, DC 20004
Phone: (202) 524-5322

#129
Clyde's Of Gallery Place
Category: American
Average Price: Modest
Address: 707 7th St NW
Washington, DC 20001
Phone: (202) 349-3700

#130
El Centro DF - Georgetown
Category: Bar
Average Price: Modest
Address: 1218 Wisconsin Ave NW
Washington, DC 20007
Phone: (202) 333-4100

#131
American Ice Company
Category: Barbeque
Average Price: Modest
Address: 917 V St NW
Washington, DC 20001
Phone: (202) 758-3562

#132
Madhatter
Category: Bar
Average Price: Modest
Address: 1321 Connecticut Ave NW
Washington, DC 20036
Phone: (202) 833-1495

#133
H Street Country Club
Category: Mexican
Average Price: Modest
Address: 1335 H Street NE
Washington, DC 20002
Phone: (202) 399-4722

#134
Thally
Category: American
Average Price: Expensive
Address: 1316 9th St NW
Washington, DC 20001
Phone: (202) 733-3849

#135
Nanny O'Brien's Irish Pub
Category: Pub
Average Price: Inexpensive
Address: 3319 Connecticut Ave NW
Washington, DC 20008
Phone: (202) 686-9189

#136
The Corner Store
Category: Art Gallery
Average Price: Inexpensive
Address: 900 S Carolina Ave SE
Washington, DC 20003
Phone: (202) 544-5807

#137
Local 16
Category: Lounge
Average Price: Modest
Address: 1602 U St NW
Washington, DC 20009
Phone: (202) 265-2828

#138
Veritas Wine Bar
Category: Wine Bar
Average Price: Modest
Address: 2031 Florida Ave NW
Washington, DC 20009
Phone: (202) 265-6270

#139
The 51st State Tavern
Category: Sports Bar
Average Price: Inexpensive
Address: 2512 L St NW
Washington, DC 20037
Phone: (202) 625-2444

#140
National Gallery Of Art - Friday Jazz In The Garden Series
Category: Jazz, Blues
Average Price: Inexpensive
Address: 700 Constitution Ave NW
Washington, DC 20004
Phone: (202) 289-3360

#141
Ghibellina
Category: Italian
Average Price: Expensive
Address: 1610 14th St NW
Washington, DC 20009
Phone: (202) 803-2389

#142
Jack Rose Dining Saloon
Category: Bar
Average Price: Modest
Address: 2007 18th St NW
Washington, DC 20009
Phone: (202) 588-7388

#143
Rocket Bar
Category: Pool Hall
Average Price: Modest
Address: 714 7th St NW
Washington, DC 20001
Phone: (202) 628-7665

#144
Irish Whiskey Public House
Category: Irish
Average Price: Modest
Address: 1207 19th St NW
Washington, DC 20036
Phone: (202) 463-3010

#145
Donovan House Rooftop
Category: Lounge
Average Price: Expensive
Address: 1155 14th St NW
Washington, DC 20005
Phone: (202) 737-1200

#146
Secret Pleasures Boutique
Category: Adult Entertainment
Average Price: Modest
Address: 1510 U St NW
Washington, DC 20009
Phone: (202) 664-1476

#147
Rappahannock Oyster Bar
Category: Seafood
Average Price: Modest
Address: 1309 5th St NE
Washington, DC 20002
Phone: (202) 544-4702

#148
Helix Lounge
Category: Lounge
Average Price: Modest
Address: 1430 Rhode Island Ave
Washington, DC 20005
Phone: (202) 462-9001

#149
Bossa
Category: Lounge
Average Price: Modest
Address: 2463 18th St NW
Washington, DC 20009
Phone: (202) 667-0088

#150
A Lounge
Category: Lounge
Average Price: Modest
Address: 1710 H St NW
Washington, DC 20006
Phone: (202) 904-2500

#151
Stoney's On L
Category: American
Average Price: Modest
Address: 2101 L St NW
Washington, DC 20037
Phone: (202) 721-0019

#152
Dirty Bar
Category: Dance Club
Average Price: Modest
Address: 1223 Connecticut Ave NW
Washington, DC 20036
Phone: (202) 503-2640

#153
**Tonic At Quigley's Bar
And Restaurant**
Category: American
Average Price: Modest
Address: 2036 G St NW
Washington, DC 20036
Phone: (202) 296-0211

#154
Acre 121
Category: Southern
Average Price: Modest
Address: 1400 Irving St NW
Washington, DC 20010
Phone: (202) 328-0121

#155
Penn Social
Category: Bar
Average Price: Modest
Address: 801 E St NW
Washington, DC 20004
Phone: (202) 697-4900

#156
Bar Dupont
Category: Bar
Average Price: Expensive
Address: 1500 New Hampshire Ave NW
Washington, DC 20036
Phone: (202) 797-0169

#157
Black Fox Lounge
Category: Lounge
Average Price: Modest
Address: 1723 Connecticut Ave NW
Washington, DC 20009
Phone: (202) 483-1723

#158
Bar 7
Category: Lounge
Average Price: Modest
Address: 1015 1/2 7th St NW
Washington, DC 20001
Phone: (202) 347-4343

#159
Black Whiskey
Category: Bar
Average Price: Modest
Address: 1410 14th St NW
Washington, DC 20005
Phone: (202) 800-8103

#160
Elephant & Castle
Category: British
Average Price: Modest
Address: 1201 Pennsylvania Ave NW
Washington, DC 20004
Phone: (202) 347-7707

#161
Beacon Rooftop Sky Bar
Category: Bar
Average Price: Modest
Address: 1615 Rhode Island Ave NW
Washington, DC 20036
Phone: (202) 872-1126

#162
Marx Cafe
Category: Bar
Average Price: Modest
Address: 3203 Mt Pleasant St NW
Washington, DC 20010
Phone: (202) 518-7600

#163
The Brixton
Category: Bar
Average Price: Modest
Address: 901 U St NW
Washington, DC 20001
Phone: (202) 560-5045

#164
Zoo Bar Cafe
Category: Restaurant
Average Price: Modest
Address: 3000 Connecticut Ave NW
Washington, DC 20008
Phone: (202) 232-4225

#165
Stadium Club
Category: Adult Entertainment
Average Price: Expensive
Address: 2127 Queens Chapel Rd NE
Washington, DC 20018
Phone: (202) 509-2348

#166
Redline
Category: American
Average Price: Modest
Address: 707 G St NW
Washington, DC 20001
Phone: (202) 347-8683

#167
Chi-Cha Lounge
Category: Latin American
Average Price: Modest
Address: 1624 U St NW
Washington, DC 20009
Phone: (202) 234-8400

#168
Beau Thai - Mount Pleasant
Category: Thai
Average Price: Modest
Address: 3162 Mt Pleasant St
Washington, DC 20010
Phone: (202) 450-5317

#169
GBD
Category: Bar
Average Price: Modest
Address: 1323 Connecticut Ave NW
Washington, DC 20036
Phone: (202) 524-5210

#170
Logan Tavern
Category: Bar
Average Price: Modest
Address: 1423 P St NW
Washington, DC 20005
Phone: (202) 332-3710

#171
St. Arnold's On Jefferson
Category: Belgian
Average Price: Modest
Address: 1827 Jefferson Pl NW
Washington, DC 20036
Phone: (202) 833-1321

#172
Station 4
Category: American
Average Price: Modest
Address: 1101 4th St SW
Washington, DC 20024
Phone: (202) 488-0987

#173
Larry's Lounge
Category: Lounge
Average Price: Modest
Address: 1840 18th St NW
Washington, DC 20009
Phone: (202) 483-1483

#174
Satellite Room
Category: Bar
Average Price: Modest
Address: 2047 9th St NW
Washington, DC 20001
Phone: (202) 506-2496

#175
The Elroy
Category: Lounge
Average Price: Modest
Address: 1423 H St NE
Washington, DC 20002
Phone: (202) 735-5300

#176
Rhino Bar & Pumphouse
Category: Bar
Average Price: Modest
Address: 3295 M St NW
Washington, DC 20007
Phone: (202) 333-3150

#177
Acacia Bistro & Wine Bar
Category: Wine Bar
Average Price: Modest
Address: 4340 Connecticut Ave NW
Washington, DC 20008
Phone: (202) 537-1040

#178
Vegas Lounge
Category: Jazz, Blues
Average Price: Modest
Address: 1415 P St NW
Washington, DC 20005
Phone: (202) 483-3971

#179
Eden DC
Category: Dance Club
Average Price: Modest
Address: 1716 I St NW
Washington, DC 20007
Phone: (202) 905-9300

#180
Empress Lounge
Category: Jazz, Blues
Average Price: Modest
Address: 1330 Maryland Ave Sw
Washington, DC 20024
Phone: (202) 787-6042

#181
Tunnicliff's Tavern
Category: American
Average Price: Modest
Address: 222 7th St SE
Washington, DC 20003
Phone: (202) 544-5680

#182
The Blaguard
Category: Sports Bar
Average Price: Modest
Address: 2003 18th St NW
Washington, DC 20009
Phone: (202) 232-9005

#183
The Rooftop Bar And Lounge
Category: Lounge
Average Price: Expensive
Address: 1075 Thomas Jefferson St NW
Washington, DC 20007
Phone: (202) 337-0900

#184
Ziegfeld's/Secrets
Category: Gay Bar
Average Price: Modest
Address: 1824 Half St SW
Washington, DC 20024
Phone: (202) 863-0670

#185
Merlot's Masterpiece
Category: Art Classes
Average Price: Expensive
Address: 1512 U St NW
Washington, DC 20009
Phone: (202) 387-4278

#186
Po Boy Jim
Category: Cajun/Creole
Average Price: Modest
Address: 709 H St NE
Washington, DC 20002
Phone: (202) 621-7071

#187
MOVA Lounge DC
Category: Lounge
Average Price: Modest
Address: 2204 14th St NW
Washington, DC 20009
Phone: (202) 629-3859

#188
Penthouse Pool Club
Category: Swimming Pool
Average Price: Exclusive
Address: 1612 U St NW
Washington, DC 20009
Phone: (202) 939-2563

#189
Dirty Martini
Category: American
Average Price: Modest
Address: 1223 Connecticut Ave NW
Washington, DC 20036
Phone: (202) 503-2640

#190
Old Glory
Category: Barbeque
Average Price: Modest
Address: 3139 M St NW
Washington, DC 20007
Phone: (202) 337-3406

#191
Josephine
Category: Dance Club
Average Price: Expensive
Address: 1008 Vermont Ave NW
Washington, DC 20005
Phone: (202) 347-8601

#192
Good Guys Club
Category: Adult Entertainment
Average Price: Expensive
Address: 2311 Wisconsin Ave NW
Washington, DC 20007
Phone: (202) 333-0128

#193
Carriage House
Category: American
Average Price: Modest
Address: 2333 18th St NW
Washington, DC 20009
Phone: (202) 817-3255

#194
The Big Board
Category: Burgers
Average Price: Modest
Address: 421 H St NE
Washington, DC 20002
Phone: (202) 543-3630

#195
The Tombs
Category: Pub
Average Price: Modest
Address: 1226 36th St NW
Washington, DC 20007
Phone: (202) 337-6668

#196
Duke's Grocery
Category: Bar
Average Price: Modest
Address: 1513 17th St NW
Washington, DC 20036
Phone: (202) 733-5623

#197
Lucky Bar
Category: Pub
Average Price: Modest
Address: 1221 Connecticut Ave NW
Washington, DC 20036
Phone: (202) 331-3733

#198
Chez Billy
Category: Restaurant
Average Price: Expensive
Address: 3815 Georgia Ave NW
Washington, DC 20011
Phone: (202) 506-2080

#199
Cosmos Club
Category: Bar
Average Price: Expensive
Address: 2121 Massachusetts Ave NW
Washington, DC 20008
Phone: (202) 387-7783

#200
Dram & Grain
Category: Cocktail Bar
Average Price: Expensive
Address: 2007 18th St NW
Washington, DC 20009
Phone: (202) 607-1572

#201
The Bier Baron Tavern
Category: Pub
Average Price: Modest
Address: 1523 22nd St NW
Washington, DC 20037
Phone: (202) 293-1887

#202
Vetro
Category: Dance Club
Average Price: Exclusive
Address: 1401 K St NW
Washington, DC 20005
Phone: (202) 789-2800

#203
Union Pub
Category: Pub
Average Price: Modest
Address: 201 Massachusetts Ave NE
Washington, DC 20002
Phone: (202) 546-7200

#204
Menu- Market, Bistrobar, Kitchen
Category: Restaurant
Average Price: Expensive
Address: 405 8th St NW
Washington, DC 20004
Phone: (202) 347-7491

#205
Muzette Karaoke & Restaurant
Category: Karaoke
Average Price: Modest
Address: 2305 18th St NW
Washington, DC 20009
Phone: (202) 758-2971

#206
Pure Lounge
Category: Lounge
Average Price: Inexpensive
Address: 1326 U St NW
Washington, DC 20009
Phone: (202) 290-7058

#207
Uniontown Bar And Grill
Category: American
Average Price: Modest
Address: 2200 Martin Luther King Jr Ave SE
Washington, DC 20020
Phone: (202) 450-2536

#208
Park Tavern
Category: Bar
Average Price: Modest
Address: 202 M St SE
Washington, DC 20003
Phone: (202) 554-0005

#209
Lou's City Bar
Category: Sports Bar
Average Price: Modest
Address: 1400 Irving St NW
Washington, DC 20010
Phone: (202) 518-5687

#210
Wok And Roll
Category: Karaoke
Average Price: Modest
Address: 604 H St NW
Washington, DC 20001
Phone: (202) 347-4656

#211
Petworth Citizen
Category: Bar
Average Price: Modest
Address: 829 Upshur St NW
Washington, DC 20011
Phone: (202) 722-2939

#212
Mission
Category: Mexican
Average Price: Modest
Address: 1606 20th St
Washington, DC 20009
Phone: (202) 525-2010

#213
Recessions
Category: Dive Bar
Average Price: Inexpensive
Address: 1823 L St NW
Washington, DC 20036
Phone: (202) 296-6686

#214
Dahlak Restaurant
Category: Ethiopian
Average Price: Modest
Address: 1771 U St NW
Washington, DC 20009
Phone: (202) 332-2110

#215
Ibiza Night Club
Category: Dance Club
Average Price: Expensive
Address: 1222 1st St NE
Washington, DC 20002
Phone: (888) 424-9232

#216
The Gryphon
Category: Seafood
Average Price: Modest
Address: 1337 Connecticut Ave NW
Washington, DC 20036
Phone: (202) 827-8980

#217
Red Light
Category: Cocktail Bar
Average Price: Modest
Address: 1401 R St NW
Washington, DC 20009
Phone: (202) 234-0400

#218
Duffy's Irish Restaurant & Pub
Category: Pub
Average Price: Modest
Address: 2106 Vermont Ave NW
Washington, DC 20001
Phone: (202) 265-3413

#219
Town Danceboutique
Category: Dance Club
Average Price: Modest
Address: 2009 8th St Nw
Washington, DC 20001
Phone: (202) 234-8696

#220
Club Heaven & Hell
Category: Bar
Average Price: Modest
Address: 2327 18th St NW
Washington, DC 20009
Phone: (202) 667-4355

#221
Molly Malone's
Category: Irish
Average Price: Modest
Address: 713 8th St SE
Washington, DC 20003
Phone: (202) 547-1222

#222
Froggy Bottom Pub
Category: Vietnamese
Average Price: Modest
Address: 2021 K St NW
Washington, DC 20554
Phone: (202) 338-3000

#223
El Centro DF - 14th St
Category: Mexican
Average Price: Modest
Address: 1819 14th St NW
Washington, DC 20009
Phone: (202) 328-3131

#224
1331 Bar & Lounge
Category: American
Average Price: Modest
Address: 1331 Pennsylvania Ave NW
Washington, DC 20004
Phone: (202) 393-2000

#225
The Dubliner
Category: Pub
Average Price: Modest
Address: 520 N Capitol St NW
Washington, DC 20001
Phone: (202) 737-3773

#226
Harry's Restaurant
Category: Dive Bar
Average Price: Modest
Address: 436 11th St NW
Washington, DC 20004
Phone: (202) 624-0053

#227
14 K Restaurant & Lounge
Category: American
Average Price: Modest
Address: 1001 14th St NW
Washington, DC 20005
Phone: (202) 218-7575

#228
Boveda
Category: Lounge
Average Price: Modest
Address: 2350 M St NW
Washington, DC 20037
Phone: (202) 448-1000

#229
Justin's Cafe
Category: American
Average Price: Modest
Address: 1025 1st St SE
Washington, DC 20003
Phone: (202) 652-1009

#230
Rural Society
Category: Argentine
Average Price: Expensive
Address: 1177 15th St NW
Washington, DC 20005
Phone: (202) 587-2629

#231
Crew Club
Category: Adult Entertainment
Average Price: Exclusive
Address: 1321 14th St NW
Washington, DC 20005
Phone: (202) 319-1333

#232
Murphy's Of DC
Category: Pub
Average Price: Modest
Address: 2609 24th St NW
Washington, DC 20008
Phone: (202) 462-7171

#233
Clyde's Of Georgetown
Category: American
Average Price: Modest
Address: 3236 M St NW
Washington, DC 20007
Phone: (202) 333-9180

#234
The Pursuit Wine Bar
Category: Wine Bar
Average Price: Modest
Address: 1421 H St Ne
Washington, DC 20002
Phone: (202) 758-2139

#235
Maple
Category: Wine Bar
Average Price: Modest
Address: 3418 11th St NW
Washington, DC 20010
Phone: (202) 588-7442

#236
Simple Bar & Grill
Category: Bar
Average Price: Modest
Address: 5828 Georgia Ave NW
Washington, DC 20011
Phone: (202) 316-9171

#237
Bandolero
Category: Mexican
Average Price: Expensive
Address: 3241 M St NW
Washington, DC 20007
Phone: (202) 625-4488

#238
Public Bar
Category: Sports Bar
Average Price: Modest
Address: 1214 18th St NW
Washington, DC 20036
Phone: (202) 223-2200

#239
Vinoteca
Category: Wine Bar
Average Price: Modest
Address: 1940 11th St NW
Washington, DC 20001
Phone: (202) 332-9463

#240
Crackle Bar
Category: Bar
Average Price: Inexpensive
Address: 3245 M St NW
Washington, DC 20007
Phone: (202) 337-8269

#241
Bidwell
Category: Bar
Average Price: Modest
Address: 1309 5th St NE
Washington, DC 20002
Phone: (202) 547-0172

#242
Vitaminwater Uncapped Live
Category: Art Gallery
Average Price: Modest
Address: 2217 14th St NW
Washington, DC 20009
Phone: (707) 726-2246

#243
Love Night Club
Category: Dance Club
Average Price: Expensive
Address: 1350 Okie St NE
Washington, DC 20002
Phone: (202) 636-9030

#244
Carter Barron Amphitheatre
Category: Music Venues
Average Price: Inexpensive
Address: 4850 Colorado Ave, N.W.
Washington, DC 20011
Phone: (202) 426-0486

#245
Ultrabar
Category: Bar
Average Price: Modest
Address: 911 F St NW
Washington, DC 20004
Phone: (202) 638-4663

#246
The House
Category: Adult Entertainment
Average Price: Expensive
Address: 3530 Georgia Ave NW
Washington, DC 20010
Phone: (202) 882-2014

#247
Takoma Station Tavern
Category: Music Venues
Average Price: Modest
Address: 6914 4th St NW
Washington, DC 20012
Phone: (202) 829-1999

#248
Twins Jazz
Category: Jazz, Blues
Average Price: Modest
Address: 1344 U St NW
Washington, DC 20009
Phone: (202) 234-0072

#249
Mason Inn
Category: Southern
Average Price: Inexpensive
Address: 2408 Wisconsin Ave NW
Washington, DC 20007
Phone: (202) 337-1313

#250
Post Pub
Category: Pub
Average Price: Modest
Address: 1422 L St NW
Washington, DC 20005
Phone: (202) 628-2111

#251
Ping Pong Dim Sum
Category: Dim Sum
Average Price: Modest
Address: 1 Dupont Circle
Washington, DC 20036
Phone: (202) 293-1268

#252
Lillies Restaurant & Bar
Category: Mediterranean
Average Price: Modest
Address: 2915 Connecticut Ave NW
Washington, DC 20008
Phone: (202) 450-4824

#253
Old Dominion Brewhouse
Category: Pub
Average Price: Modest
Address: 1219 9th St NW
Washington, DC 20001
Phone: (202) 289-8158

#254
Catch 15
Category: Tapas
Average Price: Modest
Address: 1518 K St N W
Washington, DC 20005
Phone: (202) 969-2858

#255
Bar Louie DC
Category: Bar
Average Price: Modest
Address: 701 7th St NW
Washington, DC 20001
Phone: (202) 638-2460

#256
Public Bar Tenley
Category: Sports Bar
Average Price: Modest
Address: 4611 41st St NW
Washington, DC 20016
Phone: (202) 237-1783

#257
Capitol Lounge
Category: Bar
Average Price: Modest
Address: 229 Pennsylvania Ave SE
Washington, DC 20003
Phone: (202) 547-2098

#258
M Bar
Category: Bar
Average Price: Modest
Address: 1143 New Hampshire Ave NW
Washington, DC 20037
Phone: (202) 775-0800

#259
Marvin
Category: Lounge
Average Price: Modest
Address: 2007 14th St NW
Washington, DC 20009
Phone: (202) 797-7171

#260
Grand Slam Sports Bar
Category: Sports Bar
Average Price: Modest
Address: 1000 H St NW
Washington, DC 20001
Phone: (202) 637-4789

#261
Jin
Category: Lounge
Average Price: Modest
Address: 2017 14th St NW
Washington, DC 20050
Phone: (202) 332-2104

#262
The Bar At The Ritz-Carlton
Category: Lounge
Average Price: Modest
Address: 1150 22nd St NW
Washington, DC 20037
Phone: (202) 835-0500

#263
Mirrors
Category: Restaurant
Average Price: Inexpensive
Address: 33 New York Avenue NE
Washington, DC 20002
Phone: (202) 326-0774

#264
Smith Point
Category: Lounge
Average Price: Modest
Address: 1338 Wisconsin Ave NW
Washington, DC 20007
Phone: (202) 333-9003

#265
F Street Bistro
Category: American
Average Price: Modest
Address: 2116 F St NW
Washington, DC 20037
Phone: (202) 328-9355

#266
Chaplin's
Category: Cocktail Bar
Average Price: Modest
Address: 1501 9th St NW
Washington, DC 20001
Phone: (202) 644-8806

#267
Shenanigans Irish Pub
Category: Pub
Average Price: Inexpensive
Address: 2450 18th St NW
Washington, DC 20009
Phone: (202) 588-7405

#268
Liv
Category: Dance Club
Average Price: Modest
Address: 2001 11th St NW
Washington, DC 20009
Phone: (202) 299-0800

#269
President's Sports Bar
Category: Bar
Average Price: Modest
Address: 999 9th St NW
Washington, DC 20001
Phone: (202) 898-9000

#270
Red Lounge
Category: Lounge
Average Price: Modest
Address: 2013 14th St NW
Washington, DC 20009
Phone: (202) 232-5788

#271
Uptown Tap House
Category: Bar
Average Price: Modest
Address: 3412 Connecticut Ave
Washington, DC 20008
Phone: (202) 244-2030

#272
Phase One
Category: Gay Bar
Average Price: Inexpensive
Address: 525 8th St SE
Washington, DC 20003
Phone: (202) 544-6831

#273
Bound
Category: Dance Club
Average Price: Modest
Address: 411 New York Ave NE
Washington, DC 20002
Phone: (703) 303-9470

#274
The Town Tavern
Category: Bar
Average Price: Inexpensive
Address: 2323 18th St NW
Washington, DC 20009
Phone: (202) 387-8696

#275
Steel Plate
Category: Cocktail Bar
Average Price: Modest
Address: 3523 12th St NE
Washington, DC 20017
Phone: (202) 290-2310

#276
Rebellion
Category: Bar
Average Price: Modest
Address: 1836 18th St NW
Washington, DC 20009
Phone: (202) 299-0399

#277
Hawk N' Dove
Category: Bar
Average Price: Modest
Address: 329 Pennsylvania Ave SE
Washington, DC 20003
Phone: (202) 547-0030

#278
Rendezvous Lounge
Category: Lounge
Average Price: Inexpensive
Address: 2226 18th St NW
Washington, DC 20009
Phone: (202) 462-1238

#279
Jake's American Grille
Category: American
Average Price: Modest
Address: 5018 Connecticut Ave NW
Washington, DC 20008
Phone: (202) 966-5253

#280
The Meeting Place
Category: American
Average Price: Inexpensive
Address: 1707 L St NW
Washington, DC 20005
Phone: (202) 293-7755

#281
Roxanne
Category: Restaurant
Average Price: Modest
Address: 2319 18th St NW
Washington, DC 20009
Phone: (202) 518-7575

#282
M.I.A. Lounge
Category: Lounge
Average Price: Expensive
Address: 1214 18th St NW
Washington, DC 20036
Phone: (202) 785-9525

#283
Cleveland Park Bar And Grill
Category: Sports Bar
Average Price: Modest
Address: 3421 Connecticut Ave NW
Washington, DC 20008
Phone: (202) 806-8940

#284
Poste
Category: French
Average Price: Expensive
Address: 555 8th St NW
Washington, DC 20002
Phone: (202) 783-6060

#285
Angles Bar & Billiards
Category: Pool Hall
Average Price: Modest
Address: 2339 18th St NW
Washington, DC 20009
Phone: (202) 462-8100

#286
Rose's Dream
Category: Lounge
Average Price: Modest
Address: 1370 H St NE
Washington, DC 20002
Phone: (202) 398-5700

#287
Pier 7 Restaurant
Category: Seafood
Average Price: Modest
Address: 650 Water St SW
Washington, DC 20024
Phone: (202) 554-2500

#288
Archibald's
Category: Adult Entertainment
Average Price: Expensive
Address: 1520 K St NW
Washington, DC 20005
Phone: (202) 638-5112

#289
Mcfadden's Restaurant And Saloon
Category: Restaurant
Average Price: Modest
Address: 2401 Pennsylvania Ave NW
Washington, DC 20037
Phone: (202) 223-2338

#290
Kiss Lounge
Category: Lounge
Average Price: Modest
Address: 1608 7th St NW
Washington, DC 20001
Phone: (202) 460-6124

#291
The Queen Vic
Category: Pub
Average Price: Modest
Address: 1206 H St NE
Washington, DC 20002
Phone: (202) 396-2001

#292
9:30 Club Backbar
Category: Dive Bar
Average Price: Inexpensive
Address: 815 V St NW
Washington, DC 20001
Phone: (202) 265-0930

#293
Shadowroom
Category: Dance Club
Average Price: Expensive
Address: 2131 K St NW
Washington, DC 20050
Phone: (202) 887-1200

#294
District Underground
Category: Bar
Average Price: Modest
Address: 2477 18th St NW Adams Morgan
Washington, DC 20009
Phone: (202) 518-9820

#295
Twelve Restaurant & Lounge
Category: American
Average Price: Modest
Address: 1123 H St NE
Washington, DC 20002
Phone: (202) 398-2655

#296
Sonoma Restaurant & Wine Bar
Category: American
Average Price: Expensive
Address: 223 Pennsylvania Ave SE
Washington, DC 20003
Phone: (202) 544-8088

#297
Fast Eddie's Billiard Cafe
Category: Pool Hall
Average Price: Modest
Address: 1520 K St NW
Washington, DC 20005
Phone: (202) 638-6800

#298
Solly's Tavern
Category: Music Venues
Average Price: Inexpensive
Address: 1942 11th St NW
Washington, DC 20001
Phone: (202) 232-6590

#299
The FAB Lounge
Category: Dance Club
Average Price: Inexpensive
Address: 1805 Connecticut Ave NW
Washington, DC 20009
Phone: (202) 797-1122

#300
Muse Lounge
Category: Dance Club
Average Price: Expensive
Address: 717 6th St NW
Washington, DC 20001
Phone: (202) 842-9800

#301
The Players Lounge
Category: Restaurant
Average Price: Modest
Address: 2737 Martin Luther King Jr Ave SE
Washington, DC 20032
Phone: (202) 574-1331

#302
Lyman's Tavern
Category: Bar
Average Price: Inexpensive
Address: 3720 14th St NW
Washington, DC 20005
Phone: (202) 723-0502

#303
Bar Charley
Category: Bar
Average Price: Modest
Address: 1825 18th St NW
Washington, DC 20009
Phone: (202) 627-2183

#304
Capitale
Category: Bar
Average Price: Modest
Address: 1301 K St NW
Washington, DC 20533
Phone: (202) 962-3933

#305
Duplex Diner
Category: Bar
Average Price: Modest
Address: 2004 18th St NW
Washington, DC 20009
Phone: (202) 265-7828

#306
Mixx
Category: Bar
Average Price: Modest
Address: 999 9th St NW
Washington, DC 20001
Phone: (202) 898-9000

#307
ENO
Category: Wine Bar
Average Price: Modest
Address: 2810 Pennsylvania Ave NW
Washington, DC 20007
Phone: (202) 295-2826

#308
Sweet Spot
Category: Dance Club
Average Price: Modest
Address: 1140 19th St NW
Washington, DC 20036
Phone: (202) 775-0668

#309
Billy Goat Tavern
Category: Bar
Average Price: Inexpensive
Address: 500 New Jersey Ave NW
Washington, DC 20001
Phone: (202) 783-2123

#310
Dunya Restaurant And Bar
Category: Mediterranean
Average Price: Modest
Address: 801 Florida Ave NW
Washington, DC 20001
Phone: (202) 332-0207

#311
L'Enfant Cafe & Bar
Category: Bar
Average Price: Modest
Address: 2000 18th St NW
Washington, DC 20009
Phone: (202) 319-1800

#312
Zeke Sport Cafe
Category: Hookah Bar
Average Price: Modest
Address: 7711 Georgia Ave NW
Washington, DC 20012
Phone: (202) 541-9499

#313
Tel'Veh Cafe & Wine Bar
Category: Wine Bar
Average Price: Modest
Address: 401 Massachusetts Ave NW
Washington, DC 20001
Phone: (202) 758-2929

#314
Cafe Saint-Ex
Category: Pub
Average Price: Modest
Address: 1847 14th St NW
Washington, DC 20009
Phone: (202) 265-7839

#315
Grand Central
Category: Bar
Average Price: Modest
Address: 2447 18th St NW
Washington, DC 20009
Phone: (202) 986-1742

#316
Sweet Mango Cafe
Category: Caribbean
Average Price: Modest
Address: 3701 New Hampshire Ave NW
Washington, DC 20010
Phone: (202) 726-2646

#317
The Cantina @ Darlington House
Category: Pub
Average Price: Modest
Address: 1610 20th St NW
Washington, DC 20009
Phone: (202) 332-3722

#318
Columbia Station
Category: Jazz, Blues
Average Price: Modest
Address: 2325 18th St NW
Washington, DC 20009
Phone: (202) 462-6040

#319
The Fireplace
Category: Gay Bar
Average Price: Inexpensive
Address: 2161 P St NW
Washington, DC 20037
Phone: (202) 293-1293

#320
Park View Patio
Category: Bar
Average Price: Modest
Address: 3632 Georgia Ave
Washington, DC 20010
Phone: (202) 291-2182

#321
Optimism Bar & Lounge
Category: American
Average Price: Inexpensive
Address: 3301 12th St NE
Washington, DC 20017
Phone: (202) 526-0100

#322
Expo DC Bar And Lounge
Category: Ethiopian
Average Price: Inexpensive
Address: 1928 9th St NW
Washington, DC 20001
Phone: (202) 681-1277

#323
Camelot Show Bar
Category: Adult Entertainment
Average Price: Modest
Address: 1823 M St NW
Washington, DC 20036
Phone: (202) 887-5966

#324
Buffalo Billiards
Category: Pool Hall
Average Price: Modest
Address: 1330 19th St NW
Washington, DC 20036
Phone: (202) 331-7665

#325
The Sheppard
Category: Bar
Average Price: Expensive
Address: 1337 Connecticut Ave NW
Washington, DC 20036
Phone: (202) 744-4253

#326
The Lodge At Redrocks
Category: Music Venues
Average Price: Modest
Address: 1348 H St NE
Washington, DC 20002
Phone: (202) 621-7300

#327
Acuario
Category: Bar
Average Price: Inexpensive
Address: 3410 11th St NW
Washington, DC 20010
Phone: (202) 328-1425

#328
The Embassy Row Hotel
Category: Hotel
Average Price: Modest
Address: 2015 Massachusetts Ave NW
Washington, DC 20036
Phone: (202) 265-1600

#329
The St Regis Bar
Category: Lounge
Average Price: Modest
Address: 923 16th St NW
Washington, DC 20006
Phone: (202) 879-6900

#330
Spot Lounge DC
Category: Lounge
Average Price: Modest
Address: 1214 18th St NW
Washington, DC 20036
Phone: (202) 785-2922

#331
Bravo Bravo
Category: Bar
Average Price: Inexpensive
Address: 1001 Connecticut Ave NW
Washington, DC 20036
Phone: (202) 223-5330

#332
Opera Ultra Lounge
Category: Dance Club
Average Price: Expensive
Address: 1400 I St NW
Washington, DC 20005
Phone: (202) 289-1400

#333
Lux Lounge
Category: Lounge
Average Price: Expensive
Address: 649 New York Ave
Washington, DC 20005
Phone: (202) 347-8100

#334
Top Of The Hill
Category: Bar
Average Price: Modest
Address: 319 Pennsylvania Ave SE
Washington, DC 20050
Phone: (202) 546-7782

#335
Leeloo Lounge & Restaurant
Category: Nightlife
Average Price: Modest
Address: 521 G St NW
Washington, DC 20001
Phone: (202) 289-1600

#336
Tree House Lounge
Category: Lounge
Average Price: Modest
Address: 1006 Florida Ave NE
Washington, DC 20002
Phone: (202) 398-7700

#337
Epicurean And Company
Category: Deli
Average Price: Modest
Address: 3800 Reservoir Rd NW
Washington, DC 20057
Phone: (202) 625-2222

#338
STIR Lounge
Category: Dance Club
Average Price: Expensive
Address: 705 G St NW
Washington, DC 20001
Phone: (202) 333-2538

#339
Kelly's Irish Times
Category: Dive Bar
Average Price: Modest
Address: 14 F St NW
Washington, DC 20001
Phone: (202) 543-5433

#340
Federal Restaurant & Lounge
Category: Southern
Average Price: Modest
Address: 2477 18th St NW
Washington, DC 20009
Phone: (202) 506-4314

#341
Blackfinn
Category: Sports Bar
Average Price: Modest
Address: 1620 I St NW
Washington, DC 20006
Phone: (202) 429-4350

#342
Article One Lounge
Category: Lounge
Average Price: Modest
Address: 400 New Jersey Ave NW
Washington, DC 20001
Phone: (202) 719-8478

#343
Bobby Lew's Saloon
Category: Bar
Average Price: Modest
Address: 2006 18th St NW
Washington, DC 20009
Phone: (202) 234-5397

#344
Brookland Pint
Category: Bar
Average Price: Modest
Address: 716 Monroe St NE
Washington, DC 20017
Phone: (202) 758-2757

#345
Pasha Lounge
Category: Dance Club
Average Price: Modest
Address: 2147 P St NW
Washington, DC 20037
Phone: (202) 775-1883

#346
Mellow Mushroom
Category: Pizza
Average Price: Modest
Address: 2436 18th St NW
Washington, DC 20009
Phone: (202) 290-2778

#347
Brass Monkey
Category: Bar
Average Price: Modest
Address: 2317 18th St NW
Washington, DC 20009
Phone: (202) 667-7800

#348
Expo Lounge
Category: Lounge
Average Price: Modest
Address: 1928 9th St
Washington, DC 20001
Phone: (323) 639-0513

#349
Prince Café
Category: Middle Eastern
Average Price: Modest
Address: 2400 18th St NW
Washington, DC 20009
Phone: (202) 667-1400

#350
Phase 1 Dupont
Category: Dance Club
Average Price: Modest
Address: 1415 22nd St NW
Washington, DC 20037
Phone: (202) 974-6832

#351
Hank's Oyster Bar
Category: Seafood
Average Price: Modest
Address: 633 Pennsylvania Ave SE
Washington, DC 20003
Phone: (202) 733-1971

#352
Lotus Lounge
Category: Dance Club
Average Price: Expensive
Address: 1420 K St NW
Washington, DC 20005
Phone: (202) 289-4222

#353
Flava At Wa-Zo-Bia
Category: Caribbean
Average Price: Modest
Address: 618 T St NW
Washington, DC 20001
Phone: (202) 232-2225

#354
Bachelors Mill
Category: Gay Bar
Average Price: Inexpensive
Address: 1104 8th St SE
Washington, DC 20003
Phone: (202) 546-5979

#355
Prince Cafe
Category: Middle Eastern
Average Price: Modest
Address: 1042 Wisconsin Ave NW
Washington, DC 20007
Phone: (202) 625-6400

#356
Da Luft Restaurant & Lounge
Category: Lounge
Average Price: Modest
Address: 1242 H St Ne
Washington, DC 20002
Phone: (202) 388-1200

#357
Midtown
Category: Dance Club
Average Price: Modest
Address: 1219 Connecticut Ave
Washington, DC 20036
Phone: (202) 466-7529

#358
**Prince Cafe Restaurant
And Lounge**
Category: Hookah Bar
Average Price: Inexpensive
Address: 3205 Prospect St NW
Washington, DC 20007
Phone: (202) 625-6400

#359
Lounge Of Three
Category: Lounge
Average Price: Modest
Address: 1013 U St NW
Washington, DC 20001
Phone: (202) 387-3333

#360
Maraki Restaurant & Lounge
Category: American
Average Price: Modest
Address: 1930 9th St NW
Washington, DC 20001
Phone: (202) 518-1161

#361
Handsome Cock
Category: Dive Bar
Average Price: Inexpensive
Address: 1334 U St NW
Washington, DC 20001
Phone: (202) 265-0708

#362
Charlies Bar & Grill
Category: Dive Bar
Average Price: Inexpensive
Address: 7307 Georgia Ave NW
Washington, DC 20012
Phone: (202) 726-3567

#363
Ultimo Lounge
Category: Lounge
Average Price: Modest
Address: 1633 17th St NW
Washington, DC 20009
Phone: (202) 232-0437

#364
Rosebar Current Lounge
Category: Japanese
Average Price: Expensive
Address: 1215 Connecticut Ave NW
Washington, DC 20036
Phone: (202) 955-5525

#365
Oxygen The Venue
Category: Dance Club
Average Price: Modest
Address: 2122 24th Pl NE
Washington, DC 20018
Phone: (202) 621-6957

#366
Bayou
Category: Music Venues
Average Price: Modest
Address: 2519 Pennsylvania Ave NW
Washington, DC 20037
Phone: (202) 223-6941

#367
Flight Wine Bar
Category: Wine Bar
Average Price: Modest
Address: 777 6th St NW
Washington, DC 20001
Phone: (202) 864-6445

#368
Dr. Clock's Nowhere Bar
Category: Dive Bar
Average Price: Inexpensive
Address: 2226 18th St NW
Washington, DC 20009
Phone: (202) 487-4615

#369
PH9
Category: Tapas
Average Price: Expensive
Address: 1318 9th St NW
Washington, DC 20001
Phone: (202) 629-8443

#370
Aqua Resturant & Bar
Category: Dance Club
Average Price: Modest
Address: 1818 New York Ave NE
Washington, DC 20002
Phone: (202) 832-4878

#371
The Macombo Lounge
Category: Adult Entertainment
Average Price: Modest
Address: 5335 Georgia Ave NW
Washington, DC 20011
Phone: (202) 726-2880

#372
Chuck & Billy's Bar & Carryout
Category: Restaurant
Average Price: Modest
Address: 2718 Georgia Ave NW
Washington, DC 20001
Phone: (202) 234-5870

#373
Royal Palace
Category: Adult Entertainment
Average Price: Expensive
Address: 1805 Connecticut Ave NW
Washington, DC 20009
Phone: (202) 462-2623

#374
Etto
Category: Bar
Average Price: Modest
Address: 1541 14th St NW
Washington, DC 20005
Phone: (202) 232-0920

#375
Midtown Loft
Category: Lounge
Average Price: Expensive
Address: 1219 Connecticut Ave NW
Washington, DC 20036
Phone: (202) 466-7529

#376
High Velocity
Category: Sports Bar
Average Price: Modest
Address: 901 Massachusetts Ave NW
Washington, DC 20001
Phone: (202) 824-9200

#377
Fuego Salvaje
Category: Gay Bar
Average Price: Modest
Address: 1720 I St NW
Washington, DC 20006
Phone: (202) 486-6117

#378
Charlie Palmer Steak
Category: Steakhouse
Average Price: Exclusive
Address: 101 Constitution Avenue Northwest
Washington, DC 20001
Phone: (202) 547-8100

#379
Delta Elite Social Club
Category: Adult Entertainment
Average Price: Expensive
Address: 3734 10th St NE
Washington, DC 20017
Phone: (202) 529-0626

#380
Safari DC
Category: American
Average Price: Modest
Address: 4306 Georgia Ave NW
Washington, DC 20011
Phone: (202) 722-7300

#381
Adams Morgan Spaghetti Garden
Category: Dive Bar
Average Price: Modest
Address: 2317 18th St NW
Washington, DC 20009
Phone: (202) 232-2929

#382
Lima Restaurant & Lounge
Category: Latin American
Average Price: Expensive
Address: 1401 K St NW
Washington, DC 20005
Phone: (202) 789-2800

#383
Azela Cafe
Category: Coffee, Tea
Average Price: Inexpensive
Address: 2118 18th St NW
Washington, DC 20009
Phone: (202) 797-0778

#384
Queen's Café & Hookah
Category: Hookah Bar
Average Price: Modest
Address: 2405 18th St NW
Washington, DC 20009
Phone: (202) 629-8924

#385
Axum's Level X Lounge
Category: Music Venues
Average Price: Expensive
Address: 1934 9th St NW
Washington, DC 20001
Phone: (202) 387-0765

#386
Lucky Strike
Category: Lounge
Average Price: Expensive
Address: 701 7th St NW
Washington, DC 20001
Phone: (202) 347-1021

#387
Signature Lounge
Category: Hookah Bar
Average Price: Modest
Address: 1920 9th St NW
Washington, DC 20001
Phone: (202) 372-6861

#388
Peyote Cafe
Category: Karaoke
Average Price: Inexpensive
Address: 2319 18th St NW
Washington, DC 20009
Phone: (202) 265-6665

#389
Ripple
Category: Wine Bar
Average Price: Expensive
Address: 3417 Connecticut Ave NW
Washington, DC 20008
Phone: (202) 244-7995

#390
Karma
Category: Middle Eastern
Average Price: Modest
Address: 1900 I St NW
Washington, DC 20006
Phone: (202) 331-5800

#391
Millie & Al's
Category: Pizza
Average Price: Inexpensive
Address: 2440 18th St NW
Washington, DC 20009
Phone: (202) 387-8131

#392
TASTE Restaurant And Lounge
Category: African
Average Price: Modest
Address: 1812 Hamlin St NE
Washington, DC 20018
Phone: (202) 269-3335

#393
Avenue Cafe & Lounge
Category: Lounge
Average Price: Modest
Address: 1501 Rhode Island Ave NW
Washington, DC 20005
Phone: (202) 483-2000

#394
Soussi Restaurant
Category: Hookah Bar
Average Price: Modest
Address: 2228 18th St NW
Washington, DC 20009
Phone: (202) 299-9314

#395
Ventnor Sports Cafe
Category: Sports Bar
Average Price: Modest
Address: 2411 18th St NW
Washington, DC 20009
Phone: (202) 234-3070

#396
Beacon Bar And Grill
Category: Bar
Average Price: Modest
Address: 1615 Rhode Island Ave NW
Washington, DC 20036
Phone: (202) 872-1126

#397
Sign Of The Whale
Category: Dive Bar
Average Price: Modest
Address: 1825 M St NW
Washington, DC 20036
Phone: (202) 785-1110

#398
Roofers Union
Category: Bar
Average Price: Modest
Address: 2446 18th St NW
Washington, DC 20009
Phone: (202) 232-7663

#399
Halftime Sports Bar
Category: Sports Bar
Average Price: Modest
Address: 1427 H St NE
Washington, DC 20002
Phone: (240) 832-8526

#400
Lyman's Tavern
Category: Dive Bar
Average Price: Inexpensive
Address: 3720 14th St NW
Washington, DC 20005
Phone: (202) 723-0502

#401
Empire Lounge & Restaurant
Category: Ethiopian
Average Price: Inexpensive
Address: 5333 Georgia Ave
Washington, DC 20011
Phone: (240) 476-9806

#402
Stetson's Famous Bar & Grill
Category: Bar
Average Price: Inexpensive
Address: 1610 U St NW
Washington, DC 20009
Phone: (202) 667-6295

#403
Topaz Bar
Category: Bar
Average Price: Modest
Address: 1733 N St.
Washington, DC 20036
Phone: (202) 393-3000

#404
Portico Restaurant
Category: Lounge
Average Price: Modest
Address: 1914 9th St NW
Washington, DC 20001
Phone: (202) 234-7511

#405
Russia House Restaurant
& Lounge
Category: Lounge
Average Price: Expensive
Address: 1800 Connecticut Ave NW
Washington, DC 20009
Phone: (202) 234-9433

#406
Ozio
Category: Lounge
Average Price: Modest
Address: 1813 M St NW
Washington, DC 20036
Phone: (202) 822-6000

#407
Turntable Restaurant & Disco
Category: Dance Club
Average Price: Inexpensive
Address: 5802 Georgia Ave NW
Washington, DC 20011
Phone: (202) 726-3322

#408
Fringetree
Category: Bar
Average Price: Modest
Address: 1400 M St Nw
Washington, DC 20005
Phone: (202) 429-1700

#409
Vita Lounge DC
Category: Lounge
Average Price: Modest
Address: 1318 9th St NW
Washington, DC 20001
Phone: (202) 332-0170

#410
Serengeti Resturaunt & Lounge
Category: Dive Bar
Average Price: Modest
Address: 6210 Georgia Ave NW
Washington, DC 20011
Phone: (202) 723-0190

#411
The Atlas Room
Category: Bar
Average Price: Expensive
Address: 1015 H St NE
Washington, DC 20002
Phone: (202) 388-4020

#412
Tattoo Bar
Category: Bar
Average Price: Expensive
Address: 1413 K St NW
Washington, DC 20005
Phone: (202) 408-9444

#413
Proof Restaurant
Category: American
Average Price: Expensive
Address: 775 G St NW
Washington, DC 20001
Phone: (202) 737-7663

#414
Balletto
Category: Lounge
Average Price: Inexpensive
Address: 1708 L St NW
Washington, DC 20036
Phone: (202) 296-7640

#415
Carolina
Category: Dance Club
Average Price: Modest
Address: 3700 14th St NW
Washington, DC 20010
Phone: (202) 829-4668

#416
Look Restaurant & Lounge
Category: Italian
Average Price: Modest
Address: 1909 K St NW
Washington, DC 20006
Phone: (202) 331-1050

#417
Foggy Brewpub
Category: American
Average Price: Modest
Address: 480 L'Enfant Plaza SW
Washington, DC 20024
Phone: (202) 484-1000

#418
T.G.I. Friday's
Category: Bar
Average Price: Modest
Address: 2100 Pennsylvania Ave NW
Washington, DC 20037
Phone: (202) 872-4344

#419
DC Star Nightclub
Category: Dance Club
Average Price: Expensive
Address: 2135 Queens Chapel Rd NE
Washington, DC 20018
Phone: (202) 635-0089

#420
The Exchange Sports Saloon
Category: Sports Bar
Average Price: Modest
Address: 1719 G St NW
Washington, DC 20006
Phone: (202) 393-4690

#421
Round Robin Bar
Category: Lounge
Average Price: Expensive
Address: 1401 Pennsylvania Ave NW
Washington, DC 20004
Phone: (202) 628-9100

#422
Number Nine
Category: Gay Bar
Average Price: Modest
Address: 1435 P St
Washington, DC 20005
Phone: (202) 986-0999

#423
Policy
Category: American
Average Price: Modest
Address: 1904 14th St NW
Washington, DC 20009
Phone: (202) 387-7654

#424
PX
Category: Lounge
Average Price: Expensive
Address: 728 King St
Alexandria, VA 22314
Phone: (703) 299-8385

#425
Galaxy Hut
Category: Dive Bar
Average Price: Modest
Address: 2711 Wilson Blvd
Arlington, VA 22201
Phone: (703) 525-8646

#426
The Arsenal At Bluejacket
Category: Bar
Average Price: Modest
Address: 300 Tingey Street SE
Washington, DC 20003
Phone: (202) 524-4862

#427
Museum
Category: Nightlife
Average Price: Expensive
Address: 915 F St NW
Washington, DC 20004
Phone: (202) 638-1234

#428
Nellie's Sports Bar
Category: Gay Bar
Average Price: Modest
Address: 900 U St NW
Washington, DC 20001
Phone: (202) 332-6355

#429
Maddy's Bar & Grille
Category: Bar
Average Price: Modest
Address: 1726 Connecticut Ave NW
Washington, DC 20009
Phone: (202) 483-2266

#430
Sidebar
Category: Bar
Average Price: Modest
Address: 8081 Georgia Ave
Silver Spring, MD 20910
Phone: (301) 565-9700

#431
Cafe Milano
Category: Italian
Average Price: Expensive
Address: 3251 Prospect St NW
Washington, DC 20007
Phone: (202) 333-6183

#432
Majestic Lounge
Category: Lounge
Average Price: Modest
Address: 2000 Mount Vernon Ave
Alexandria, VA 22301
Phone: (703) 549-5051

#433
Spacebar
Category: Bar
Average Price: Modest
Address: 709 W Broad St
Falls Church, VA 22046
Phone: (703) 992-0777

#434
Midtown Partyplex
Category: Nightlife
Average Price: Expensive
Address: 1219 Connecticut Ave NW
Washington, DC 20036
Phone: (202) 681-1219

#435
IOTA Club & Cafe
Category: Music Venues
Average Price: Modest
Address: 2832 Wilson Blvd
Arlington, VA 22201
Phone: (703) 522-8340

#436
The Cue Club
Category: Pool Hall
Average Price: Modest
Address: 7014 Columbia Pike
Annandale, VA 22003
Phone: (703) 941-7665

#437
Freddie's Beach Bar & Restaurant
Category: American
Average Price: Modest
Address: 555 23rd St S
Arlington, VA 22202
Phone: (703) 685-0555

#438
Odds Restaurant & Bar
Category: Dance Club
Average Price: Modest
Address: 1160 20th St
Washington, DC 20036
Phone: (202) 296-8644

#439
Penn Quarter Sports Tavern
Category: Sports Bar
Average Price: Modest
Address: 639 Indiana Ave NW
Washington, DC 20004
Phone: (202) 347-6666

#440
The Fainting Goat
Category: American
Average Price: Modest
Address: 1330 U Street NW
Washington, DC 20009
Phone: (202) 735-0344

#441
Quarry House Tavern
Category: Dive Bar
Average Price: Inexpensive
Address: 8401 Georgia Ave
Silver Spring, MD 20910
Phone: (301) 587-8350

#442
Napoleon
Category: Breakfast & Brunch
Average Price: Modest
Address: 1847 Columbia Rd NW
Washington, DC 20009
Phone: (202) 299-9630

#443
Screwtop Wine Bar
Category: Wine Bar
Average Price: Modest
Address: 1025 N Fillmore St
Arlington, VA 22201
Phone: (703) 888-0845

#444
Velvet Lounge
Category: Music Venues
Average Price: Inexpensive
Address: 915 U St NW
Washington, DC 20001
Phone: (202) 462-3213

#445
Music Center At Strathmore
Category: Art Gallery
Average Price: Modest
Address: 5301 Tuckerman Lane
N. Bethesda, MD 20852
Phone: (301) 581-5100

#446
Bin 1301 Wine Bar
Category: Wine Bar
Average Price: Modest
Address: 1301 U St NW
Washington, DC 20009
Phone: (202) 506-7716

#447
Hamilton's Bar & Grill
Category: Sports Bar
Average Price: Modest
Address: 233 2nd St NW
Washington, DC 20001
Phone: (202) 347-6555

#448
Hank's Oyster Bar
Category: Seafood
Average Price: Modest
Address: 1624 Q St NW
Washington, DC 20009
Phone: (202) 462-4265

#449
Basin Street Lounge
Category: Lounge
Average Price: Modest
Address: 219 King St
Alexandria, VA 22314
Phone: (703) 549-1141

#450
701 Pennsylvania Avenue Restaurant & Bar
Category: American
Average Price: Expensive
Address: 701 Pennsylvania Ave NW
Washington, DC 20004
Phone: (202) 393-0701

#451
Chasin' Tails
Category: Cajun/Creole
Average Price: Modest
Address: 2200 N Westmoreland St
Arlington, VA 22213
Phone: (703) 538-2565

#452
Arlington Cinema & Drafthouse
Category: Cinema
Average Price: Modest
Address: 2903 Columbia Pike
Arlington, VA 22204
Phone: (703) 486-2345

#453
DAR Constitution Hall
Category: Performing Arts
Average Price: Expensive
Address: 18Th & C Streets N.W.
Washington, DC 20006
Phone: (202) 347-1581

#454
TNT Bar
Category: Bar
Average Price: Modest
Address: 2413 Columbia Pike
Arlington, VA 22204
Phone: (703) 920-0315

#455
Olive Lounge & Grill
Category: American
Average Price: Modest
Address: 7006 Carroll Ave
Takoma Park, MD 20912
Phone: (301) 270-5154

#456
Black's Bar & Kitchen
Category: American
Average Price: Expensive
Address: 7750 Woodmont Ave
Bethesda, MD 20814
Phone: (301) 652-5525

#457
Irish Channel Restaurant & Pub
Category: Pub
Average Price: Modest
Address: 500 H St NW
Washington, DC 20001
Phone: (202) 216-0046

#458
The National Capital Barbecue Battle
Category: Local Flavor
Average Price: Inexpensive
Address: 9th Street NW And Pennsylvania Ave NW Washington, DC 20005
Phone: (202) 828-3099

#459
Birchmere
Category: Music Venues
Average Price: Modest
Address: 3701 Mt. Vernon Ave
Alexandria, VA 22305
Phone: (703) 549-7500

#460
Black Rooster Pub
Category: Pub
Average Price: Modest
Address: 1919 L St NW
Washington, DC 20036
Phone: (202) 659-4431

#461
Zed's Cafe
Category: Coffee, Tea
Average Price: Inexpensive
Address: 8225 Georgia Ave
Silver Spring, MD 20910
Phone: (301) 495-5614

#462
Menomale Pizza Napoletana
Category: Bar
Average Price: Modest
Address: 2711 12th St NE
Washington, DC 20018
Phone: (202) 248-3946

#463
Social Reform Kitchen & Bar
Category: Bar
Average Price: Expensive
Address: 401 9th St NW
Washington, DC 20004
Phone: (202) 393-1300

#464
The Fillmore
Category: Music Venues
Average Price: Modest
Address: 8656 Colesville Rd
Silver Spring, MD 20910
Phone: (301) 960-9999

#465
**Parthenon Restaurant
& Chevy Chase Lounge**
Category: Nightlife
Average Price: Modest
Address: 5510 Connecticut Ave NW
Washington, DC 20015
Phone: (202) 966-7600

#466
Mckeever's Pub
Category: Pub
Average Price: Modest
Address: 6625 Old Dominion Dr
Mclean, VA 22101
Phone: (703) 790-9453

#467
O'Shaughnessy's Pub
Category: Dive Bar
Average Price: Inexpensive
Address: 1324 King St.
Alexandria, VA 22314
Phone: (703) 836-7885

#468
Cuba Libre Restaurant & Rum Bar
Category: Cuban
Average Price: Modest
Address: 801 9th St NW
Washington, DC 20001
Phone: (202) 408-1600

#469
The State Theatre
Category: Venues, Event Space
Average Price: Modest
Address: 220 N Washington St
Falls Church, VA 22046
Phone: (703) 237-0300

#470
A-Town Bar & Grill
Category: American
Average Price: Modest
Address: 4100 N Fairfax Dr
Arlington, VA 22203
Phone: (703) 528-1110

#471
New Town Kitchen & Bar
Category: American
Average Price: Modest
Address: 1336 U St NW
Washington, DC 20009
Phone: (202) 265-0966

#472
Bobby Mckey's Dueling Piano Bar
Category: Bar
Average Price: Modest
Address: 172 Fleet St
National Harbor, MD 20745
Phone: (301) 602-2209

#473
Shooters Sports Bar
Category: Sports Bar
Average Price: Modest
Address: 7052 Spring Garden Dr
Springfield, VA 22150
Phone: (703) 942-6130

#474
Crystal City Sports Pub
Category: Sports Bar
Average Price: Modest
Address: 529 23rd St S
Arlington, VA 22202
Phone: (703) 521-8215

#475
Slate Wine Bar + Bistro
Category: Wine Bar
Average Price: Modest
Address: 2404 Wisconsin Ave NW
Washington, DC 20007
Phone: (202) 333-4304

#476
Pose Ultra Lounge & Nightclub
Category: Dance Club
Average Price: Expensive
Address: 201 Waterfront St
National Harbor, MD 20745
Phone: (301) 965-4000

#477
Westover Beer Garden & Haus
Category: Dive Bar
Average Price: Modest
Address: 5863 N Washington Blvd
Arlington, VA 22205
Phone: (703) 536-5040

#478
Gringos & Mariachis
Category: Mexican
Average Price: Modest
Address: 4928 Cordell Ave
Bethesda, MD 20814
Phone: (240) 800-4266

#479
Whitlow's On Wilson
Category: Bar
Average Price: Modest
Address: 2854 Wilson Blvd
Arlington, VA 22201
Phone: (703) 276-9693

#480
Ireland's Four Courts
Category: Breakfast & Brunch
Average Price: Modest
Address: 2051 Wilson Blvd
Arlington, VA 22201
Phone: (703) 525-3600

#481
Eatbar
Category: Bar
Average Price: Modest
Address: 2761 Washington Blvd
Arlington, VA 22201
Phone: (703) 778-9951

#482
Blackfinn Ameripub
Category: American
Average Price: Modest
Address: 2750 Gallows Rd
Merrifield, VA 22180
Phone: (703) 207-0100

#483
Dietle's Tavern
Category: Bar
Average Price: Inexpensive
Address: 11010 Rockville Pike
Rockville, MD 20852
Phone: (301) 881-8711

#484
The Light Horse
Category: Bar
Average Price: Modest
Address: 715 King St
Alexandria, VA 22314
Phone: (703) 549-0533

#485
Bistro La Bonne
Category: French
Average Price: Modest
Address: 1340 U St NW
Washington, DC 20009
Phone: (202) 758-3413

#486
Republic
Category: Bar
Average Price: Modest
Address: 6939 Laurel Ave
Takoma Park, MD 20912
Phone: (301) 270-3000

#487
Union Street Public House
Category: Pub
Average Price: Modest
Address: 121 S Union St
Alexandria, VA 22314
Phone: (703) 548-1785

#488
Continental Bar & Billiards
Category: Pool Hall
Average Price: Modest
Address: 1911 N Fort Myer Dr
Arlington, VA 22209
Phone: (703) 465-7675

#489
T.J. Stone's
Category: Bar
Average Price: Modest
Address: 608 Montgomery St
Alexandria, VA 22314
Phone: (703) 548-1004

#490
Laugh Riot At The Hyatt
Category: Arts, Entertainment
Average Price: Modest
Address: 7400 Wisconsin Ave
Bethesda, MD 20814
Phone: (301) 946-1102

#491
Dogwood Tavern
Category: American
Average Price: Modest
Address: 132 W Broad St
Falls Church, VA 22046
Phone: (703) 237-8333

#492
4935 Bar And Kitchen
Category: American
Average Price: Expensive
Address: 4935 Cordell Ave
Bethesda, MD 20814
Phone: (301) 951-4935

#493
Shooter Mcgee's
Category: American
Average Price: Modest
Address: 5239 Duke St
Alexandria, VA 22304
Phone: (703) 751-9266

#494
Bistrot Lepic
Category: French
Average Price: Expensive
Address: 1736 Wisconsin Ave NW
Washington, DC 20007
Phone: (202) 333-0111

#495
Harry's Pub
Category: Pub
Average Price: Modest
Address: 2660 Woodley Rd NW
Washington, DC 20008
Phone: (202) 328-2900

#496
Ragtime
Category: Pub
Average Price: Modest
Address: 1345 N Court House Rd
Arlington, VA 22201
Phone: (703) 243-4003

#497
Rumors
Category: Bar
Average Price: Modest
Address: 1900 M St NW
Washington, DC 20036
Phone: (202) 466-7378

#498
The Codmother
Category: Pub
Average Price: Inexpensive
Address: 1334 U St NW
Washington, DC 20009
Phone: (202) 245-0571

#499
Iris Lounge
Category: American
Average Price: Modest
Address: 1524 Spring Hill Rd
Mclean, VA 22102
Phone: (703) 760-9000

#500
Rhodeside Grill
Category: American
Average Price: Modest
Address: 1836 Wilson Blvd
Arlington, VA 22201
Phone: (703) 243-0145

Made in the USA
Middletown, DE
28 June 2017